Reforming Economics and Economics Teaching in the Transition Economies

Partial financial support for the development of this volume was provided by the US Department of Education through grants to the National Council on Economic Education for the International Education Exchange Program (PR Award # R304A970001-00), and by a grant from the Calvin K. Kazanjian Economics Foundation. Any opinions, findings, conclusions, or recommendations expressed in this publication are those of the authors and do not necessarily reflect the view of the US Department of Education or the Calvin K. Kazanjian Economics Foundation.

Reforming Economics and Economics Teaching in the Transition Economies

From Marx to Markets in the Classroom

Edited by

Michael Watts
Purdue University

William B. Walstad
University of Nebraska-Lincoln

Edward Elgar
Cheltenham, UK • Northampton, MA, USA

Published by
Edward Elgar Publishing Limited
Glensanda House
Montpellier Parade
Cheltenham
Glos GL50 1UA
UK

Edward Elgar Publishing, Inc.
136 West Street
Suite 202
Northampton
Massachusetts 01060
USA

A catalogue record for this book
is available from the British Library

Library of Congress Cataloguing in Publication Data

Reforming economics and economics teaching in the transition economies /
edited by Michael Watts, William B. Walstad.
   p.cm
   Includes index
   1. Economics–Study and teaching–Europe, Eastern. 2. Economics–Study and
   teaching–Former Soviet republics. 3. Europe, Eastern–Economics
   –1989-4. Former Soviet republics–Economic conditions. I. Watts, Michael. II.
   Walstad, William B.

   HB74.9.E852 R44 2002
   330'.071'147–dc21

                                                                2002072160

   ISBN 1 84064 541 5
   Printed and bound in Great Britain by MPG Books Ltd, Bodmin, Cornwall

Contents

PART THREE: CONCLUSION

Tables

Contributors

Nataliya Aksenenko is a Program Coordinator for the Kyrgyz National Council on Economic Education. Since 1995 she has offered workshops and other teacher training programs for secondary and elementary school teachers in Kyrgyzstan. She has also taught economics and mathematics in private schools in Bishkek.

Veronika Bikse is the Head of the Department of Economics at the University of Latvia, where she is also one of the founding members of the Center for Economic Education and now serves as its Director. Since 1996 she has organized and taught teacher training programs for Latvian teachers and participated in conferences in eastern Europe, Israel, and the United States.

Jacek (Jack) Brant is Subject Leader in Business and Economics Education at the Institute of Education, University of London. He has a background of teaching in business education, with previous experience in manufacturing industry. He has lectured in Poland (Gdansk, Krakow, and Warsaw), both to practicing teachers and to undergraduates, and he has also presented papers at international conferences held in Poland (Zakopane and Lodz). He is especially interested in the role of subject knowledge and creativity in the education process.

Mikhail Chepikov has been a Professor in the Department of Economics at Belarus State University since 1991 and serves as the General Accountant of the Belarusian Economics Association.

Steven L. Cobb is Associate Professor and Chair of Economics at the University of North Texas, where he also serves as Director of the Center for Economic Education. Since 1994 he has participated in 16 training programs and conferences in eastern Europe, central Asia, and the former Soviet Union, offered for university professors, secondary economics teachers, and teacher trainers.

James Dick is Professor of Teacher Education and Co-director of the Center for Economic Education at the University of Nebraska at Omaha. He completed a Fulbright lectureship in Cherkassy, Ukraine in the fall of 2000 and has participated in several other teaching activities in Ukraine. including training programs for university and secondary educators, study tours for teachers, and Ukrainian conferences on economic education.

James Grunloh is Professor of Economics and Director of the Center for Economic Education at the University of Wisconsin Oshkosh. Since 1994 he has participated in more than 25 economic education training programs and conferences in eastern Europe and central Asia offered for university and college professors, secondary economics teachers, and pedagogical faculty.

Anatoli Kovalenko has been a Professor in the Department of Economics at Belarus State University since 1981 and serves as the Executive Director of the Belarusian Economics Association.

Alexander Kovzik was a Professor in the Department of Economics at Belarus State University from 1981-2001 and has held Fulbright and other visiting positions at universities in the United States and Germany. He is the President of the Belarusian Economics Association.

David Lines is Professor and Head of the Centre for the Enhancement of Learning and Teaching at the Robert Gordon University in Aberdeen, Scotland. For more than a decade he has provided training in economics and business education for a wide range of interested parties, ranging from politicians, civil servants, and administrators through practicing teachers to those in initial training. This work has taken him to the Far East, Australia, North America, the Russian Republic, western Europe, and the emerging countries of eastern Europe, especially Poland.

Jane S. Lopus is Professor of Economics and Director of the Center for Economic Education at California State University, Hayward. She has conducted 14 programs to train economics teachers in nine formerly communist countries, including a program in Romania in 1999. She is currently working on a project to design an economics curriculum for middle school students in Romania.

Craig R. MacPhee is Paul C. Burmeister College Professor of Economics at the University of Nebraska-Lincoln. In recent years he has served as an advisor on educational reform in Russia and Poland and as an advisor on economic policy in the republics of Georgia and Montenegro.

Thomas McKinnon is University Professor of Economics and Director of the Bessie Moore Center for Economic Education at the University of Arkansas. He has participated in 12 training programs and conferences in eastern Europe and the former Soviet Union for teachers, teacher trainers, and business people.

Volodymyr Melnyk is the Director of the Ukrainian Council for Economic Education, and formerly served as an administrator at the International Renaissance Foundation in Kiev, and before that in the Kiev city government.

Sandra Odorzynski is Professor of Economics and Director of the Center for Economic Education at St. Norbert College in De Pere, Wisconsin. She has served as a faculty member in workshops for teachers and teacher trainers in Belarus, Estonia, Lithuania, Russia, and Ukraine.

Barbara J. Phipps is Associate Professor of Teaching and Leadership and Director of the Center for Economic Education at the University of Kansas. Since 1997 she has taught in more than 15 training programs and seminars for educators in eastern Europe and the former Soviet Union. In 1999-2000 she was a Fulbright Scholar at Sofia University in Bulgaria.

Sergei Ravitchev is Director of the International Center for Economic and Business Education in Moscow, Russia. He organized the Center and coordinates the work of 55 affiliated regional Centers for Economic Education throughout Russia.

Alexander Skiba is a student in the Ph.D. program in economics at Purdue University. He received his undergraduate degree in economics from Rivne State Technical University in Ukraine.

Dan Christian Stoicescu is working toward a Ph.D. in education administration at Pennsylvania State University. His field of interest is financial public education. He was a high school economics teacher in Romania from 1981-91, and a research fellow at the Institute for Educational Sciences in Bucharest from 1991-97.

Stefania Szczurkowska is an Assistant Professor at the Pedagogical University of the Polish Association for Adult Education and a Senior Researcher at the Institute for Educational Research in Warsaw. She has also worked at the International Institute for Educational Planning (UNESCO, Paris), in several educational institutions in Great Britain, and at the Brigham Young University School of Education.

Antoanetta Voikova is the Chief Economic Education Expert in Bulgaria's Ministry of Education and Science. For 12 years she taught students and economics teachers at the secondary level and is the author of six economics books. She has been the President of the Bulgarian Council on Economic Education since its inception in 2000.

George Vredeveld is a Professor of Economics and Director of the Center for Economic Education at the University of Cincinnati. Since 1990 he has worked extensively with Bulgarians to strengthen their economics instruction. He also has taught economics seminars in eastern Europe and the former Soviet Union.

William B. Walstad is a Professor of Economics at the University of Nebraska-Lincoln. He serves as Chair of the Committee on Economic Education of the American Economic Association and as an Associate Editor of the *Journal of Economic Education*. He is the editor of *An International Perspective on Economic Education* (Kluwer, 1994), and began his work in transition economies in 1992 as an instructor for a seminar on the reform of the principles of economics courses at Moscow State University.

Michael Watts is Professor of Economics and Director of the Center for Economic Education at Purdue University, and an Associate Editor of the *Journal of Economic Education*. Since 1992 he has participated in over 30 training programs and conferences in eastern Europe, central Asia, and the former Soviet Union, offered for university professors, secondary economics teachers and teacher trainers, and for legislators, government officials, and journalists.

Foreword

For more than 70 years ideology drove education in the vast Soviet empire. With the breakup of the Soviet Union education reformers faced a daunting task. With only the textbooks from the past and their own Marxist training, school teachers from Vilnius to Vladivostock and from the Barents Sea to the Black Sea were unprepared to help their students understand the economic and political reforms their countries were undergoing.

This book tells the remarkable story of how university professors, school teachers, and other educators from the new independent states of the former Soviet Union and from central and eastern Europe have responded to the challenge of teaching economics under dramatically changed economic, political, legal, and educational systems. An important part of this compelling story is the role played by US educators – as well as colleagues from western Europe – in supporting these reforms.

We are especially pleased that the United States government supports educators who played – and still play – a meaningful role in contributing to this transformation. The United States Congress had the foresight to anticipate these challenges, and it first funded the International Education Exchange Program (IEEP) in economics and civics in 1995. This unique program continues to be administered through the US Department of Education, in cooperation with the Department of State.

The Congress recognized that the United States, and for that matter the rest of the world, had an important stake in helping these countries make the difficult transition to democracy and market economies. Educational programs were immediately seen as a key part of this assistance because, if the reforms were to be sustained, ordinary citizens would have to support them and elect leaders who supported them.

The IEEP legislation grew out of the conviction that economic and civic education would help young people in transition countries grow up with a sound understanding of market economies and democracy. Moreover, the program gives US teachers an opportunity to contribute to education reform beyond their own borders, and to bring these experiences back to their own students and classrooms. This, too, is important, because such historic changes in educational

Foreword

and economic systems are rare, and the opportunity to participate and observe those changes provides a remarkable chance to learn and grow, as well as teach.

THAD COCHRAN
United States Senator

DALE E. KILDEE
Member of Congress

Acknowledgements

The inspiration for this project began in 1992, when we were invited to participate in separate projects in Russia to help university economists and educators working with secondary schools reform the content and teaching of economics. We realized at that time that a remarkable story was unfolding, not only in Russia but in all the nations of the former Soviet Union and eastern Europe that were making the transition from socialism and central planning to democratic market economies. As we participated in many other projects with participants from over 20 nations, and observed what our colleagues were doing in various nations to reform economic education in elementary and secondary schools and in universities, we became even more convinced that this enormous undertaking should be described in a edited book.

Given the range of countries, institutions, and topics covered in this volume, we expected it be an especially difficult book to organize, write, and edit, which is why we delayed starting work on the volume for so many years. The wait did not make the task of producing an edited volume any easier, and in fact may have made it harder because there is so much more to analyze and describe. If we hadn't believed the academic reform of economics and economics teaching in the transition economies to be so important, we wouldn't have begun, let alone completed, the book.

When we finally decided to accept the challenge, we were very fortunate to receive, very quickly, generous and enthusiastic support from the two financial sponsors named below and from Edward Elgar Publishing Ltd. In presenting a proposal to the publisher, we decided it would be crucial for most chapters to be written by teams of authors, pairing at least one economist or educator from a wide range of the transition economies with one or more western economists and educators who had worked extensively in the countries. That also made the project more difficult in some ways, but we firmly believe it was also what ultimately made the project feasible and the results that appear here far more credible. Accordingly, our first thanks go to the contributing authors. They were asked to summarize sweeping changes in relatively few pages, report evidence that was typically difficult to find and document, and also to offer insights and conclusions reflecting their own personal experiences. The authors were exceedingly patient and understanding in working through multiple drafts and revisions. For their important contributions we offer our sincere thanks.

Major funding for the volume was provided by two organizations. The first is the US Department of Education through grants to the National Council on Economic Education for the International Education Exchange Program (IEEP). In cooperation with the US Department of State, the Department of Education has supported programs on economic and civic education in the transition economies since 1995. Dr. Ram N. Singh, Senior Associate in the Office of Educational Research and Improvement (OERI), has served as the program officer for the IEEP in economics. At the National Council on Economic Education, Dr. Patricia Elder, Vice President of EconomicsInternational and Governmental Relations, and Barbara DeVita, Director of EconomicsInternational, not only supported the idea of this volume but provided information on the extensive range of NCEE programs in the transition economies to many of our chapter authors.

Generous financial support for the development of the volume was also provided by the Calvin K. Kazanjian Economics Foundation, Inc. We are indebted to the Foundation's Board and to its Managing Director, Dr. Michael MacDowell.

Many other organizations – far too many to list separately here – also provided information to our authors on national programs in specific transition economies, including the national Soros Foundations, Junior Achievement programs, Ministries of Education, colleges and universities, national Councils and regional and local Centers for Economic Education, and the US Agency for International Development.

Julie Huffer at Purdue University and Sharon Nemeth at the University of Nebraska-Lincoln spent untold hours typing, formatting, revising, and proofreading every page of the volume. We are most grateful for their skillful assistance with this challenging work, which helped us produce a much better volume. Finally, we benefited substantially from the strong support we received from Deirdre Watts and Tammie Fischer as we worked through each phase of this project – one that went on longer than we expected.

We make no claim that this volume tells the complete story of what happened to economics and the teaching of economics in these transition economies, but each of the chapters gives readers a history and a framework for understanding these substantial changes in the content and teaching of economics in the transition economies.

PART ONE

The Academic and Public Policy Transition in
Teaching Market Economics

1. The Academic Transition from Marxian to Market Economics

Michael Watts and William B. Walstad

Shortly before the formal breakup of the former Soviet Union, the central planners in Moscow arranged for a Russian translation of the best-selling US college textbook on the principles of economics, and for the publication and distribution of 500,000 copies of the translated text.[1] The handwriting was, in effect, now plainly written on the Kremlin wall – market economics could no longer be withheld from university faculty members and students, or for that matter from the public at large.

When Germany reunified, professors of Soviet-style economics were fired and replaced in the economics departments at universities in the former East Germany. In the other transition economies that didn't happen, partly because of more severe financial constraints at universities in those countries, but largely because it would have been far more difficult to find enough qualified replacements in those nations – although some were found in mathematics departments and among younger faculty members in economics departments who turned out to be eager to learn and teach western economics openly. There was substantial resistance, however, from some professors who truly believed what they had taught about Marx and Lenin, from others who did not believe that markets or market-based economics could flourish in their nations until major reforms had been made in political and economic institutions, and from some who were simply too old or unprepared to learn a new way of teaching economics.

In elementary and secondary schools there were different and in some ways bigger questions about what to do about the teaching of economics, because much less had been done in terms of presenting Marxist economics as a formal course in the school during the Soviet era.[2] Consequently, in most of the transition economies the academic transition at this level of education was not simply a matter of substituting a course or unit in western economics for a course or unit in Marxian economics. Instead, economics courses had to be justified as an acceptable new subject for the school curriculum.

Some administrators and ministries resisted initiatives to teach market economics at the elementary and secondary levels, where (as in many western countries) the curriculum is already crowded with 'core' courses and few teachers have been trained to teach economics. Financial constraints and the paucity of instructional materials and curriculum guidelines in economics were far more serious problems in the transition economies than in the West. But demands for such instruction kept growing as economic and political reforms started to take hold, and as reforms in the content and teaching of economics at universities all across the transition economies, and at the elementary and secondary levels in some of these nations, began to take hold, too.

Compared to the far more wide-ranging economic and political reforms that were starting to occur across the newly independent nations of eastern Europe and central Asia, what happened to the teaching of economics in the university and elementary and secondary classrooms was far less dramatic and newsworthy. There were no riots and demonstrations for or against the academic reforms; no guns were fired; and apparently nobody was killed or physically injured. But over the past decade there have been many fundamental changes in this area of academia, some with serious repercussions that were sometimes sudden and swift, but more often gradual and even sporadic, and in most cases still unfolding. We believe these events make it clear that the reform of economic education can be a key element or building block in the transition to a market economy, for students at all levels of education and, over time, for the general public.

This volume is the first extensive treatment of this academic transition. Most of the chapters are written by teams of US or UK economists and educators who have traveled and worked extensively in the transition economies, paired with economists and educators who live, work, and were trained in each of the nations that are discussed. That mix of knowledge and perspectives permeates the chapters and the overall volume, and the combination adds richness to the discussion and analysis of changes in the transition economies.

Chapter 2, by Michael Watts, William Walstad, and Alexander Skiba, summarizes public opinion surveys conducted by economists, political scientists, and sociologists in transition economies, primarily during the 1990s and especially in the early years of political and market reforms. The major purpose of this review is to assess reactions to market reforms in the transition economies and whenever possible compare attitudes on economic issues and policies in those countries to survey responses collected in western nations. It is important to note that there was some decline in the originally optimistic outlook for economic reforms and public acceptance of a market economy because of the initial deterioration in the economic performance of these economies. But an important underlying theme in this chapter is that economic education through coursework and public education affects people's views on economic issues and their degree of support for market-based solutions, as well as democratic political reforms.

As noted above, one of the earliest and most important transitions in education was the reform of undergraduate economics instruction. In Chapter 3, Alexander Kovzik and Michael Watts offer a detailed description of the changes at the leading universities in the three core nations of the former Soviet Union – Russia, Belarus, and Ukraine. Changes at these flagship universities, and especially at Moscow State University, sent important signals and, in effect, marching orders, to other universities in the transition economies. But even at these three preeminent universities, financial and personnel constraints shaped the reforms, with the result that while curricula now look very much like those for economics departments at leading business schools in western universities, even today there are still important differences in exactly what topics are actually taught, and especially in how they are taught and tested.

In Chapter 4 William Walstad analyzes the effects of one type of instructional program conducted in the transition economies by the National Council on Economic Education. Specifically, he studies the effects of training programs designed to improve the economic understanding and pedagogical skills of secondary economics teachers from the transition economies, and to provide them with instructional materials developed in the United States, all with the goal of increasing the economic understanding of these teachers' high school students. The study draws on data collected in five nations – Lithuania, Latvia, Ukraine, Kyrgyzstan, and Poland. Findings indicate that the economic understanding of students of these teachers is substantially enhanced beyond what would have been achieved if the teachers had not received the training and used these materials. There is also some evidence that student attitudes toward markets and a market economy become more positive as a result of this program. What makes this study unique is the data base from five transition economies. Hard data on the effect of these kinds of programs is difficult to obtain even in the United States or United Kingdom, and as might be expected even more so in the transition economies.

In Chapter 5 Craig MacPhee discusses the importance of economic education and specialized training programs for journalists, government officials, and the general public in helping to build support for specific public policies and the overall program of transition from central planning to a market economy. The chapter reflects MacPhee's personal experience working as an economic advisor to the government of Georgia, but draws several comparisons to writings by prominent economists who have worked in the policy arena as economic advisors in the United States. MacPhee identifies eight hard lessons learned by the Georgian public and government officials as they adopted market reforms. One of those lessons is that televised public service announcements providing instruction in basic principles of economics were important tools in gaining and strengthening public support for market reforms – a lesson that is especially germane to the general theme of this volume and this introduction.

The largest part of the volume is made up of eight country studies, on Belarus, Bulgaria, Kyrgyzstan, Latvia. Poland, Romania. Russia. and Ukraine. These chapters tell the stories of numerous organizations, the people who directed and staffed them, and other special circumstances that shaped the academic transition from Marxian to market economics in these nations. The primary emphasis in these chapters is on reform initiatives at the elementary and secondary levels, although some also provide comparisons to Chapter 3, on reforms in university economics instruction at Moscow State University, Belarus State University, and Kiev State University. Taken together, the chapters reveal a number of common problems, responses, and institutions working to promote economic education reforms in the transition economies. But there are key differences across countries, too, and in regions of particular countries – particularly between rural and urban elementary and secondary schools.

One of the most interesting findings is how uniform economics instruction and general educational structures were at both the college and precollege levels right up until the end of the Soviet period. That educational system was, indeed, a classic case of central educational planning and instruction. But after 1991 that uniformity quickly began to crack and erode, with different countries choosing different paths, facing different constraints, and receiving (or accepting) different levels of assistance from several western organizations. And while there is no doubt that economic education under the Soviet system was unique, the process of educational reform in the content and teaching of economics since the breakup of the Soviet Union should be of general interest to educators who seek to promote fundamental and widespread curriculum reforms in many fields.

In virtually all of the countries represented in this volume, a number of key 'change agents' are identified in the reform process, including the ministries of education (in both the pre- and post-Soviet periods), universities, pedagogical institutes for current and future teachers, and nongovernmental organizations (NGOs) such as national Soros Foundations, national organizations of economists and economic educators, and western organizations including the National Council on Economic Education, Junior Achievement, and some educational programs and initiatives sponsored by the European Union or particular European universities.

Beyond those organizations and differences in educational policies, differences in history, geography, and politics also shaped, and continue to shape, the academic transition in economics in these countries. For example:

- Politically and economically, Belarus still looks to Russia more than the West, and quite possibly still to the Russian Soviet legacy more than the Russia of post-1991 reforms.
- Bulgaria's educational reforms have been characterized by a series of starts and stops, to an even greater degree than what is commonly found in the transition economies. This was also one of the few republics in which a secondary economics course was required during the Soviet period and has now been replaced by required coursework on market-based economics.
- Kyrgyzstan's history. location. and ethnic mix make its story different from the other nations discussed in the volume, but so too does its attempts to move rapidly with both economic and educational reforms, especially in moving quickly to mandate a secondary course in western-style economics.
- Latvia, like Kyrgyzstan, moved rapidly to offer and mandate economics courses at the precollege level, but with far more university involvement in that process and less binding financial constraints.

- Poland's story is different because of its geographic and historical western orientation, and the rapid pace of its economic reform and growth since 1991.
- Romania's turbulent political history around the time of the breakup of the former Soviet Union shaped its educational policies and reforms, and in many ways created special problems that are still being addressed today. Romania was also one of the few Soviet Republics to require a secondary course on economics.
- Russia's story is, of course, unique because of its size, scope, and political influence, both during the Soviet period and today.
- Like Russia, Ukraine's economic and educational reforms have lagged behind eastern Europe, partly reflecting more severe economic constraints, but also regional and ethnic differences in eastern and western Ukraine, and in urban and rural areas of the country.

The final chapter offers our general summary and conclusions, based on the findings from these chapters on nine different nations (eight country studies plus MacPhee's chapter on economic policy reforms in Georgia) and our own work and travel in many more of the transition economies. The chapter describes the major change agents across the nations and offers an assessment of their influence and effectiveness. Most of all we hope that a sense of the historic nature of the political and economic reforms, and the related changes in how economics is being taught in these nations, comes through loud and clear. That sense of history is still palpable in these nations, and so is the sense that, however important economic education is· in the United States, the United Kingdom, and other western economies, it is even more important just now in the transition economies.

NOTES

1. *Economics: Principles, Problems, and Policies* (11th edition) by Campbell R. McConnell and Stanley L. Brue (McGraw-Hill, 1990).
2. Two exceptions to this were Bulgaria and Romania.

2. Attitudes Toward Markets and Market Reforms in the Former Soviet Union and Eastern Europe

Michael Watts, William B. Walstad, and Alexander Skiba

Public opinion is a key factor in establishing support for economic reforms and increasing the politically feasible rate of economic change in the transition economies. The sense of a historic watershed that underlaid the process of economic reforms in these nations through the 1990s was evident, but so too was the 40-70 year heritage of Soviet control, the Cold War, and being part of one of the world's two military superpowers. That history and the uncertain prospects for the sweeping reform programs led researchers from around the world to investigate how people in the transition economies formed their attitudes on economic issues and viewed new economic structures and policies in their countries. Researchers also tried to determine whether the attitudes of ordinary citizens and national leaders were mainly shaped by looking to the West or the East, and to the future or the past.

Intertwined with the uncertain direction and pace of the economic changes in these nations were major political reforms promoting democratic rule and creating new political institutions. These simultaneous initiatives on the economic and political fronts made the study of economic attitudes in these nations even more compelling because of their potential influence on the support for democratic institutions. Consequently, political scientists conducted many studies on how economic attitudes in transition economies shaped perspectives on politics, political institutions, and voting. In an early example of this type of study Duch (1993) concluded 'political evaluations are shaped primarily by evaluations of overall economic performance' (p. 591) and also found that attitudes towards a market economy affect support for multiparty, democratic elections:

Given these economic and political concerns, the level of public support for, or opposition to, market-based reforms in the transition economies has been measured by hundreds of public opinion surveys conducted over the past 10-15 years, with dozens published in leading academic journals in several fields. In some cases these results were compared to responses on similar questions or statements in surveys conducted in the United States, the European Union, or other western nations with market economies. Much of this work was conducted during the early years following the breakup of the former Soviet Union as newly independent nations struggled to establish or reestablish decentralized forms of government, private ownership, and a national system of markets.

This work is relevant to this volume because one expected outcome of economic education programs in the transition economies is to influence public knowledge and attitudes about economic issues, institutions, and public policies. Earlier research in the United States has shown that as teachers and high school students learn more economics their attitudes on economic issues change, becoming more like the responses found in surveys of academic economists (Allgood and Walstad, 1999; Becker, Walstad, and Watts, 1994).[1] There is also robust evidence from multiple public opinion surveys of adults in the United States that the greater the level of economic knowledge, the more likely adults are to hold opinions that would be similar to the views of most economists on a range of micro- and macroeconomic issues (Walstad, 1997; Walstad and Rebeck, 2002). In fact, in the studies cited economic knowledge was the only factor that consistently affected opinions on different economic issues (and not age, gender, education level, household income, or even political party affiliation). Perhaps the most important finding, especially in light of this chapter's focus on public opinion in nations undergoing economic transition, is that adults with more knowledge about economics were more willing to accept economic change and more optimistic about future prospects in a market economy (see Walstad and Rebeck, 2002).

While the US research indicates that changing people's knowledge of conceptual understandings in economics leads to changes in their attitudes about economic issues and policies, the reverse is not necessarily true. That is, changing a person's attitude towards economics and economic issues is not likely to affect their level of economic understanding or literacy (Beron, 1990; Walstad, 1987; Walstad, 1996). The rationale for this unidirectional result is that changes in economic knowledge occur primarily by receiving more information and more instruction, and then transforming what is read, heard, or taught into greater knowledge. Being more positive about economics or being willing to accept economic views may establish initial conditions for such learning, but does not replace the necessary cognitive process or substitute for information and instruction that enables a person to increase their knowledge.

As noted in several other chapters of this book, economic education programs that have been offered in the transition economies since the early 1990s have often measured, to some extent, the effects of that training on participants' economic understanding and attitudes. Those programs have usually targeted specific audiences such as teachers, students, or university faculty members who educate teachers. As a result, the effects of these programs on widespread public opinion will be limited, at least in the short run. In the long run, there is greater expectation that an investment in educating teachers about economics and the use of new instructional materials will increase the economic knowledge of precollege and college students, who will in turn significantly influence public opinion as they mature.

Contemporary public opinion is not likely to be influenced by such economic education programs, however. Public opinion is more likely to be shaped by perceptions of the success or failure of market reform initiatives, by the distribution of the benefits and costs of such reforms, by economic conditions facing individuals and nations, and by the media coverage of those issues. These factors have, of course, varied considerably across the different transition economies, but they have generally affected public views of the economic transformation in each nation.

This chapter reviews selected findings from some of the more important and insightful published surveys of public opinion on major economic issues in the transition economies. Our basic purpose is to investigate public support for market reforms and public opinion on related economic policies that advance the market reforms. Whenever possible, comparisons are made to the findings from surveys conducted in the United States, the European Union, or other market economies. Our secondary purpose is to establish the context for understanding the essential role that economic education has played, and continues to play, in helping these nations develop widespread public awareness, knowledge, and understanding of how markets, systems of markets, and their own national economies work. As many of the authors in other chapters of this volume conclude, such education will be essential in insuring the long-term success of the economic reforms in these nations.

I. PUBLIC SUPPORT FOR MARKET REFORMS

Several surveys conducted in the early 1990s found widespread – but certainly not unanimous – support for market reforms in eastern Europe and the former Soviet Union (FSU), and extensive disenchantment with Soviet-style planning and socialism. Duch (1993) reported on surveys of approximately 1500 people from European nations in the Soviet Union in May 1990, asking about perceptions on the need for radical economic reforms, willingness to allow prices to be set by supply and demand, and allowing a system of private ownership in exchange for the availability of high quality consumer goods, even if those goods are not available to everyone as a result of higher prices and increased levels of income inequality (Table 2.1).

Clarke (1993, pp. 626-8) reports findings from a number of surveys conducted in Russia from mid-1990 to mid-1991 by survey organizations. He argues that these surveys were far more reliable than surveys conducted independently or by contract in Russia shortly after the breakup of the FSU. A May 1990 survey found general support for the transition to a market economy. A November 1990 poll reported more public opposition to market reform than previous surveys, but most of the public still supported the move to a market economy. Another poll conducted that November found a majority of those surveyed were generally in

Table 2.1: Support for economic reform (in percent)

Item	Support market reforms	Not sure	Oppose market reforms
Radical economic reform is necessary	54.3	20.3	25.4
Favor an economy in which prices are set by supply and demand	48.0	22.1	29.9
Favor private ownership with high quality goods, but higher prices and income inequality	50.9	22.6	26.5

Source: Duch (1993, p. 595) using 1990 data.

favor of the radical '500 days' program for the rapid transition to the market economy that was adopted by the Russian Federation. Finally, a December 1990 survey found that 60 percent of the population favored the transition to the market. About 20 percent of this sample were in favor of a transfer to the market as rapidly as possible, and only 16 percent were against such a rapid change.

What is especially noteworthy in the Clarke study are the public perceptions of when the benefits would accrue (see Table 2.2). While only a relatively small fraction (about one in five) of respondents felt that reforms would bring benefits to a majority of the population within five years, about the same number felt that those benefits would never occur, and about a third had no idea about whether or when they might occur. Those with higher levels of education were more likely to believe that the majority of the population would eventually benefit, but were also more likely to say that those benefits would be longer in coming. Clarke concluded that 'the Soviet population had no illusions about the benefits that would flow from the market economy' (p. 626).

Table 2.2: Expected years until market reforms will help a majority (in percent)

		EDUCATIONAL LEVEL		
	All	Higher	Middle Special	Middle	9 class or less
1-2 years	3	4	3	1	2
3-5 years	18	25	16	20	17
At least 10 years	19	28	23	17	14
At least 15 years	7	10	7	6	6
Never	14	6	14	15	16
I think that it will never begin	6	5	6	7	5
Difficult to answer	33	22	31	34	38

Question: When will the transition to the market give positive results for a majority of the population?
Source: Clarke (1993, p. 627) using 1990 data.

Reporting on a survey conducted as part of the International Social Justice Program in mid-1991,[2] Mason (1995) also found considerable support for market reforms in Russia and seven of the eastern European transition economies. These results are shown in Table 2.3. There was variation in the levels of support and opposition across these nations, but the general pattern held in all of the nations: More people supported a market economy than opposed it.

Table 2.3: Support for a market economy by country (in percent)

Country	Strongly agree	Somewhat agree	Neither agree nor disagree	Somewhat disagree	Strongly disagree	N
Bulgaria	44.0	24.7	14.1	10.7	6.6	1,229
Czechoslovakia	51.8	31.1	11.9	4.0	1.3	1,087
Estonia	40.9	32.1	18.8	5.0	3.1	897
Poland	26.5	46.0	15.3	8.0	4.1	1,343
Russia	36.0	34.5	9.2	11.3	9.0	1,283
Slovenia	73.7	20.7	4.3	1.0	0.3	1,287

Question: Please tell me how much you agree or disagree with the following statement: A free market economy is essential to our economic development.
Source: Mason (1995, p. 388) using 1991 data.

An essentially opposite way of looking at this issue is to ask whether people support or oppose socialism (see Table 2.4). In this case less than a fourth of the survey respondents in each nation very much or somewhat favored the socialist system, while a majority or plurality in each nation (from a low of 33 percent in Slovenia to a high of 53 percent in Estonia) were somewhat against or totally against such a system. These findings are consistent with the findings on questions about support for a market system, and lend some validity to the idea that there was widespread opposition to the socialist system and general support for market reforms. Nevertheless, a substantial number of respondents were agnostic on these issues, on questions asked in either format.

Stability and Pace of Reform

One issue raised in these studies during the early years of reform was whether the movement to capitalism and democracy in these nations was likely to be abandoned because of deteriorating economic conditions, often including high inflation, high unemployment, and a stagnant or declining standard of living. In a second study, Duch (1995) used survey data from 1990 in the European portion of the Soviet Union and 1991 survey data from Hungary, Poland, and Czechoslovakia

Table 2.4: Views about socialism by country (in percent)

Country	Very much in favor	Somewhat in favor	Neither for nor against	Somewhat against	Totally against	N
Bulgaria	8.1	16.1	24.2	19.2	32.4	1,286
Czechoslovakia	2.4	12.4	34.8	24.1	26.3	1,119
East Germany	1.6	16.6	39.2	27.6	14.9	986
Estonia	2.3	18.5	26.1	18.2	35.0	875
Poland	1.8	9.2	43.2	20.2	25.7	1,418
Russia	9.6	17.0	29.7	21.4	22.2	1,385
Slovenia	4.8	16.2	46.0	15.5	17.5	1,249

Question: People have different views about socialism. Based on your experience in (country name) of socialism, would you say that you are very much in favor, somewhat in favor, neither for nor against, somewhat against, or totally against socialism?
Source: Mason (1995, p. 388) using 1991 data.

to conduct a regression analysis of factors affecting public support for democracy and a market economy. He concluded that the economic chaos experienced in these nations during this early period of transition would not cause citizens in these nations to abandon the shift to capitalism and democracy, and that public preferences for these new economic and political institutions were not transient but relatively stable despite the economic difficulties these nations were experiencing. This conclusion is consistent with findings in a study of 1993 voting in Poland by Powers and Cox (1997), who reported that support for economic transition was only weakly affected by assessments of personal economic circumstances and instead mostly influenced by perceptions about the past and the blame assigned to the failed communist system.

Other studies did find changes in public support for capitalism after the early years of reform. Following an initial period with substantial support for radical reform, as economic conditions worsened public opinion shifted to some degree. Whitefield and Evans (1994) suggested '...the transition experience itself has reoriented public opinion away from utopian expectations about the market and democracy, which were characteristic of the period when the old system was collapsing, toward a more informed and certainly more cautious outlook' (p. 58). Of course, this statement conflicts with the conclusion drawn by Clarke (1993, quoted above), that the Soviet population was not at all utopian in its views about the timing or level of benefits associated with political and economic reform programs.

What probably changed most in the mind of the public from the early years of reform was not general support for a market economy or utopian expectations about the timing and level of benefits, but public support for a rapid pace of reform. Colton (2000), for example, conducted an extensive study of Russian voters in the State Duma elections in 1995 and the presidential election in 1996. The survey results were based on 2,841 weighted cases in 1995 and 2,472 weighted cases in 1996. One survey item asked about views on the market economy. As shown in Table 2.5, there was strong support for a market economy in Russia from about two-thirds of the respondents in each year, but minimal support for a rapid movement to a market economy and broadest support for a gradual approach.[3]

Table 2.5: Russian support for a market economy (in percent)

Response	1995	1996
You are for a market economy and believe the transition to the market should be quick	6	8
You are for a market economy and believe the transition to the market should be gradual	58	61
You are against the transition to a market economy	21	16
Don't know	11	8

Question: What is your view of the transition to a market economy in Russia? Which of the opinions that I shall now read out is closest to your opinion?
Source: Colton (2000, p. 245) using 1995 and 1996 data.

Colton's findings are similar to those of Gerber (2000), who also finds qualified support for market reforms in Russia. Gerber used survey data collected in January 1996 by VTsIOM from 2,321 Russian adults. One question asked which economic system seemed best, one with state planning and distribution, one with private property and markets, or whether it was hard to chose. About a third selected each of the three responses: state planning (34 percent), a market economy (31 percent), and hard to say (35 percent). Concerning the appropriate pace for the transition to a market economy, 46 percent said it should be gradual, only 15 percent thought it should be fast, with the other respondents replying that it was hard to say (26 percent) or that no change should be made (13 percent). When asked whether the reforms should be continued, 37 percent agreed, 38 percent said it was hard to say, and 25 percent said they should be stopped.[4]

Political and Economic Attitudes

There have also been debates among political scientists and sociologists about whether or not attitudes toward democracy and capitalism were directly linked in the transition economies. Finifter and Mickiewicz (1992) argued that they were not; Miller, Hesli, and Reisinger (1994) claimed that they were. Finifter and Mickiewicz used survey data collected in 1989 in the Soviet Union and found no relation between attitudes towards political democracy and attitudes towards individual responsibility for social well-being. Miller, Helsi, and Reisinger based their study on public opinion data collected in Russia, Ukraine, and Lithuania in 1990-92 and discovered a strong positive association between preferences for individual responsibility for social well-being and support for political reform. A follow-up study by Finifter (1996) reanalyzed their 1989 data and found that the relationship varied by republic, and by the level of education and the place of residence of the respondent.

This debate is reminiscent of debates between economists such as Milton Friedman and Paul Samuelson about the strength of the relationship between capitalism and democracy and political freedoms. For decades, Friedman, Hayek, and other conservative economists argued that there was a clear, unbreakable link between capitalism and democracy, pointing to Hong Kong and the United States on the one hand, and to India and the Soviet Union on the other hand, to support their claims. Samuelson and others pointed to the Scandinavian welfare states as counterexamples, and noted the extensive range in the size of government even among the industrialized western democracies. The nature of this controversy leads us to ask whether these arguments are primarily a matter of the eye of the beholder or based on different political persuasions. It could also be that in survey research results often depend on how survey items are framed and measured by social scientists. In fact, in the debate over the association between democratic and market attitudes in transition economies, Finifter (1996) concluded that large differences in sampling and measurement procedures and major economic and political changes in these nations over time contributed to the different results.

A study by Gibson (1996) on the relationships between attitudes towards democracy and a market economy reports on a unique panel study of 700 individuals in Russia and Ukraine, who were surveyed on their attitudes toward market and political reforms in 1990 and then again in 1992. Other individuals also participated in one or the other surveys, with a total of over 2,200 respondents from Russia and over 840 from Ukraine. Gibson finds that political attitudes remained basically constant in these two countries over these years, but there was some 'crystallization' of economic attitudes, which moved in the direction of closer alignment with individuals' political attitudes. Like Duch (1993) and others, Gibson (1996) finds 'a fairly strong relationship between support for democratic institutions and processes and support for market-based institutions and processes' (p. 967), with simple Pearson correlation coefficients of 0.50 in Russia and 0.48 in Ukraine. But that correlation means that only about 25 percent of the variance in the two variables is shared, and Gibson finds it surprising that the correlations are not stronger.

The central question in Gibson's study is to explore the direction of causation between political and economic attitudes. After extensive analysis of such factors as respondents' level of education, measures of economic and social dissatisfaction, knowledge of western European political institutions, and measures of individuals' resistance to change and social conservatism, Gibson concluded that in Russia 'attitudes toward democratic institutions have a greater influence over economic attitudes than economic attitudes have over attitudes toward democracy' (p. 973). In Ukraine, however, there were 'roughly equal' effects of political and economic attitudes on each other. To help explain these differences, Gibson noted that Russia adopted considerably more reforms during these years than Ukraine, and that well educated people in Russia during these years probably had wider access to information about western political and economic arrangements.[5]

II. GROUPS THAT SUPPORT MARKET REFORMS

Both sociologists and political scientists have tried to identify which groups in transition economies are more likely to support market reforms, and to support either rapid or gradual reforms. Clarke (1993) reported on several surveys conducted across Russia from November of 1990 to June of 1991, and concluded that 'a majority of the population welcomed the transition to a market economy as the only means of freeing themselves from an oppressive system' (p. 619), albeit with some reservations. He also reported results by a wide range of occupational subgroups (Table 2.6), although many of the sample sizes for the occupational subgroups are small and thus are only suggestive of what is likely to have been found if larger samples had been surveyed.

Table 2.6: Support for rapid or gradual transition to a market economy in Russia,
            by occupation (in percent)

Groups	Support rapid transition	Support gradual transition	Oppose	Undecided
Directors of enterprises, organizations, managers	26	45	19	10
Specialists with higher education	26	42	23	9
White-collar	20	26	42	12
Skilled blue-collar	14	33	33	20
Unskilled blue-collar	18	12	6	64
Pensioners	8	30	34	28
Students	23	51	11	15
Overall	18	34	28	20

Source: Clarke (1993, p. 628) using data from 1990.

Clarke (1993) also examined the differences in support for the market reforms among demographic subgroups. In response to the question 'Do you support the transition to a market economy?' 48 percent either said yes or on the whole, 34 percent either said no or not on the whole, and 18 percent said it was difficult to say. Table 2.7 shows the responses of those for and against the economic transition by demographic groups. Although the same concern about sample sizes noted for the occupation data also holds for the demographic subgroups, Clarke concludes that in many different surveys of various groups 'there was ... a close correlation between support for the market and educational or socio-economic status, with pensioners and peasants being on balance opposed to the market, while the ruling stratum was strongly in favor of it' (pp. 629-30). Attitudes were also clearly related to the age of respondents, with younger people far more supportive of market reforms than the elderly.

Table 2.7:   Support for transition to a market economy in Russia, by demographic factors and occupation (in percent)

Group	Pro	Con	Group	Pro	Con
Peasants	37	44	Non-specialist (White Collar)	49	30
Men	41	41	Men	65	24
Women	31	49	Women	44	33
Unemployed, Pensioners	39	41	Workers in Law Enforcement	50	27
Men	49	35	Teachers, Cultural Workers,	2	31
Women	32	46	Mass Media		
			ITRs and Enterprise Managers	59	22
Workers	43	38	Men	71	19
Men	53	29	Women	42	25
Women	33	47	Military Employees	67	15
Under 29	51	35	Leaseholders, Cooperative,	68	32
Over 60	25	51	Firms etc.		
			Workers in the Party Apparatus	70	19
Managers or (Economic	47	35	Students	72	22
Specialists)					
Men	55	30	Scientific and Academic	78	9
Women	35	42	Workers		
			Workers in the State Apparatus	79	10

Source: Clarke (1993, p. 629) using data from 1990.

Ironically, Clarke reports that an AON survey conducted in January of 1991 found 'apparently greater enthusiasm for the market in the Communist Party than among the general population, with 60 percent in favor of the formation of a market economy and the development of free enterprise, and only 21 percent against' (p. 628). There are, of course, many possible explanations for these findings. Party members may well have been better educated and more able, on average, than the overall population, and thus expected to do well under a market system; they may have believed they were well positioned to take advantage of new opportunities in a market system due to their political and business contacts in the Soviet Union and abroad; they may have joined the party for reasons of expediency rather than ideological commitment in the first place; or by January of 1991 they may simply have felt it was expedient to support market reforms.

In the May 1990 survey of about 1,500 people in the European nations of the former Soviet Union described earlier, Duch (1993) reports no significant differences in support for market reforms across broad occupational groups (service, farming, and industry) compared to a base group of those who received stipends from the government (primarily students and pensioners). Younger and wealthier (measured by ownership of household durable goods) respondents were more supportive of reforms, as were those with more education. Taken together, however, these variables explain less than a fifth of the overall variation in responses to the survey items on market reforms.

Firebaugh and Sandu (1998) conducted surveys in Romania in May of 1993, with a national sample of about 1,000 people. Using factor and regression analysis, they concluded that 'Marketization is most popular among the young, the more educated, the wealthier, men, and urban residents' (p. 533). Of these factors, however, only education had a substantial independent effect. And all of these factors were found to be less important predictors of respondents' support for market reforms once items measuring ideological beliefs, individuals' expectations about their own economic prospects in the next few years, and their willingness to accept risks were included in the analysis.[6]

When considering support for economic reforms, an interesting question arises as to whether cohort values are simply different for younger, wealthier, and better educated workers, or whether these groups have stronger economic incentives to support (or at least not to oppose) economic reforms. There is some debate on this point, but Duch and most other social science researchers seem to generally adopt the economic explanation, noting that younger people have more time to wait for and realize the benefits of the reform programs, and that better educated and wealthier members under the old system are likely to be more confident about succeeding in the new system, too, based on their general abilities, training, and greater knowledge of key people and institutions.

III. THE ECONOMIC ROLE OF GOVERNMENT

While the survey evidence shows general support for market reforms in nations of the former Soviet Union and the satellite nations in eastern Europe, that support is still qualified and limited in many respects. Those qualifications are most evident, when surveys ask about the role of government in these economies. particularly in dealing with employment, income, welfare, education, and other economic and social concerns. Here the socialist heritage is more evident probably because the respondents have more experience with extensive government provision of employment and social goods, and little experience with how a market economy can meet economic and social demands in a society.

The anomaly between the overall support for market reform but strong support for government intervention in the economy was recognized by Mason (1995), among others.[7] Reporting on an extensive survey conducted in 12 nations (Russia, Poland, Slovenia, Bulgaria, Hungary, Czechoslovakia, Estonia, Germany (former East and West), Holland, the United Kingdom, Japan, and the United

States) in mid-1991, he offered the following conclusion about citizens in the post-communist states:

> Having just overturned the communist system, with its authoritarianism, centralization, and inefficiencies, most people are hostile to the *idea*, at least, of socialism....
>
> Once one gets away from the ideologically loaded terms of 'socialism' and 'market,' however, this seeming consensus begins to disappear. When respondents were asked more specific questions, they tended to support important policies and values associated with the state socialist regimes they have left behind. This is perhaps most evident in widespread egalitarianism, support for a strong role for the government in the economy, and deep skepticism on the subject of a distributive system based more on merit than on need. (Mason, 1995, pp. 387-8)

Mason's evidence is based on responses to a five-point agree/disagree scale on items indicating whether respondents believed the government should guarantee everyone a minimum standard of living, put an upper limit on how much money an individual can make, and provide a job for everyone who wants a job. A 'statism index' for each country was constructed by taking the average of individuals' response values for all three questions. There was clearly more support for these government programs in the former socialist states than in the western capitalist nations, although there was considerable variance across the nations in each subgroup, too – especially in Japan and the United States (Table 2.8).[8]

Duch (1993) found similar results in his 1990 survey of people living in the European nations of the former Soviet Union and compared those results to 1987 data collected by the International Social Survey Project in eight western democratic market economies. Once again, while there was considerable variance across the western nations on items dealing with the government guaranteeing jobs and incomes, there was clearly stronger support for a more extensive role of government in the European USSR (see Table 2.9).

Further evidence on the above findings comes from a study by Listhaug and Aalberg (1999) using 1992 survey data in seven post-communist nations and 10 capitalist nations (Table 2.10). They too found a high level of public support for an activist government role to reduce income inequality, provide jobs, and guarantee a basic level of income. In response to the statement 'It is the responsibility of government to reduce the differences in income between people with high incomes and those with low incomes,' over three-fourths (76 percent) in the post-communist nations agreed, whereas just over half (58 percent) held that view in the capitalist nations. As in the studies by Mason and Duch, they discovered that there was widespread support in post-communist nations on the need for government to provide jobs (87 percent) and to guarantee a basic income (85 percent). Substantially less acceptance of these ideas was found in the capitalist nations (61 percent for job guarantees and 56 percent for income guarantees).[9]

Table 2.8: *Support for a strong role for the government in the economy (percent strongly or somewhat agreeing)*

Country	Principle			Statism Index (Rank)
	Minimum standard of living	Upper limits on money	Guaranteed jobs	
Bulgaria	93	42	87	4
East Germany	94	60	96	1
Hungary	90	58	87	2
Poland	87	47	88	5
Russia	88	34	96	6
Slovenia	92	60	88	3
Czechoslovakia	88	30	82	9
Estonia	94	32	76	8
Average for post-communist states	91	45	88	–
West Germany	85	32	71	10
Japan	83	36	86	7
Holland	86	32	53	12
Great Britain	83	39	67	11
United States	56	17	50	13
Average for capitalist states	79	31	65	–

Questions: Five point agree/disagree scale on the following statements: 1) the government should guarantee everyone a minimum standard of living; 2) the government should place an upper limit on the amount of money any one person may make; 3) the government should provide a job for everyone who wants one.
Source: Mason (1995, p. 391) using 1991 data.

Table 2.9: *Public support for government social guarantees, European USSR and western economies (percent who agree or strongly agree)*

Government should guarantee:	USSR	AUS	USA	I	UK	NL	D	CH	A
Jobs	94	39	44	81	59	75	78	49	79
Income	86	38	21	66	60	49	43	42	58
Approximate N	1,500	1,342	1,290	884	999	1,330	1,161	809	872

Column codes: USSR= European USSR; AUS = Australia; USA = United States; I = Italy; UK = United Kingdom; NL = Netherlands; D = West Germany; CH = Switzerland; A = Austria.
Source: Duch (1993, p. 598) using 1990 data.

The previous findings primarily focus on government support in guaranteeing jobs, basic incomes, and income equality in a nation. A study by Miller, White,

Table 2.10: Role of government in the economy (percent agree)

Country	Government is responsible for		
	Reducing income differences	Providing jobs	Guarantee basic income
Bulgaria	81	94	92
East Germany	89	86	92
Hungary	75	85	85
Poland	77	89	87
Russia	65	94	92
Slovenia	80	81	77
Czechoslovakia	67	78	67
Average for post-communist states	76	87	85
Australia	43	39	51
Austria	70	72	51
Canada	48	40	48
West Germany	67	66	58
Great Britain	65	56	66
Italy	80	86	69
New Zealand	53	49	61
Norway	60	86	78
Sweden	53	72	43
United States	38	47	34
Average for capitalist states	58	61	56

Source: Listhaug and Aalberg (1999. pp. 122-5) using 1992 data.

and Heywood (1998) expands the list of possible areas for government intervention in the economy to health care, housing, and price setting, in addition to jobs. They surveyed public opinion in Russia (both east and west) and Ukraine, the two principal countries of the former Soviet Union (FSU), and in Hungary, Slovakia, and the Czech Republic, three nations in east-central Europe (ECE). Their surveys were conducted at the end of 1993, with responses from 7,350 members of the general public in those nations (see Table 2.11). The results show that there is strong support for government control over prices in the economy and also for the provision of social welfare. The averages for the FSU nations and the ECE nations are essentially the same for items on health care and housing, but the FSU sample showed stronger support for the government provision of jobs (89 percent versus 72 percent) and price setting (91 percent versus 81 percent), perhaps because of the harder and rapidly deteriorating economic conditions in Russia and Ukraine at the time of the survey.[10]

Another interesting result from this study is a comparison with survey data that found British public values on selected questions to be socialist in orientation.

Table 2.11: Support for state responsibilities for social welfare (in percent)

	Health care	Jobs	Housing	Setting prices for basic goods and services
Russia	93	89	75	93
Ukraine	88	89	90	88
Czech Rep.	81	56	69	73
Slovakia	97	77	85	91
Hungary	94	84	85	78

Question: These should be mainly done by the state, rather than left mainly to private businesses and the market economy.
Note: 'Don't knows,' 'Can't decide,' etc. excluded from calculation of percentages.
Source: Miller, White, and Heywood (1998, p. 114) using 1993 data.

Almost all (98 percent) of the British public thought that government should be responsible for health care, 78 percent thought it should be responsible for full employment (jobs), and 91 percent considered the government responsible for providing adequate housing for people. Responses of politicians in Britain with their counterparts in the FSU and ECE on the same issues also found strong similarities in the support for government welfare programs. Miller, White, and Heywood concluded 'neither the public nor the politicians in the FSU and ECE looked very much more socialist than the British on social welfare aspects of socialist values – not because they lacked any commitment to socialist values but because their commitment was, on average, no greater than in Britain' (p. 393).

More recent public opinion data from Russia reconfirms the public desire for a strong role for government to provide jobs, limit income, and control prices. Colton (2000) conducted surveys before the 1995 State Duma election and before the 1996 presidential election. He asked those interviewed to indicate positions of agreement or disagreement on three statements: (1) the government ought to guarantee a job to everyone who needs one; (2) the state should set food prices; and (3) the state should limit the incomes of the rich. If people agreed or strongly agreed, he coded the response as one. The approval responses were then summed across the three items to create a 'welfarism' scale that ranged from zero to three. Almost five in ten respondents (49 percent in 1995 and 48 percent in 1996) had a score of three, which meant that they agreed or strongly agreed with all three statements. About three in ten (32 percent in 1995 and 28 percent in 1996) had a score of two, which meant that they agreed or strongly agreed with two of the three statements.[11]

East Germany also experienced the transition to a market economy, albeit in a different setting involving reunification with one of the world's wealthiest market economies. Roller (1994) reports survey data collected in East and West Germany shortly after the political reunification in October 1990 as part of the International

Social Survey Program (ISSP) and the 1991 *Allbus Base Line Study*. As shown in Table 2.12, Roller found that at that time people in former East Germany 'harbored higher expectations regarding the role of government, expectations more congruent with a planned economy' (p. 115). These differences were noted despite the fact that there were only small differences on general statements measuring support for what Roller terms 'the achievement principle of the market economy.'[12]

Table 2.12: *Responsibility of government to provide social and economic services in western and eastern Germany (in percent)*

	West	East	Difference (West–East)
Socio-economic security			
Health care for the sick	95.4	98.9	-3.5
A decent standard of living for the aged	94.7	99.2	-4.5
Appropriate housing for those who can't afford it	79.8	93.7	-13.9
A decent standard of living for the unemployed	78.4	94.1	-15.7
A job for everyone who wants one	74.2	94.9	-20.7
Socio-economic equality			
Financial support for students from low-income families	85.9	96.0	-10.1
Reduced income differences between rich and poor	63.6	84.3	-20.7
Wealth			
Price stability	69.6	90.6	-21.0
Secure growth	52.3	80.3	-28.0
Mean for all items	78.0	92.8	-14.8

Question: Should (insert item) definitely or probably be the government's responsibility to provide?
Source: Roller (1994) using 1990 data.

One of the major decisions that had to be made in transition economies was how state property would be privatized. The public's view of this issue was examined in surveys conducted in Russia in 1995 and 1996 (Colton, 2000), with responses showing fairly strong support for continuing government control of property (Table 2.13). A plurality (44 percent in 1995 and 42 percent in 1996) essentially favored state control either of all property or most property. Only about one in ten respondents thought all property in the economy should be put exclusively or for the most part in private hands.

Table 2.13: Views on privatization of state property (in percent)

Response	1995	1996
All property in the economy should be in private hands	2	1
Economic property should for the most part be in private hands	9	9
The shares of private and state property should be equal	35	41
Economic property should for the most part belong to the state	24	27
All property in the economy should belong to the state	20	15
Don't know	11	8

Question: What do you think about the privatization of state property in Russia? Please look at the card and say which alternative best corresponds to your opinion.
Source: Colton (2000, p. 246) using 1995 and 1996 data.

These findings of relatively strong opposition to privatization of state property are supported by evidence from other opinion surveys conducted in Russia. Hough and Lehmann (1998, pp. 221-2) used survey data from 1993 to 1996 on items that asked the general public whether they were for or against the privatization of large enterprises. In 1993, 36 percent said they were against this change either completely or on the whole. This opposition grew to 57 percent by 1996.[13] In addition, the great majority (75 percent in 1996) of the Russian public was against 'the free purchase and sale of land by private persons' (p. 222). This viewpoint hardly changed from 1993 to 1996. In another study using 1996 survey data from Russia, Gerber (2000) found that only about a quarter (27 percent) of the public preferred private farms over collectives for agricultural production. Size also makes a difference in public opposition to private ownership of property. Two-thirds of the public were against the private ownership of large enterprises, but only 19 percent opposed the private ownership of small enterprises.[14]

IV.   ECONOMIC INCENTIVES AND THE DISTRIBUTION OF INCOME

The use of financial incentives based on workers' productivity and the willingness to allow sizeable income differences to provide work incentives, both of which help make an economy more efficient and productive, are hard ideas for people to understand and accept in all countries. Differences of opinion often turn on questions of degree – how large will the incentives and the income differences be? But these questions can be especially difficult to face in nations with a socialist legacy, where equal wage or salary payments were often made for work regardless of the quality or productivity – although 'special' occupations did receive financial and non-financial perquisites.

Shiller, Boycko, and Korobov (1991) studied these and other issues in the former Soviet Union based on responses to a telephone survey from 391 adult residents of Moscow and 361 residents of greater New York City in 1990. They found that large majorities of adults in both Moscow and New York (90 and 86 percent, respectively) agreed with the statement 'People work better if their pay is directly tied to the quantity and quality of their work.' Nevertheless, on another item that stated 'If the government were to make sure that everyone had the same income, we would all be poor, since no one would have any material incentive to work hard,' only 41 percent of Moscow residents and 38 percent of New York residents agreed. The contradictory responses to the two questions suggest that the support for work incentives based on merit is somewhat limited. Further evidence to support this conclusion comes from results showing that a larger percentage of both groups (55 percent in Moscow and 38 percent in New York) supported a hypothetical plan to increase productivity and living standards in the overall economy, but mostly for people who responded energetically to work incentives in the plan, and only slightly for other people.

The contradictory view of work incentives and the distribution of income is also shown in the 1990 survey of the European USSR by Duch (1993). He asked respondents to indicate their willingness to use income differences as incentives to encourage individual effort and promote economic growth in the overall economy. Responses to three of these items are shown in Table 2.14. In two of the three items (1 and 3), people support the need for income differences to give people an incentive to work, but in one item (2) people are opposed (44 percent) or uncertain (29 percent) about the need for income differences for economic programs.

Table 2.14: Income inequality and economic efficiency (in percent)

Item	Agree	Uncertain	Disagree
To get people to work better, we need to increase the inequality of incomes	67.3	15.7	17.1
A great difference in incomes is necessary for the development of our society	26.9	29.2	44.0
There ought to be more equality of income even if it means that some people will not work as well as they do now	25.8	15.5	58.6

Source: Duch (1993, p. 597) using 1990 data.

Clarke (1993) reported results from a December 1990 VTsIOM survey in Russia, on the question 'Ought the state to restrict the level of personal income, and if so at what level?' The results, reproduced in Table 2.15, are generally in line with the studies by Shiller et al. and by Duch, showing some, but certainly not overwhelming, support for greater income inequality. The support rises with the level of income, but even among the most educated only slightly more than half (55 percent) oppose limits on incomes. In addition, a sizeable minority (36 percent) was in favor of either limiting the difference between high and low-income groups to ratios of three or four to one, or of limiting incomes so that there would be no millionaires.

Table 2.15: Should the Russian government limit income inequality? (in percent)

	USSR (total)	EDUCATIONAL LEVEL			
		Higher	Middle Special	Middle	9 class or less
State shouldn't limit	39	55	47	44	25
Should limit so that all have approximately equal incomes	12	5	8	11	17
Should limit so that differences are not too big (maximum 3-4:1)	18	17	15	17	19
Should limit so that we have no millionaires	18	14	18	16	21
Difficult to answer	14	9	14	13	17

Question: Ought the state to restrict the level of personal income; if so, at what level?
Source: Clarke (1993, p. 636) using 1990 data.

Like the previous studies in this section, survey data from Roller (1994) show only qualified support for permitting income differences, based on responses to two survey items used in the former East and West Germany shortly after the political reunification of late 1990. About six in ten (58 percent in East Germany and 64 percent in West Germany) agreed with the general idea of using different levels of income to motivate individual workers ('Only if the differences in income and social prestige are big enough will there be an incentive for individual efforts'). Only about half in each group (51 percent East Germany and 54 percent West Germany), however, disagreed with the proposition that incomes should not be based solely on work and that family needs should be considered ('The income one gets should not exclusively depend on one's work. Rather everybody should get what he needs for a decent living for his family').

Public support for economic incentives may become weaker because of the economic problems arising during a transition to a market economy. Kluegel, Mason, and Wegener (1999) compared survey data from 1991 and 1996 on many items related to public opinion about market justice. One question asked whether 'there is individual effort only if differences in income are large enough' (p. 280). The results for five post-communist nations (Bulgaria, Czech Republic, East Germany, Hungary, and Russia) show that the percentage of the general public agreeing with this statement dropped from an average of 63 percent to an average of 47 percent over the five years (Bulgaria: 69 to 46 percent; Czech Republic: 71 to 51 percent; East Germany: 65 to 60 percent; Hungary: 34 to 30 percent; and, Russia: 78 to 46 percent). People in these nations also became more critical of the social value of business profits. In response to the statement: 'it is [all right] if businessmen make good profits because everyone benefits in the end,' there was a fall in support from 47 percent to 27 percent, on average (Bulgaria: 38 to 14 percent; Czech Republic: 64 to 36 percent; East Germany: 36 to 27 percent; Hungary: 25 to 14 percent; and, Russia: 71 to 42 percent).

Some findings from the previous discussion of the economic role of government in the economy are also germane to the discussion of government policies in the areas of income distribution and public policies to redistribute income. There is evidence of overwhelming public support for government intervention in the transition economies to provide a minimum income for people, and even to provide a job as a way to earn an income (see Tables 2.8-2.11). The support is not nearly so strong for government actions that would reduce income inequality in these nations either through narrowing income differences (Table 2.10) or through limiting incomes (Table 2.8).[15]

Further evidence on this latter point comes from several additional survey studies conducted in Russia. A 1996 survey found that about six in ten (57 percent) of the public favored a state limit on the incomes of rich citizens, but there were also three in ten who were opposed and about one in ten who were uncertain (Hough and Lehmann, 1998, p. 222). Another survey conducted by Fleron, Hahn, and Reisinger (1997) asked 'whether an upper limit should exist on earnings so that no one accumulated more than anyone else' (p. 31). The results showed that only half agreed (51 percent in 1993 and 53 percent in 1996). Surveys in 1993 conducted in Russia and Ukraine revealed that only about half (49 percent) agreed that 'restricting the gap between rich and poor is more important than freedom to make money' (Miller, White, and Heywood, 1998, p. 117).[16]

V. PRICE CHANGES AND FAIRNESS

How prices are determined in a market economy is often difficult for people to understand without some economic education. Even if people understand why prices increase or decrease for products, they may not like the outcome if it means that they will have to pay significantly more of their income to obtain a product. Such circumstances, limited education about how markets work, and unwillingness to accept price changes that adversely affect real incomes, provide a fertile ground for populist demands that government policy makers intervene in particular markets and set prices. This issue is by no means a problem just for transition economies, because even western governments with a long tradition of general reliance on markets sometimes set particular prices to meet demands by groups of producers or consumers.[17]

A number of studies in transition economies investigated people's willingness to accept specific attributes of a market economy, such as market-determined prices or profits for businesses. As noted in the discussion of the role of government, several studies showed strong support for government setting the prices for basic goods and services. In fact, survey data from a study by Miller, White, and Heywood (1998) showed 91 percent support for price controls on basic

goods and services in Russia and Ukraine and an average of 81 percent support in
Hungary, the Czech Republic, and Slovakia (see Table 2.10). Colton (2000, p.
246) also reported strong support for price controls for food based on 1995 and
1996 surveys in Russia.

Public opinion on the fairness of price changes was investigated in a study by
Shiller, Boycko, and Korobov (1991), who found that virtually the same
percentages of respondents in Russia and the United States (66 percent in Moscow
and 68 percent in New York) felt it would be unfair for flower sellers to raise
prices on holidays when there is an unusually high demand for flowers. There was
also considerable agreement about the unfairness of a small factory raising prices
for kitchen tables 10 percent when demand was so high that the factory could not
keep up with orders, but there was no change in the factory's cost of producing the
tables. Two-thirds of the Russians responded that this was not fair, compared to
70 percent of the US respondents, although almost 60 percent of both groups
agreed that the factory should have the right to increase the price regardless of
whether or not that was fair.

Slightly more New Yorkers than Muscovites (61 versus 57 percent) felt that it
was fair for rents on summer homes to increase as a result of a new railway line
that made houses in a particular area more desirable. But many more New
Yorkers (72 versus only 46 percent Muscovites) opposed government limits on
higher prices for flowers that might result in shortages. Ten percent more of the
Moscow residents (51 versus 41 percent) felt it was unfair for a small company to
buy vegetables from rural people and resell them in the city at much higher prices,
even if the company told the growers exactly what they were doing and the rural
people voluntarily agreed to sell the vegetables to the company. A majority of
both groups (57 percent of the Russians and 64 percent of the US respondents)
preferred higher government taxes on gasoline to reduce consumption, rather than
limiting the amount of gasoline a consumer could purchase at gasoline stations.
Generally, therefore, the two groups agreed about what pricing behavior was fair
and unfair, and disagreed relatively more about how willing they were to have the
government intervene in markets to prohibit 'unfair' behavior by sellers. But in
one area sharp differences in what constituted acceptable behavior were noted.
When asked whether they would charge a friend interest on a six-month loan the
friend would use to purchase a summer home, when banks were charging three
percent interest for such loans, only six percent of the Moscow respondents said
that they would, compared to 29 percent of the New Yorkers. New York residents
were also somewhat more likely to point to speculation as a cause for higher
commodity prices and shortages than Muscovites.[18]

Whaples (1995) administered six of the questions used in the Schiller,
Boycko, and Korobov study to students in 14 sections of a semester-long
introductory economics course at Wake Forest University. Students in seven
sections took the survey at the beginning of the semester; students in the other
seven sections completed the survey at the end of the semester. Responses to these

questions for the two groups of students and the New York and Moscow
respondents in the Schiller, Boycko, and Korobov telephone surveys are shown in
Table 2.16. Even students who had not taken the Wake Forest (or any other)
economics course were more likely to view market responses such as raising
prices when demand increases as fair than the New York or Moscow respondents.
Students who answered these questions at the end of the economics course were
much more likely to accept those outcomes as fair. Whaples concluded that
'Learning economics did seem to change many students' minds about what is fair,
convincing them that market outcomes are equitable' (p. 310).

Table 2.16: Fairness of market outcomes (percent responding 'Yes')

Question	Shiller, Boycko and Korobov survey		Wake Forest students	
	Moscow	New York	No econ	After 1 course
1) Is it fair to raise rents?	57	61	88	92
2) Is it fair to raise flower prices?	34	32	82	90
3) Should government limit the increase in flower prices?	54	28	21	8
4) Is it fair to raise table prices?	34	30	76	84
5) Is it fair that middlemen make a large profit?	49	59	65	77
6) Would you be annoyed when when someone sells/buys a place in line?	69	44	44	32
Number in sample	98-132	115-120	164	158

Source: Whaples (1995, p. 310) based on student surveys in the 1993-1994 school year, and
data reported in Shiller, Boycko, and Korobov (1991).

The positive effect of economics instruction on the perceptions of market
fairness also applies to teachers in transition economies. Spiro (2000) summarized
the results of survey data collected from 416 teachers in 10 transition economies
(Ukraine, Kyrgyzstan, Lithuania, Poland, Latvia, Estonia, Bulgaria, Kazakhstan,
Uzbekistan, and Croatia). These teachers had participated in various one-week
'demonstration' workshops to improve their understanding of basic economics in
their nations between 1995 and 2000. Two items from the Shiller, Boycko, and
Korobov (1991) survey illustrate that the teachers viewed market outcomes as
more fair after instruction. On the item 'It is fair for a factory to raise the price of
tables if there is no change in the cost of production,' 57 percent agreed on the
pretest, but 75 percent agreed on the posttest. When asked 'Is it fair for flower
sellers to raise prices before a holiday?' 72 percent agreed on the pretest and 85
percent on the posttest.[19]

VI. CONCLUSIONS

The collapse of the centrally planned economies in the breakup of the former Soviet Union gave rise to popular support for a change to a market economy and democratic reforms. As the transition progressed, however, economic conditions deteriorated, resulting in falling incomes, increased unemployment, and rapid price inflation. These adverse conditions lowered the initially optimistic expectations for the outcomes of the economic reforms and how fast market-based reforms could be implemented. The changing circumstances also lent some renewed support for socialist solutions to economic and social problems. Although these post-communist nations are unlikely to return to central planning, there remains a social legacy that at least nominally supports government programs to guarantee employment, equalize incomes, provide basic goods and services, and set price limits for many products.

How far the economic reforms in the transition economies ultimately go, and the pace at which they occur, will depend to a large degree on what people in these post-communist nations think and understand about particular markets and how a market economy works. In centrally planned economies with limited personal freedom, there is perhaps less need for widespread public understanding of economics because the government makes most of the decisions and assumes most of the responsibility for the provision of basic goods and services. In a market economy, however, both the political and economic systems may work more effectively when there is widespread understanding of how markets work.

Despite John Maynard Keynes's famous warning that economics does and should not provide a 'settled body of policy conclusions,' a fairly extensive body of research from the western market economies suggests that economics coursework and other kinds of economic education programs affect people's attitudes toward a wide range of economic practices and policies, leading them to think and respond more like a majority of economists. There is also limited empirical and anecdotal evidence that similar results are observed in economic education programs that have been offered in the transition economies over the past decade.[20] Most of those programs have been targeted at students or teachers, so the short-term effect in shaping public attitudes was probably small; but over time, this may well be one of the most important outcomes of such programs. That is particularly true if, as a limited number of studies in the United States have suggested. the attitude changes are ultimately caused and backed up by underlying changes in people's levels of economic knowledge. That would appear to be a far more lasting source of changes in attitudes and behaviors than direct attempts to sway people's attitudes based on emotional or propagandistic appeals. Furthermore, several studies have shown that, even in the West, without economic education or coursework the general public often views price adjustments to changes in market conditions as inherently unfair.

Public perceptions of market reforms in the transition economies have and will continue to play a key role in determining whether or when these nations will complete their transitions. Comparisons with public opinions in the West suggest that the economic views of the public should become more supportive of market-based reforms as these reforms take effect, especially if economic education improves and people become more knowledgeable about how a market economy works. There are, of course, no guarantees that this outcome will occur, and over time there will almost certainly be unpredictable twists and turns in public thinking about economic issues that will be difficult to interpret. But as later chapters in this book will detail, the foundation has been laid for improving economic education in many of the transition economies, and that should help to create a more knowledgeable and informed public on economic issues.

NOTES

1. Watts (1994) discusses the degree of consensus and dissension among academic economists. Some educators contend that economic education as it is conducted in the United States is ideological and that it indoctrinates students (see Watts, 1987, for a critical review). The basic problem with this perspective is that the process of economic education is substantially more complex (see Walstad, 1996, pp. 178-9). Economic knowledge may change economic opinions because it increases awareness and understanding of many economic issues. This greater information and understanding, in turn, helps people develop more appreciation of other points of view, and increases the likelihood that they will change their initial opinions, or even alter their underlying attitudes. It should not be surprising then that more economic knowledge produces more positive views of a market economy or greater acceptance of the consensus position of economists on selected economic issues, on average. There is no guarantee, however, that all people with more economic knowledge will hold such opinions because even among the more informed and knowledgeable there can be differences of opinion that reflect underlying differences in economic attitudes, which are more deeply held and more difficult to change. In fact, US studies of principles of economics instruction found conflicting evidence on whether the study of economics in the United States led students to become more conservative or liberal on economic issues.
2. In Estonia the survey was conducted in 1992. National teams were responsible for conducting these surveys, with a target sample size of 1,500 adults in each nation.
3. Data from the early period of reform (1990 to 1992) reported by Miller, Hesli, and Reisinger (1994, p. 406) show Russian support for rapid reform dropping from 43 percent in 1990 to 37 percent in 1992. In Lithuania, it fell from 86 percent in 1990 to 45 percent in 1992. For Ukraine the percentage declined slightly, from 39 percent in 1990 to 37 percent in 1992. Fleron and Ahl (1998, p. 300) drew the same conclusion from various surveys on changes in Russian attitudes towards transition from 1990 to 1993: support for a rapid transition to a market eroded and support for a gradualist approach increased. Hough and Lehmann (1998) reached the same conclusion based on survey trends from 1993 to 1996. See also Mason and Sidorenko-Stephenson (1997). In eastern European nations, however, the opinions about the pace were more supportive of the transition. Hayo (1997) analyzed survey data from 1990 to 1992 and found that in Czechoslovakia people thought the change to a market economy was too slow, while respondents in Hungary and Poland were relatively satisfied with the pace of the transition.
4. Further evidence comes from Fleron and Ahl (1998, pp. 298-300). They review many studies and state: 'with respect to economic reform the weight of the evidence seems to point to the conclusion that there is only limited support for a western-style economy in Russia' (p. 300).
5. See also Gerber (2000) for a theoretical model and empirical study showing the direct influence of economic ideology on political participation.
6. Similar patterns have been found across demographic and socio-economic groups in their support for political reforms in the transition economies. For example, Gibson, Duch, and Tedin (1992) concluded: 'The best predictors of attitudes toward general democratic values were education, gender, and age' (p. 329). A good summary of the studies on attitudes toward political reforms is provided in Firebaugh and Sandu (1998).

7. Bahry (1999) also raises the issue of how the way questions are asked affects responses. In surveys conducted in Russia, she gives examples of how respondents can be viewed as being collectivist in their thinking on some questions and market-oriented in their thinking on other questions even if the questions are related to the same topic.
8. For 1996 data for Russia on these items see Mason and Sidorenko-Stephenson (1997). There is little change in these views from 1991 to 1996.
9. The support for government intervention on the income and jobs issues appears to be relatively stable over time. Survey data from 1991 and 1996 reported by Kluegel, Mason, and Wegener (1999, p. 280) showed strong support for government intervention to guarantee a basic income and provide a job remained relatively constant in five post-communist nations (Bulgaria, Czech Republic, East Germany, Hungary, and Russia). The percentages on the income and jobs issues for the post-communist nations were substantially higher than those for three western nations (Britain, Germany, and the United States) in 1991.
10. Some of the differences between the FSU and ECE nations may have to do with the extent of change in government structures and policies during the transition. Harvard economist Andrei Shleifer (1997) used survey data on attitudes toward capitalism and 'social capital,' or the idea that people in different nations appear to have different levels of willingness to trust other people, to investigate whether the different progress in reform programs in Russia and Poland occurred because, as has often been claimed, Russia is 'socially and culturally incapable of good government.' While admitting that it is difficult to identify the causes of the undeniably poor record of the Russian government, Shleifer concludes that, rather than differences in popular support or acceptance of market reforms and institutions, 'the more convincing argument is that Russia has not had as radical a change in its government, in terms of both structure and personnel, as Poland or the Czech Republic' (p. 405).
11. Lopus (1996) conducted a small sample study of Russian and US teachers' economic attitudes in 1993. She found that 'Russian teachers are more likely to agree, or to agree more strongly, that the government should control unemployment and inflation, should redistribute income and ensure product safety, and should provide health care for all citizens' (p. 247). This finding is important because teachers' attitudes and knowledge about economics can influence what students know and think.
12. The two items are reproduced in Table 2.12.
13. One possible reason for this growing aversion to privatization, however, may be that economic conditions had changed from 1993 to 1996. By 1996 many large enterprises had already been privatized, so the large enterprises left to privatize were different, and perhaps more like a public good or less amenable to privatization for other reasons.
14. Similar findings were reported by Osborn (1998, p. 42) based on 1991 surveys in Poland, Hungary, and the Czech Republic.
15. In practice, many of the governments of the transition economies have been hard pressed to provide basic services, including housing, heat, and food, to pensioners and other low-income groups. That raises questions about the true willingness of the public, and government officials, to act on these verbal expressions of public opinions, which involve no direct costs — unlike the actual policies required to act on these sentiments.
16. See Listhaug and Aalberg (1999) for similar findings on work incentives and the need for income inequality raised in this section. Kluegel, Mason, and Wegener (1999, p. 280) also provide survey data for 1991 and 1996 on these issues in five post-communist nations that support the basic conclusions in this section.
17. See Walstad (1997) and Walstad and Rebeck (2002) for examples of public opinion data from the United States on support for gas or oil price controls. Those studies show that there are positive effects of economic education on the acceptance of market-determined outcomes and less support for government intervention in markets among those with more economic education.
18. Earlier studies had noted that a majority of over 2,000 economists from the United States, France, West Germany, Austria, and Switzerland favored price adjustments to eliminate shortages or excess demand (Frey et al., 1984), but a large majority of samples from two Canadian cities (Kahneman, Knetsch, and Thaler, 1986) and from Zurich and West Berlin (Frey and Pommerehne, 1993) viewed price increases in these situations as inherently unfair, particularly if the cause was a temporary or short-term increase in demand for a product.
19. For further description of the content of these teacher workshops and their effects on the economic understanding and attitudes of students see Chapter 4 in this volume, by William B. Walstad.

20. In addition to the survey research reviewed in this chapter, see also Chapters 4 and 5 in this volume, by William B. Walstad and Craig MacPhee, respectively.

REFERENCES

Allgood, S. and W.B. Walstad (1999), 'The longitudinal effects of economic education on teachers and their students,' *Journal of Economic Education*, **30** (2), pp. 99-111.

Bahry, D. (1999), 'Comrades into citizens? Russian political culture and public support for the transition,' *Slavic Review*, **58** (4), pp. 841-53.

Becker, W.E., W.B. Walstad, and M. Watts (1994), 'A comparison of the views of economists, economic educators, teachers, and journalists on economic issues,' in W.B. Walstad (ed.), *An International Perspective on Economic Education*, Boston, Massachusetts, USA: Kluwer Academic Publishers, pp. 65-87.

Beron, K. (1990), 'Joint determination of current classroom performance and additional economics classes: A binary/continuous model,' *Journal of Economic Education*, **30** (2), pp. 99-111.

Clarke, S. (1993), 'Popular attitudes to the transition to a market economy in the Soviet Union on the eve of reform,' *Sociological Review*, **41** (4), pp. 619-52.

Colton, T.J. (2000), *Transitional Citizens: Voters and What Influences Them in the New Russia*, Cambridge, Massachusetts: Harvard University Press.

Duch, R.M. (1993), 'Tolerating economic reform: Popular support for transition to a free market in the former Soviet Union,' *American Political Science Review*, **87** (3), pp. 590-608.

Duch, R.M. (1995), 'Economic chaos and the fragility of democratic transition in former communist regimes,' *Journal of Politics*, **57** (1), pp. 121-58.

Finifter, A.W. (1996), 'Attitudes toward individual responsibility and political reform in the former Soviet Union,' *American Political Science Review*, **90** (1), pp. 138-52.

Finifter, A.W. and E. Mickiewicz (1992), 'Redefining the political system of the USSR: Mass support for political change,' *American Political Science Review*, **86** (4), pp. 857-74.

Firebaugh, G. and D. Sandu (1998), 'Who supports marketization and democratization in post-communist Romania?,' *Sociological Forum*, **13** (3), pp. 521-41.

Fleron, F., J. Hahn, and W. Reisinger (1997), 'Public opinion surveys and political culture in post-Soviet Russia,' occasional paper #266 (transcription), Washington, DC: Kennan Institute for Advanced Russian Studies, April 24.

Fleron, F.J. and R. Ahl (1998), 'Does the public matter for democratization in Russia? What we have learned from "third wave" transitions and public opinion surveys,' in H. Eckstein, F.J. Fleron, E.P. Hoffmann, and W.M. Reisinger (eds), *Can Democracy Take Root in Post-Soviet Russia: Exploration in State-Society Relations*, Lanham, Maryland: Rowman and Littlefield, pp. 287-330.

Frey, B.S. et al. (1984), 'Consensus and dissension among economists: An empirical inquiry,' *American Economic Review*, **74** (5), pp. 986-94.

Frey, B.S. and W.W. Pommerehne (1993), 'On the fairness of pricing: An empirical survey among the general population,' *Journal of Economic Behavior and Organization*, **20** (3), pp. 295-307.

Gerber, T.P. (2000), 'Market, state, or don't know? Education, economic ideology, and voting in contemporary Russia,' *Social Forces*, **79** (2), pp. 477-521.

Gibson, J.L. (1996), 'Political and economic markets: Changes in the connections between attitudes toward political democracy and a market economy within the mass culture of Russia and Ukraine,' *Journal of Politics*, **58** (4), pp. 954-84.

Gibson, J.L., R. Duch, and K. Tedin (1992), 'Democratic values and the transformation of the Soviet Union,' *Journal of Politics*, **54** (2), pp. 329-70.

Hayo, B. (1997), 'Eastern European public opinion and economic issues: Privatization and transformation,' *American Journal of Economics and Sociology*, **56** (1), pp. 86-102.

Hough, J.F. and S.G. Lehmann (1998), 'The mystery of opponents of economic reform among Yeltsin voters,' in M.S. Wyman, S. White, and S. Oates (eds), *Elections and Voters in Post-communist Russia*, Cheltenham, UK and Northampton, Massachusetts, USA: Edward Elgar, pp. 190-227.

Kahneman, D., J. Knetsch, and R. Thaler (1986), 'Fairness as constraint on profit seeking: Entitlements in the market,' *American Economic Review*, **76** (Sept.), pp. 728-41.

Kluegel, J.S, D.S. Mason, and B. Wegener (1999), 'The legitimation of capitalism in the postcommunist transition: Public opinion about market justice,' *European Sociological Review*, **15** (3), pp. 251-83.

Listhaug, O. and T. Aalberg (1999), 'Comparative public opinion on distributive justice: A study of equality ideals and attitudes toward current policies,' *International Journal of Comparative Sociology*, **40** (1), pp. 117-40.

Lopus, J. (1996), 'Russian teachers and American teachers: Attitudes about the economy,' in W.B. Walstad (ed.), *Secondary Economics and Business Education: New Developments in the United Kingdom, United States, and Other Nations*, West Essex, UK: Economics and Business Education.

Mason, D.S. (1995), 'Attitudes toward the market and political participation in postcommunist states,' *Slavic Review*, **54** (2), pp. 385-406.

Mason, D.S. and S. Sidorenko-Stephenson (1997), 'Public opinion and the 1996 elections in Russia: Nostalgic and statist, yet pro-market and pro-Yeltsin,' *Slavic Review*, **56** (4), pp. 698-717.

Miller, A.H., V.L. Hesli, and W.M. Reisinger (1994), 'Reassessing mass support for political and economic change in the former USSR,' *American Political Science Review*, **88** (2), pp. 399-411.

Miller, W.L., S. White, and P. Heywood (1998), *Values and Political Change in Postcommunist Europe*, London: Macmillan Press.

Osborn, E.A. (1998), 'Attitudes toward privatization in Poland, Hungary, and the Czech Republic,' *International Journal of Sociology*, **28** (2), pp. 36-64.

Powers, D.V. and J.H. Cox (1997), 'Echoes from the past: The relationship between satisfaction with economic reforms and voting behavior in Poland,' *American Political Science Review*, **91** (3), pp. 617-33.

Roller, E. (1994), 'Ideological bias of the market economy: Attitudes toward distribution problems and the role of government in western and eastern Germany,' *European Sociological Review*, **10** (2), pp. 105-17.

Shiller, R.J., M. Boycko, and V. Korobov (1991), 'Popular attitudes toward free markets: The Soviet Union and the United States compared,' *American Economic Review*, **81** (3), pp. 385-400.

Shleifer, A. (1997), 'Government in transition,' *European Economic Review*, **41**, pp. 385-410.

Spiro, J. (2000), *International Education Exchange Program (IEEP): Program Results, 1995-2000*, New York: Education Development Center, Inc.

Walstad, W.B. (1987), 'Applying two-stage least squares,' in W. Becker and W.B. Walstad (eds), *Econometric Modeling in Economic Education Research*, Boston: Kluwer Nijhoff Publishing, pp. 111-34.

Walstad, W.B. (1996), 'Economic knowledge and the formation of economic opinions and attitudes,' in P. Lunt and A. Furnham (eds), *Economic Socialization: The Economic Beliefs and Behaviours of Young People*, Cheltenham, UK and Brookfield, Massachusetts, USA: Edward Elgar, pp. 162-82.

Walstad, W.B. (1997), 'The effects of economic knowledge on public opinion of economic issues on teachers and their students,' *Journal of Economic Education*, **15** (3), pp. 195-210.

Walstad, W.B. and K. Rebeck (2002, forthcoming), 'Assessing the economic knowledge and economic opinions of adults,' *Quarterly Review of Economics and Finance*.

Watts, M. (1987), 'Ideology, textbooks, and the teaching of economics,' *Theory into Practice*, **26**, pp. 190-7.

Watts, M. (1994), 'Economists' ideological conflicts and consensus on economic issues. and their implications for economic education,' in W.B. Walstad (ed.), *An International Perspective on Economic Education*, Boston, Massachusetts, USA: Kluwer Academic Publishers, pp. 47-64.

Whaples, R. (1995), 'Changes in attitudes among college economics students about the fairness of the market,' *Journal of Economic Education*, **26** (4), pp. 308-13.

Whitefield, S. and G. Evans (1994), 'The Russian election of 1993: Public opinion and the transition experience,' *Post-Soviet Affairs*, **10**, pp. 38-60.

3. Reforming Undergraduate Economics Instruction in Russia, Belarus, and Ukraine: Curriculum, Personnel, and Clientele Issues

Alexander Kovzik and Michael Watts

In many respects, Russia, Belarus, and Ukraine were the 'core' nations of both the Soviet economic and educational systems. Today these three nations are still closely linked in many respects, and face many common problems in terms of economic and educational reforms. All three nations have lagged well behind the pace of economic reform and recovery in such transition economies as Poland, Hungary, and the Baltic nations; but their circumstances and policies also differ from one another in some key respects.

In this chapter we review the restructuring of undergraduate economics instruction at Moscow State University (MSU) since 1989, at the end of the Soviet period. Then we consider how closely the reforms at Moscow State are, or are not, mirrored by changes at Belarus State University (BSU) in Minsk, and at Kiev State University (KSU). We extend this discussion by offering an 'insider's' perspective on several issues related to curriculum reform that go well beyond what can be determined by looking only at published curriculum guides. Specifically, we consider such issues as the training and retraining of faculty members who teach courses in these departments; the use of translated textbooks from the United States or other western nations vs. locally-developed textbooks; problems that arise in departments where some faculty members teach western economics while others continue to teach Soviet-style economics; and a very brief discussion of some emerging trends for graduate study in economics in the former Soviet Union (FSU).[1]

The three universities we discuss are clearly the preeminent universities in these nations. During the Soviet period, MSU was recognized as *the* flagship university among all of the national flagships in the Soviet bloc. Today it continues to set educational standards and benchmarks for many other universities across the former Soviet Union. That is true even in economics, which has almost certainly faced more curriculum and staff changes than any other discipline since the breakup of the Soviet Union. Currently, undergraduate economics instruction all across Russia must meet a State educational standard that was adopted by the State Committee of Higher Education on 28 March 1994. However, as we discuss below, MSU has implemented many significant reforms in its economics program since 1994, which have been widely adopted by other Russian universities – and for that matter at many universities outside of Russia in the FSU. Belarus State University provides a clear example of such influence. The Ministry of Education for Belarus does not write its own standard for economics or other subject areas, as in Russia. Instead the ministry ranks all of the university departments in every educational field, and then the curriculum for the highest-ranked department is adopted by the ministry and becomes compulsory for all other departments in that field at other state universities. The department of economics at BSU has been selected as the highest-ranked department in economic theory. But in the introduction to the 1998 BSU curriculum guide for economics, it is noted that the BSU curriculum was developed to reflect the Russian educational standard as it is taught at MSU.

MSU has played a key leadership role in the restructuring of the undergraduate economics program in several other ways since 1989, such as hosting several international conferences on this topic.[2] But by the same token, there has been considerable decentralization in political and educational structures in the FSU countries in this period, which makes it interesting to compare the current state of the economics programs across some of these leading universities. Just as the economic transitions in these nations are providing natural experiments for institutional arrangements, incentive structures, and economic policies on a scale seldom seen, the teaching of economics at all levels in the FSU is undergoing its own transition. That transition, too, offers the chance to study institutional structures and reforms, and to understand better both academic and political views of economics in these countries.

I. A BRIEF REVIEW OF EARLIER STUDIES

Several earlier articles by western economists have traced the long and erratic history of bringing mainstream western economics into the curriculum of universities in the FSU. Those initiatives date back at least to a highly restricted distribution of a translation of Paul Samuelson's principles textbook, *Economics*, in the 1960s (see Gerschenkorn, 1978). Of course, officially the purpose of that 'reform' was to permit better critiques of market economics, not to change the training or teaching of future generations of Soviet economists.

Until the late 1980s the state policies establishing a uniquely Soviet style of economics were, for the most part, achieved. In their article 'Economics in the Former Soviet Union,' Michael Alexeev, Clifford Gaddy, and Jim Leitzel (1992, pp. 138-9) concluded that 'in the mid-1980s, the principle role of Soviet economists had been to explain why the policies which the state had already implemented were in fact optimal.' And they found that even in the early 1990s, 'In reality, the training of economists in the Soviet Union and the United States is fundamentally different. The average Soviet economist has less in common with an American economist than do American economists with American sociologists or other social scientists.'

There were two major types of economics training and research under the Soviet system, and these two groups are still represented in most university economics departments in the former Soviet Union today. Under the old economic and academic systems, the title 'economist' generally referred to practitioners from the first and far larger group of political economists, whose work was typically

> historical and descriptive, and completely devoid of mathematics. It uses a conceptual framework that is derived from the 'historical materialism' of previous decades of Soviet economics. There is no behavioral modeling, nor any appeal to individual rational economic behavior... (Alexeev et al., p. 141)

In contrast, after 1960 a much smaller group of Soviet mathematical economists followed the work pioneered by L.V. Kantorovich, V.S. Nemchinov, and V.V. Novozhilov. Generally, this work features proofs and other sophisticated mathematics, often with very little verbal discussion. Two particular branches of this work deal with forecasting featuring non-behavioral models (such as Kondratiev waves), and models of the system of optimal functioning of the socialist economy (SOFE) that deal with

> optimization methods of production, efficiency concerns, information flows among subsystems, and shadow price calculations. Traditionally, the system-wide objective function has been assumed to be determined by the highest level of the hierarchy, the central planners. Shadow prices generated within the optimization models of SOFE provided a guide toward economic reform proposals, but the system-wide objective function limited the scope of the proposals to the framework of a centrally planned economy. (Alexeev et al., p. 142)

Not surprisingly, there have been many disputes between these two groups of Soviet economists about the usefulness or lack of success of each approach. That dispute includes charges against both approaches that are similar, in some ways, to recent complaints about the overemphasis of mathematics and statistics in the US graduate training of Ph.D. students in economics (see Krueger et al., 1991 and Hansen, 1991). Nevertheless, from a western and more general perspective, in early 1992 Alexeev et al. concluded that

> while political economists have significant institutional knowledge, and mathematical economists have outstanding quantitative skills, neither variety of Soviet economist has the mindset of a typical economist from a market-oriented country. Almost all Soviet economists that we talked with agreed that Soviet economists in general do not understand even the basic principles of the workings of markets. (p. 145)

But many things began to change for economics departments in the FSU during the period of *perestroika*, and especially during the mid- to late-1990s. Ironically, one of the last acts of the communist government in the FSU was the approval to translate, publish, and use in the universities a basic textbook on market economics (see Brue and MacPhee, 1995, p. 182). A team of eight Russian economists, headed by Anatoly Porokhovsky, spent two years translating the 1990 edition of the best-selling US principles textbook, *Economics*, by Campbell McConnell and Stanley Brue. Unlike the limited distribution of the Samuelson translation some 30 years earlier, 500,000 copies of the McConnell and Brue textbook were published for widespread use at Russian universities, and pirated copies were soon available to the general public in bookstores and from street vendors. Many other textbooks at the secondary and university level, and a later edition of McConnell and Brue, have now been translated and widely distributed. For a partial list of these materials see Rushing (1994).

Changes in the curriculum for economics degrees have also been made. Comparing course requirements at Moscow State University in 1992 to those that prevailed a few years earlier, Brue and MacPhee concluded:

> Gone is the Marxist-Lenninist beginning course. Gone are the special seminars on Marx's *Capital*, the theory of imperialism, and the political economy of socialism. Gone are the state exams. It is relatively easy to substitute a standard western title for each of the courses in the listing. That was not true for the old curriculum. (pp. 189-90)

In 1992 and now, there were and are several important caveats to this rather optimistic appraisal. First, there were still some courses in the MSU curriculum, such as a required course on the history of religion (in the Soviet curriculum, this was the course on scientific atheism), which had no counterparts in most western universities' economics majors. Second, the people teaching the courses in the new curriculum were, for the most part (with departments in the former East Germany providing a notable exception) the same people who taught economics courses in the old curriculum. What ultimately matters, of course, is what is actually taught in the curriculum, not just the new titles of various courses. Using instructors with little or no formal training in western economics, and indeed who were trained in very different and often conflicting approaches may be, as Brue and MacPhee noted, 'like assigning a creationist to teach evolution' (1995, p. 189). Third, using translations of US or western textbooks to teach courses in Russia or eastern Europe solves some problems, but creates others in terms of the relevance of examples used in the books and discussions of institutions, public policies, and economic circumstances. Fourth, there is considerable bureaucratic and individual faculty opposition to the wholesale and uncritical adoption of western economics. Generally, as Rushing and others have pointed out (for example, see the discussion of a 1992 survey by Boeva and Shironin in Lipton and Sachs, 1992), there is more support for market reforms among younger segments of the population in eastern Europe and the FSU than there is among older groups. That is hardly surprising, and in economics departments the pattern is even more expected given costs and benefits related to training, retraining, and the obsolescence of human capital built up under the Soviet system.

One response to these factors represents, at best, a more diplomatic reaction than outright rejection of curriculum reforms, while searching for a path that is feasible for and more acceptable to the majority of faculty members who were trained as political economists. There have been frequent and persistent discussions about developing a new, 'third way' for teaching economics that endorses neither capitalism nor socialism. At the very least, it is argued, the new economics curriculum must stress historical and current conditions and institutions in Russia and the other transition economies. Some possible approaches to this 'third way' were outlined as early as 1990 by A.R. Markov, who was then assistant dean of the school of economics at MSU. The potential problems with these third-way solutions are easy to see, and Alexeev et al. (1992) noted that the two such approaches described by Markov 'sound suspiciously like a minor repackaging of the political economy of socialism' (p. 147).

II. CURRENT DEGREE REQUIREMENTS

Moscow State University

Appendix 3.A lists required and elective courses for the four-year general economics program at MSU for the 1998-99 and 1999-2000 academic years. There are numerous changes here compared to the 1992 curriculum for MSU reported by Brue and MacPhee (1995, p.189). As noted in the curriculum guide published in 1995, many of those changes took place from 1994-95 when the MSU economics department worked with representatives from the London School of Economics, the Sorborne University in Paris, and the University of Tilburg in the Netherlands, with the explicit aim of bringing the MSU curriculum as closely in line with international standards as possible.

But many additional changes were made after 1995. For example, in 1995 students had to choose areas of specialization in either general economics or mathematical economics. Now there is a common program for all students until the seventh and eighth semesters, at which time students can choose to specialize in one of the six different areas listed at the end of Appendix 3.A.

In 1995 the baccalaureate program in general economic theory required coursework in two areas that were largely unrelated: (1) micro- and macroeconomics (148 hours) and (2) the theory of the transition economy (90 hours).[3] After completing those courses students took further coursework on economic theory and mathematical methods (166 hours). The current program requires separate courses on microeconomics (I and II), macroeconomics (I and II), and the theory of the transitional economy. In all of the micro and macro theory courses, students can choose from two alternative programs, featuring different emphasis on mathematics. All the required micro and macro theory courses use translated American textbooks. For instance, in microeconomics I students use the principles textbook by McConnell and Brue *and* an intermediate textbook (either David Hyman's or Hal Varian's *Intermediate Economics*). Even more noteworthy, perhaps, is that the course on the theory of transition economies has become more focused on coverage of the same basic concepts, featuring textbooks written by MSU faculty with such titles as *The Theory of Transitional Economy: Macroeconomics* and *The Theory of Transitional Economy: Microeconomics.*

Although the introductory course on Marxist-Leninist theory was dropped in the 1992 curriculum, as Brue and MacPhee (1995) pointed out as late as the 1995 curriculum there was still a seminar on *Das Kapital* (96 hours). In the description of this course in the 1995 curriculum guide, Professor A.I. Yudkin and his colleagues stressed that 'the method of *Das Kapital* allows one to get into the inside structure of bourgeois society and to understand the logic of modern social-economic processes' (p. 125). Two other seemingly quite different seminars, on Alfred Marshall (51 hours) and J.M. Keynes (48 hours), were in fact taught by the same group of professors who taught the course on Marx. So it is likely that in these courses, too, the method of *Das Kapital* helped instructors and students to understand the logic and inside workings of the major works by Marshall and Keynes. In the latest curriculum guide all these seminars are gone, although the elective course titled 'Introduction to Political Economy' is still taught from the Marxist perspective.

Other holdovers from the old (Soviet) system of instruction are found in the required course on the history of economic thought. In this area the only western textbook that has been translated into Russian is Marc Blaug's *History of Economic Analysis*. Consequently, students still read Russian textbooks written in the 1960s and 1970s, obviously in the Marxist tradition. But imagine the different effect of such readings and courses on students today, who were four or five years old when *perestroika* began, and who now take these courses after completing courses on western, market-oriented micro- and macroeconomics.

There are numerous other reforms that have taken place at the level of topic coverage in specific courses. For example, in the 1995 MSU curriculum guide the course description for economic history featured such terms as Lenin's 'monopolistic capitalism.' In the current guide many of those terms are gone.

The other major development is the first appearance of a wide range of new required and elective courses on such topics as international economics, industrial organization, and the economics of the public sector. These courses are taught using translated textbooks by Peter Lindert, F.M. Scherer and David Ross, and Joseph Stiglitz, respectively. It is indeed now difficult to think of major topics covered in undergraduate economics programs at US and other western universities that are not reflected directly in the MSU curriculum. The introduction of these courses and textbooks has also played a crucial role in changing the content and approach in some other courses that still sound different from US course offerings. For example, the course on socioeconomic statistics now features a detailed description of the system of national income accounts that reflects mainstream international standards.

There is a heavy emphasis on mathematics in the current undergraduate program at MSU, which generally exceeds that found in US and other western departments. Actually, this is not a new feature – during the Soviet period candidates for departments of political economy were expected to pass rigorous entrance exams in mathematics and then to complete approximately the same number of credit hours in mathematics courses as are currently required. But that led many students to ask *why* there was such an emphasis on mathematics, because there was never a connection between the math courses they were required to take and their courses on political economy. Nor were they ever expected to use mathematics after they graduated and went on to teach or work as political economists. Instead, given the level of precollege mathematics education in the Soviet system, the high math requirements served as a way to screen out weaker students and promote the 'scientific' status of political economy. Today students can readily see the connection between the mathematics they take and their intermediate and advanced courses in economic theory, which often feature prerequisites in mathematics. There is also a new feature in the most recent MSU curriculum, in allowing students to take elective courses on various mathematical methods.

In the preface of the latest edition of the MSU curriculum guide, vice-dean A. Khodzhaev writes that the new curriculum is based on basic economic concepts and theory, but offers a much broader range of electives and specializations than the previous curriculum. He also notes that the faculty at MSU worked very diligently to insure both 'vertical and horizontal coordination' between subjects. The long-time dean of the MSU Economics Department, Vasily Kolesov, then notes that there are many new institutions in the Russian educational market, offering 'international' diplomas and attracting students using courses with exotic titles. But Kolesov believes that, in truth, the level of instruction provided at these new institutions is well below international standards. It is clear to us that the level of economics instruction at MSU today is far above the average in the FSU.

Belarus State University

Appendix 3.B shows course requirements for the two basic economics degree programs now offered at Belarus State University. BSU continues to use a five-year curriculum for students majoring in economics. While the BSU program is less influential than the MSU program, it is perhaps also more representative in terms of the typical pattern of course offerings and requirements and the level of rigor of undergraduate economics instruction in the FSU.

The economic theory specialization at BSU is the program that evolved from the political economy program of the Soviet period, which was then offered by the Philosophical Economics Department. That department offered two other majors during the Soviet period: sociology and philosophy. About 1995, following the revised structure at Moscow State University and other leading universities in the FSU, the department at Belarus State also began to offer a specialization or major in management. Finally, in 1999, the economics group completely separated from the philosophy department. Related to that reorganization, a new dean (a mathematician who had worked for the national government with the National Bank of Belarus) decided to offer another new specialization, in economics. It is not yet fully clear what will be included in this specialization, compared to the specialization in economic theory; but in general terms economic theory appears to be a mixture of economics and political economy, while economics is described as a mixture of economics, mathematical economics, and applied economics.

The first students were admitted to the new BSU specialization in economics in the summer of 1999. At that time, to help distinguish between the two specializations, the dean announced that the economic theory major is intended for future teachers of economic sciences (basically future university teachers), while the 'economics' major is more appropriate training for economic analysts who will work for the government or firms.[4] This process – which has left even BSU faculty members uncertain about what courses will be taught in each specialization, and who will teach them – might suggest a lower degree of faculty governance at Belarus State than might be observed at many US universities. But on the other hand that may be more a matter of appearance and process than practical reality, if one considers how fast deans in US universities can have new courses and majors approved when they really want them.

As in the MSU curriculum, there are several required basic theory courses in the BSU curriculum: principles of economics (70 hours), microeconomics (140 hours), macroeconomics (72 hours), and international economics (68 hours). Half of these hours are lectures and half are seminars or recitation sections. The main textbook for the principles course is the translated version of McConnell and Brue. In the first semester students cover the sections of the book dealing with fundamental concepts and microeconomics. The emphasis is more on intuition and the structure of the discipline, rather than technical matters such as graphs and algebra – but it is important to remember that these students generally are much better prepared in mathematics than their US counterparts. The second semester is devoted to macroeconomics and the world economy. At the end of each semester students must pass an oral exam to demonstrate their understanding of the main topics in the course and textbook.

During the second and third semesters students study microeconomics using a translated version of *Modern Microeconomics* by Hyman. or for those who understand English, *Microeconomics* by Katz and Rosen. In seminars/recitation sections, students solve questions from the study guides and workbooks for these texts. Sophomores are also required to choose one major topic from the course and write an overview of the available literature on the topic in a 25 to 30-page term paper.

Starting in the third semester, students study intermediate macroeconomics using Russian translations of the textbooks by Mankiw and by Dornbusch and Fisher. Then students take a course on international economics that is closely correlated with the coursework on macroeconomics, and based on a translated version of Lindert's textbook. Third-year students have further coursework on macroeconomics, in which they work with macroeconomic data for Belarus. To pass these courses students must receive high scores on written final exams.

Other upper-level courses complement this stress on mainstream economics. Since 1999, BSU students have also been required to take a one-semester course in industrial organization using a translated version of the textbook by Scherer and Ross. Since 1997 there has been a required, one-semester course on the economics of the public sector using the textbook by Stiglitz. The course on the economy in transition, which deals with problems of economic policy in the FSU, is closely linked to the macroeconomics and international economics courses. In this course seniors are required to prepare an essay or case study on the economic role of government. Their basic task in this paper is to apply theoretical models to the real-world problems facing transition economies.

There are many frustrations facing the BSU professors who teach courses on labor economics, the economics of the firm (or enterprise), and agricultural economics. Substantively, they would like to change their course content to fit the new emphasis on economic theory, but the unavailability of suitable textbooks is a major obstacle. Some courses, such as the course on basic principles of entrepreneurship and management, are taught by professors whose background is definitely not in these areas. Such problems remain very common at almost every university in the FSU.

As in the MSU curriculum, the Marxist courses on political economy and the seminar on *Das Kapital* are still taught in the economic theory specialty (for future university economists) at BSU, the first as a required course and the second in the specialization in history of economic thought. Furthermore, the course on economic policy in the economic theory specialization has nothing in common with economic policy courses that are taught in the West – instead it is based partly on articles and books by Lenin. In the economics specialization, the economic policy and transition economy courses are taught from a western perspective. Again as at MSU, the courses in the specialty area on the history of economic thought (208 hours) are still taught using textbooks written from 1960 to the 1980s, featuring Soviet-style economics.[5]

Kiev State University

Appendix 3.C shows course requirements for the economics program at Kiev State University. Except for courses that deal specifically with Ukraine rather than Russia or Belarus, and the addition of an internship, the program is very similar to those at BSU and MSU. Indeed, many of the same Russian and western textbooks are used in key courses. The same courses on Marx's *Das Kapital* and the history of economic thought are still included as a specialty area. Some apparent differences are, in fact, only a matter of differences in course titles, rather than content. For example, the KSU course on 'theory of finance' covers the same material as the BSU course on 'economics of the public sector.'

Summarizing our comparison of the three programs, we find that while there are minor differences relating to general education requirements, courses on national institutions and policies, and the length of the degree programs, all three programs are very much alike in terms of the amount of 'holdover material' from the Soviet period, and how much western economics – and even what western textbooks – are covered. In those key respects it is almost as if there were no borders between three countries. But in fact it is probably more accurate to say that MSU is still the flagship that other leading universities in the FSU emulate, just as they did 10-20 years ago.

III. ISSUES BEYOND COURSE REQUIREMENTS

There were three required ideological disciplines in the curriculum of every university in the USSR: political economy, Marxist-Leninist philosophy, and scientific communism. The textbook for coursework on the political economy of capitalism was nothing more than a simplified version of *Das Kapital*, with descriptions of some modern problems and issues. The principal goal of this textbook and coursework was to prove that all of Marx's major conclusions about the failures of capitalism and its inherent exploitation of labor still held.

If you examine any thesis that was defended as a doctoral dissertation in political economy anywhere in the USSR, you will read in the conclusion that the author claims to have found some new evidence of the deepening crisis of capitalism. Over time this left Soviet professors of political economy in a rather remarkable position that provided the subject for a lot of jokes among students: the professors taught courses criticizing capitalism, but most of them had never been in any capitalist country even once to see these deepening crises firsthand.

Economics Professors in the FSU

It is important for western observers trying to understand the current reform of economics in the FSU to realize that there were two different groups of Soviet professors of political economy, especially after the late 1970s and early 1980s. The first group truly believed what they wrote and taught, and for them *Das Kapital* was a kind of religious text. The second group was far more pragmatic: they taught Marxist-Leninist political economy only because that was what they were required to teach. This group was, admittedly, in a pretty two-faced position, because 'in the kitchen' they told very different stories about the western economy to each other, or even to their students. But predictably, the readiness to reform economics coursework and curriculums at the beginning of the 1990s differed greatly among these two groups.

In many key respects the professors of political economy who were disenchanted with the Soviet curriculum were the natural choice to teach the restructured courses. As students and professors they worked in courses on the history of economic thought. Ideologically these courses had to prove the crises of the bourgeois political economy, but perhaps even more important, as it turned out, these were the only courses where the names and ideas of Marshall, Keynes, Joan Robinson, and other western economists were discussed. In the BSU Department of Political Economy, for example, in the late 1970s the history of thought courses entailed 110 hours of lectures and 110 hours of seminars. At least half of this time was devoted to western economists. Students in these courses could also attend a special, 36-hour course on consumer behavior, which covered some basic topics of mainstream economics.

Therefore, while it may seem paradoxical, when the time came to teach economics using the McConnell and Brue textbook in the early 1990s, the vanguard of supporters of mainstream economics was largely made up of professors who had specialized previously in the critique of bourgeois political economy. These professors were also the first group to translate and edit western textbooks for use in Russia, and to publish their own articles on teaching, student guides, and so on. Many of these professors had also studied English, which naturally gave them a major advantage in reading western economics.

Course Content and Textbooks

When governments in the FSU nations proclaimed the transition to a market economy as a main goal of society in the early 1990s, it became untenable for Marxist political economy to maintain its former place in the university curriculum. Most departments of political economy were soon renamed as departments of economic theory. But then the problem became one of defining what was really meant by economic theory. There is still a strong belief among some faculty that it is more important for students to know 'Why is the economy structured as it is?' rather than 'How does the economy work?' These faculty members also claim that western economics does not provide 'economic laws' to explain the transition from one kind of economic system to another. They therefore do not agree to treat mainstream economics as a substitute for Soviet-style political economy in the curriculum. Instead, they often try to incorporate some current topics into the old political economy textbooks and publish them as 'Economic Theory.' Such books were widely published in Russia, Ukraine, and Belarus in the early 1990s.

One example of such a textbook is a second edition of an economic theory textbook that was published in Belarus in 1999 by some members of the faculty of Belarus State Economic University (not BSU), and approved by the Ministry of Education as a textbook for students majoring in economics and business. There are four sections in the book: fundamentals of economic theory, microeconomics, macroeconomics, and international economics. The chapters comprising the fundamentals section are:

Chapter 1.   Economic theory as a science.
Chapter 2.   Economic system of society.
Chapter 3.   The social and economic essence of property relations.
Chapter 4.   Production: main features, factors, and results.
             Reproduction (investment) and its phases.
Chapter 5.   Types of formations (the natural economy and the
             commodity economy).
Chapter 6.   Markets: functions and structure.
Chapter 7.   Transition economies: essence, peculiarities, and
             tendencies. The role of government.

It is obvious that this section of the textbook was written by Marxist economists. The labor theory of value and surplus value are still central to the analysis, and it is stated flatly that 'the methods of economic theory are based on dialectical materialism' (p. 15). Commodities, money, and the reproduction and circulation of the aggregate stock of social capital are described as they always were in Marxist textbooks. In 140 pages, there is only one graph. But there is one very important difference to note, compared to Marxist textbooks written in earlier decades: the authors include many quotes from western economists *without* criticizing them. In fact, this is done so often that it appears the authors are not so much opposed to the market system as they are unable to explain it, except in the ways they were taught to do so 30 or 40 years ago.

Certainly this section of the textbook does not prepare students to read the three later sections. In truth, it is often the case for this kind of textbook that the different sections are written by different authors, with little or no coordination and cross-referencing across sections. Typically, the fundamental and methodological parts of the book are written by professors who are 60 years old or older, who either fear, do not know, or simply do not want to dive into all the graphs and math of western economics. The micro- and macroeconomic theory sections are usually written by economists who are about 40 years old, and mostly self-educated in mainstream economics.

Personnel Issues

In the former East Germany Soviet-style professors of political economy were simply fired and replaced, but in the rest of the FSU these professors are still on the faculty. Occasionally they still fight to teach Marx and Soviet-style economics, but more often they simply try to hold on to their jobs until they can retire. In either situation this makes it more difficult to reform and restructure the curriculum. For that matter, so too does the continuing influence of communists in the national legislative bodies of these three countries, and throughout society. In Belarus, the president himself is often openly pro-Soviet and anti-western – certainly not someone likely to fire or accept the firing of Soviet-style economists at state universities. As a result university economics departments in these nations must face a long, and sometimes contentious, period of transition to teaching only mainstream economics.

In considering these personnel issues, it is also very important to consider the different backgrounds and roles of mathematical and political economists. In the early 1990s economists and lawyers were in great demand across the FSU. A large number of private colleges and universities sprouted like mushrooms offering only two majors, business and law. This provided more lucrative career opportunities for economics and law professors, although the new positions were often taken on a part-time basis while maintaining a full-time position at the established and more prestigious state universities. During this same period the demand for specialists in natural sciences, physics, and mathematics sharply decreased, partly due to changing patterns of government expenditures, particularly in the area of national defense and defense-related scientific research. Many of these displaced academics desperately tried to find new positions – it was not at all uncommon for western visitors in the FSU to find that their driver was a Ph.D. physicist. Moving to economics departments offered a better substitute for some mathematicians, who claimed it was appropriate for them to teach economics because they understood algebra, graphs, and advanced mathematics better than political economists, and were not tainted by a history of teaching Marxist ideology. There was some truth in that, as we have suggested above; but not surprisingly (especially to economists), there was also self-interest and rivalry. Initially the position of political economists seemed more favored, especially in terms of teaching at the principles level. But soon, at the intermediate level and beyond, they began to lose ground to the mathematicians.

Today, if you look at the composition of the faculty for departments of economic theory at any major university in the FSU, you will almost always find at least several professors whose university training (and often whose first career) was in mathematics. The extent of the role for mathematics in a department's curriculum, and in terms of what kind of person (mathematician or political economist) will be assigned to teach a particular course, often depends on the background or beliefs of the chief of the department. At MSU most of the intermediate and advanced courses in economics are taught by mathematicians. There is also a strong chair in mathematical methods of economic analysis that offers students the option of enrolling in mathematically-based courses in microeconomics I and II, and macroeconomics I and II.

Testing

Many of the required courses at MSU now also require students to take quizzes and mid-term and final exams that feature multiple choice questions, problems, and essay questions. This change occurred largely because of the increased mathematics orientation of departments. The final grade/score in courses depends on the scores of all the tests and home assignments taken during the semester. This is common in the US and other western universities, but it differs sharply from common practice during the Soviet period. The new practice, together with rigorous entry requirements, helps to insure that seniors at MSU are able to get high scores on the GRE field exam in economics.

At most universities in the FSU that use a five-year degree program, there is still a final state exam for students who major in economic theory.[6] Although these are called state exams because they are officially approved by the Ministry of Education, and because the chief of the state examining commission must be an outsider – usually a professor from another institution who is appointed by the ministry – in practice the exams are written and administered by the faculty of the economic theory department at each university. Not surprisingly, the structure and content of the exam typically reflects the balance of power between Marxist and market-oriented professors in the department. To consider one such case, it took several years for professors at BSU to implement changes in the procedures for the state exam. Currently the exam consists of two parts. First, students take a written exam that includes 50 multiple choice questions that are essentially identical to the questions from the GRE field exam in economics. Then, on the next day, students must pass an oral exam that includes questions from classical political economy (mainly Marxist economics), microeconomics, macroeconomics, international economics, economic policy, applied economics, and the history of economic thought. The state commission that administers the oral exam includes five professors, at least two of whom do not teach economics. Strong answers are required for a passing score, but the questions posed to an individual student are chosen at random. Therefore, it is possible for a student to receive a high score on the written exam, to be very familiar with microeconomics and macroeconomics, but fail the oral exam because she is given a question on the oral exam dealing with the structure and logic of the second volume of *Das Kapital*. Ironically, in recent years some students who received low grades on the BSU state exam for this reason were later admitted to prestigious graduate programs in Great Britain or the United States.

It is also worth noting that some members of the state commission whose field is political economy are not really able to evaluate students taking the exams, because they have only a basic level of knowledge on market-based economics. This was an especially severe problem during the early 1990s, when most faculty members in economics departments were rewriting their courses, restructuring departmental curricula, and intensely engaging in self-training or retraining. Because economics departments in the FSU are highly specialized and include business subjects, some professors were working on various fields of economics, others on management, others on statistics, and so on. But while professors were retraining in one highly specialized area, students were taking the revised courses in all of the subject areas. Therefore, by the time a fifth-year student took the state exam, he or she often had better general training than some of the members of the examining commission. Students also often complained – then and now – that there was poor coordination of content across different courses and subject areas, resulting in both coverage gaps and redundancies.

Formal Training and Retraining Programs

There was a law in the USSR requiring university professors to take a one-semester retraining course every five years. This was a strictly enforced requirement for keeping a position in a university chair. Several retraining institutes dealing with humanities education were opened at the largest universities in Moscow, Leningrad, Kiev, Minsk, and some other capital cities. In the area of political economy these retraining institutes played very important ideological and methodological roles. Faculty members from smaller cities and universities used these opportunities to obtain new publications, teaching materials, and course syllabuses.

Usually the best professors in political economy were invited to give the lectures at the retraining programs. Therefore, when the Economic Development Institute (EDI) of the World Bank launched its own retraining program (titled 'Introduction to Market Economy: Principles and Policy') in 1992, it was quite natural for them to affiliate with the leading retraining institutes.

The primary goal of the World Bank program was to present instruction on the basic features of market economies for government officials from economic ministries across the FSU. But first, teams of professors from the FSU nations were invited to Washington DC for several seminars at the World Bank and the International Monetary Fund (IMF), providing intensive instruction on teaching micro- and macroeconomics. The EDI retraining centers were then established in various countries at the retraining institutes, and the programs for ministry officials were taught jointly by World Bank and IMF economists, and by university economists from these nations who had been trained in the first phase of the program. Eventually, at least in some nations, the training programs were taught only by local economists.

These programs had very good multiplier effects in several dimensions. In Belarus, for example, four BSU professors were involved in the EDI retraining programs. They immediately redirected their own courses and students towards textbooks that were recommended by the EDI staff and at the Joint Vienna Institute. They also tried to involve as many of their colleagues as possible in several retraining activities, although there are still many courses at BSU that are taught very traditionally (that is, as in the Soviet period). The Minsk EDI center has, to date, conducted 20 three-week courses for government officials, and also organized a two-year retraining program for university and college professors, and for high school economics teachers. These programs greatly helped to accelerate and smooth the restructuring of economics courses and curricula at most Belarusian universities, and at other educational institutions.

The Moscow EDI office, which is affiliated with the MSU retraining institute, played an even more significant role in restructuring the economics curriculum. As discussed in the following section, several MSU professors have translated western economics textbooks into Russian, and/or have published their own textbooks, which are very popular in Russia and across the FSU. Not surprisingly, many of these same professors are involved in numerous international projects in economics. The same group of professors also prepared the first Russian Internet textbook on economics.

Current Textbooks

Many authors in the FSU, especially in Russia, now write economics textbooks with no ideological or methodological influence from Soviet-style political economy. Good examples of this include textbooks on *Microeconomics* by M. Loukin and R. Emtsov, on *Macroeconomics* by T. Agapova and S. Seregina, and on *International Economics* by N. Miklashevskaya and A. Kholopov. All of these economists were involved in the EDI retraining programs for university professors and government officials. For several years they taught micro and macroeconomics at MSU using translated versions of the textbooks by Katz and Rosen and Mankiw. In fact, Emtsov was the chief editor of the Mankiw translation. With this background it is easy to see why the textbooks these authors have written in Russian feature content and structures that are very similar to these US textbooks.

Not all of the new textbooks written in Russian, Ukrainian, or Belarusian meet these high standards, however. In fact, most are probably still of lower quality than American textbooks, so it often makes sense to continue to use translations in many courses, and even to translate additional western books in many other subfields. This is a controversial topic in the FSU, however, with many economists claiming that US textbooks do not explain the current FSU reality, and arguing that it is therefore necessary to cover the main topics in the US textbooks using local examples. But all too often, in practice, local examples only mean that instead of John and Mary authors talk about Ivan and Maria. In the textbook on economic theory written by faculty from the Belarus State Economics University, described earlier, there are only five or six rather minor examples dealing with the FSU in 330 pages of material on micro- and macroeconomics.

It is also important to remember that textbooks on economic theory are not textbooks for the FSU courses on the economy in transition. Rather, these texts and courses play a different role in the curriculum by demonstrating how to construct and use the most basic models of rational economic behavior. That is, of course, the same role that these courses and books play in the United States, or in any other mainstream economics curriculum, so the importance of local examples, institutions, and data should not be overstated.

Another important issue related to the use of translated or locally written textbooks in the FSU, which is probably not widely appreciated in the West, is the relative prices of these books. In Minsk in August 1999, the price of the textbook written by Belarusian faculty members was 374,000BLR, the price for a Russian textbook published in Russia was 1,550,000BLR, and the price for a translated US textbook was about 4,000,000BLR.[7] In many cases, these relative prices are also a reasonably accurate measure of the relative quality of these textbooks.

The demand for these different kinds of textbooks varies greatly, depending on whether students are majoring in economic theory or some other field. There is almost no demand for the higher priced and higher quality textbooks from students who are not in economics departments, and even among that group there is quite limited demand from the students who specialize in business. Most non-economics majors try to use the simplest and cheapest textbooks on economics. In other words, the students majoring in economic theory departments, and of course the professors who teach economics courses, are the main consumers of the translated textbooks. Even among this group not all can afford the translated volumes.

Workbooks present several additional problems. First, the traditional pedagogical method of Soviet instruction was even more heavily lecture-oriented than US teaching of economics – without discussion or student questions in class, and few if any written assignments or mid-term quizzes or exams. Political economy was taught like a catechism, not as something to be used to solve practical problems. Today, many professors who now teach market-based economics still teach in the same manner: once I prove the law of demand, why waste time solving multiple-choice questions? This naturally affects the demand for workbooks.

Another problem limiting the use of workbooks is that some faculty members are not psychologically or technically prepared to solve the questions and problems themselves. In the retraining programs described above, it was soon evident that test scores for university professors were not always higher than most student scores on the same exams.

Even when workbook materials are available and a professor wants to use them, there are serious problems in distributing the materials. Students who can barely afford textbooks are even more reluctant to buy workbooks. And aside from any copyright concerns, duplicating copies of such materials to hand out to students is beyond the budget for most departments. As a result, it is not unusual now to find professors reading multiple-choice questions to their students, in some cases for up to half of a class period.

Faculty and Student Issues Concerning Graduate Study

We conclude by very briefly discussing how the restructuring of undergraduate economics programs in the FSU has affected the opportunities for students at these universities to pursue graduate-level instruction. There are currently three main options:

1. Some universities in the FSU, particularly those that have gone from five-year to four-year undergraduate programs, have recently launched master's programs. By 1996 MSU offered master's programs in economic theory, international economics and management, mathematical methods of economic analysis, and state policy and management. Kiev National Economic

University has master's programs in all the major fields, including: the economics of the firm/enterprise, finance, banking, auditing, marketing, institutional management, management of labor resources, economic statistics, economic cybernetics, international economics, and business law. BSU briefly offered a one-year master's program in economic theory to supplement its five-year undergraduate program, but soon dropped the program.

2. Some universities have joint master's programs with British and American universities. Often students in these programs can take some coursework at their home university and part abroad (for example, in the joint program of Novosibirsk State University and the University of Maryland, or in a program on the Management of Technology offered by the BSU Management of Technology Institute and the Economics Institute at the University of Colorado). In other cases FSU universities invite foreign professors to teach courses for these programs on site.

3. Today, the best undergraduate students across the FSU usually study English or occasionally some other western language, and devote considerable effort to preparing themselves for the GRE and TOEFL exams. They obviously hope to do their graduate study abroad, and many are able to do so. This has led to a serious 'brain drain' problem for graduate programs at FSU universities that is particularly pronounced in economics and business. It is also a serious long-term concern for the FSU nations, because few of the students who go abroad for graduate study return to their home nations after completing their advanced degrees.

IV. CONCLUSIONS

While remarkable progress has been made in restructuring economics courses and curricula at the leading universities in the FSU that progress is not uniform, nor is the process complete. It has been hampered by resistance from those professors of political economy who truly believed what they taught under the Soviet system, and by the substantial costs of retraining other faculty members both in areas of content and pedagogy. It has also been impeded by the substantial costs of translating, developing, and distributing new instructional materials. Furthermore, while student populations at these universities are typically very well prepared by their elementary and secondary educational programs, particularly when compared to their western counterparts, the FSU universities' financial positions are very strained – reflecting economic conditions in these nations. This has led some faculty and many graduate students to seek more rewarding careers, including positions at western universities.

APPENDIX 3.A: Coursework for the general economics degree
at Moscow State University, 1998-2000
(hours of coursework shown in parentheses)

Required courses

Microeconomics I (102)
Microeconomics II (68)
Macroeconomics I (96)
Macroeconomics II (64)
Theory of the transitional economy
(68)
History of economic thought (132)
Economic history (115)
International economics (68)
Industrial organization (68)
Institutional economics (30)
Economics of public sector (68)
Environmental economics (64)
Economics of agrarian sector (30)
Economics of the firm (68)
Accounting (64)
Financial markets (64)
Firm's finance (68) [corporate
finance]
Banking (40)
Economics of population and
demography (64)
Economics of labor and labor
resources (68)

Management (32)
State regulation of national economy
[macroeconomic forecasting and
stabilization policies] (64)
Economics of foreign countries (64)
Econometrics (66)
Statistics (general theory) (68)
Statistics (socioeconomic statistics) (64)
Mathematical statistics (64)
Operations research (64 + 68)
Game theory (34)
Economic cybernetics (32)
Mathematical analysis (132 + 132)
Linear algebra (115)
Probability theory (68)
Informatics [management information
systems] (132)
Economic geography (68)
History of the Fatherland (51)
Political logic (40)
Philosophy (68)
Foreign languages (636)

Elective courses

Natural science for economists (64)
Discrete mathematics (64)
Introduction to political economy
(64)
History of world civilizations (64)
Economic systems in the economic
structure (68)
Theoretical analysis of economic
systems (132)
Theoretical seminar on transitional
economy (64)

Theory of economic development (68)
Multidimensional statistical analysis
(68)
Applied operations analysis (64)
Introduction to project analysis (64)
Basics of risk management and
insurance (64)
Sociology (64)
Mathematical sociology (64)
Modern system of market economy (51)
Economics of services (51)

APPENDIX 3.A (continued)

Areas of Specialization (7th and 8th semesters)

Economic theory (216)
Mathematical methods of economic
   analysis (216)
Economic and social policy (216)

International economics (216)
Financial economics (216)
Economics of the firm and
   industrial organization (216)

APPENDIX 3.B: Coursework for the general economics degrees at Belarus State University, 1999-2000 (hours of coursework shown in parentheses)

SPECIALIZATION IN ECONOMIC THEORY (for future teachers of university economics)

General Humanities and Social Courses

Philosophy (88)
Logic (36)
Political history (34)
Political logic (36)
Ethics (72)
Social psychology (54)
Religion (34)
International law (36)

Pedagogics (54)
Cultural logic (36)
Foreign language (770)
Civic law (34)
History and ethnology of Belarus (34)
Physical training (210)

Mathematics and Science Courses

Principles of ecology (34)
Mathematics (210)
Probability theory and mathematical statistics (104)

Informatics [management information systems] (104)
Modern technologies (34)

General Professional and Special Courses

Economic sociology (34)
Environmental economics (34)
Economic history of Belarus and foreign countries (104)
Economics of countries and regions (72)
History of economic thought (208)
Economic statistics (122)
Principles of marketing (34)
Principles of management (72)
Pricing (54)
Economic psychology (34)
Introduction to the specialty (18)
Introduction to economics (36)

Econometrics (68)
Principles of economics (70)
Microeconomics (140)
Macroeconomics (72)
International economics (68)
Economics of the firm (enterprise) (122)
Economics of agrarian sector (72)
Accounting and audits (122)
Labor economics (54)
Money, banks, and credit (68)
Political economy (54)
Business analysis (68)
Macroeconomic planning (104)

APPENDIX 3.B (continued)

Financial law (34)
Business law (36)
Finance (of state and enterprise) (72)
Economic policy (68)

Methods of teaching economic
   sciences (54)
Economics of public sector (68)
Courses recommended by the
   University Council (72)

Specialization (610 hours)

Specialization in 'Economic Policy'
Macroeconomic problems of
   transitional economies
Antimonopoly regulation
Economic education and literacy
   (analysis of investment projects)
Theory and practice of taxation

*Specialization in 'History of
   Economic Thought'*
Institutional economics
Seminar on A. Marshall, J.M.
   Keynes, A.C. Pigou, V. Leontiev
Seminar on Marx's *Das Kapital*
Internet in teaching economics

Elective Courses

Modern Belarusian language (20)
System of state regulation (20)

Regional integration (20)
Theory of state debt (20)

SPECIALIZATION IN ECONOMICS (for government or firm economic analysts)
General Humanities and Social Courses (1174 hours)

Philosophy (102)
Logic (34)
History and culture of Belarus (34)
Political logic (34)
Ethics of business relations (68)
Social psychology (52)
Economic sociology (68)

International law (34)
Pedagogics (34)
Demography (34)
Foreign language (408)
Civic law (68)
Physical training (204)

Mathematics and Science Courses (486 hours)

Analysis (204)
Algebra, geometry, and
   programming (170)
Economic informatics [management
   information systems] (154)
Probability theory and mathematical
   statistics (102)

Numerical methods in economics
   (102)
Operations research, optimization,
   and games (136)
Computer mathematics for
   economists (68)
Ecology and environmental
   economics (52)

APPENDIX 3.B (continued)

General Professional and Special Courses (2102 hours)

Economic history (136)
Economic geography (68)
Principles of economics (86)
Microeconomics (136)
Macroeconomics (102)
History of economic thought (136)
Introduction to the speciality (18)
Econometrics and forecasting (68)
International economics and finance
  (102)
Management (68)
Economics of the firm (102)
Statistics (120)
Marketing (68)
Money, banks, and credit (102)
Economic policy and the theory of
  transitional economy (68)

Pricing (52)
Agricultural economics (68)
Accounting and financial analysis
  (136)
Labor economics and management
  of labor resources (52)
Strategic planning (86)
Business law (34)
Tax and budget system (68)
Financial markets and investments
  (68)
Financial law (34)
Mathematical economics (72)
Courses recommended by the
  University Council (72)

Specialization (692 hours)

Special courses (276)
Special seminars (208)
Laboratory work (208)
*Specialization in 'National
  Economics'*
Theory of transitional economies
Budget planning
Indicative planning and forecasting
Foreign markets
State funds
Urban economics
Industrial policy
Analysis of economic development
Economics of the public sector
System of state regulation
Regional integration

*Specialization in 'Economics of the
  Firm'*
Economic theory of the firm
Production management
Personnel management
Controlling
Business analysis
Logistics
Labor law
Taxation
Industrial policy
Analysis of investment projects
Business planning
Economic informatics

APPENDIX 3.B (continued)

Specialization in 'Banking and Financial Economics'
Actuary mathematics
Investment and financial markets
Analysis of investments
Insurance and risk
Financial analysis
Evaluating bank performance
Capital management
Financial programming
Credit risks and business plan analysis
Bank management
Financial informatics

Specialization in 'Economics of Foreign Trade'
Customs policy
International trade and banking law
State regulation of international economic relations
World economy
International marketing and world markets
Balance of payments and state debt analysis

Elective Courses

Modern Belarusian language (20)   Methods of teaching economics (68)

APPENDIX 3.C: Coursework for the general economics degree at Kiev State University, 1999-2000 (hours of coursework shown in parentheses)

Humanities (1656 hours)

History of Ukraine (108)
Ukrainian business language (54)
Ukrainian and foreign culture (108)
Philosophy (108)
Basics of psychology and pedagogy (54)
Religion (54)

Political logic (108)
Basics of law (54)
Foreign language (630)
Sociology (54)
Basics of constitution law (54)
Logic (54)
Physical training (54)

Fundamental Courses (3439 hours)

Economic theory (315)
Microeconomics (135)
Macroeconomics (135)
History of economic thought (181)
Economic history (108)
Mathematics for economists (432)
Mathematics (216)
Probability theory (108)
Mathematical methods of operations research (108)
Econometrics (81)
Theory of statistics (108)
Economic statistics (108)
Informatics [management information systems] (216)
Systems of processing of economic information (81)
Economics of the firm (enterprise) (162)

Management (108)
Marketing (108)
Theory of money (54)
Theory of finance (81)
Theory of credit (81)
Firm's finance (54) [corporate finance]
Theory of accounting (108)
Accounting of the enterprise (108)
Economic analysis (81)
Insurance (81)
Investments (81)
Allocation of productive resources (81)
Labor economics (81)
International economics (108)
Industrial organization (68)
Business law (81)
State regulation of the economy (81)

Professional Courses (987 hours)

Modern economic systems (108)
Ukrainian economy in transition (108)
Microeconomics: Analysis of market behavior (108)

Economic history of Ukraine (90)
History of Ukrainian economic thought (60)
Information systems and technologies in macroeconomics (81)

APPENDIX 3.C (continued)

Macroeconomic analysis (108)
Economic policy (108)
Economic integration and global
  problems (54)

Philosophy and methodology of
  scientific cognition (81)
Methods of teaching economic
  sciences (81)

KSU-selected Elective Courses (792 hours)

Introduction to the specialty (54)
Institutional economics (81)
Welfare economics (135)
Basics of environmental economics
  (108)
Economic risk and methods of its
  calculation (108)

Special seminar on J.M. Keynes
  (108)
Special seminar on *Das Kapital*
  (108)
International economic relations (90)

Student-selected Elective Courses (417 hours)

Theory of economic development
  (81) or Economic systems of
  theoretical analysis
Social policy (108) or Concept of
  human development
Small and medium business (108) or
  Enterprise

Theory and practice of competition
  (60)
Inflation and unemployment
Foreign investments (60) or Finances
  of foreign countries

Internships (468 hours)

NOTES

We thank Mikhail Chepıkov at Belarus State University, Vera Rube at Moscow State University, and Sergei Gassanov at Kiev State University for their help in obtaining and sometimes interpreting curriculum guidelines from their respective institutions. Francis W. Rushing provided helpful comments on an earlier version of this work, presented at the meetings of the American Economic Association in Boston, Massachusetts, in January, 2000. A shorter version of this work appeared in the Winter 2001 issue of *The Journal of Economic Education*. William B. Walstad provided helpful comments on this version.

1. Many leading universities in the former Soviet Union continue to use a five-year program with no distinction for bachelor's and master's programs, although Moscow State and Kiev State now use four-year programs. Regardless of the length of their baccalaureate program, the best students can apply directly to Ph.D. programs across the former Soviet Union, which typically do not assume that students have completed any specific courses. Ph.D. students majoring in economic theory are then required to pass a series of exams and to defend a dissertation.
2. Some of these conferences have been described in the earlier papers on the economics curriculum at MSU.
3. Hours reported are total hours of class meetings in a course. Undergraduates in the FSU typically spend 40 or more hours a week in class meetings. Historically, they took few or no exams or quizzes until the end of the term; but that practice is changing in many courses.
4. Both specializations are taught by the BSU *fakultet* of economics, which is equivalent to a western department of economics. Within the BSU *fakultet* there are currently three areas, or *otdeleniya*, which the faculty at BSU refer to as departments: economic theory, economics, and management. Students must apply to one of these three specializations, which have separate entrance exams and degree requirements. We do not consider the management specialization in this paper.
5. Some of this may change very soon. The economic policy course was taught by the former head of the department, a 75-year old man who was not likely to retrain in western economics, but who is now deceased.
6. The state exam still appeared in the 1995 MSU curriculum guide, but is not mentioned in the current guide. Nor is such an exam mentioned in the current KSU guide. This may well reflect the fact that both of these universities have now adopted four-year degree programs.
7. At that time, based on current exchange rates, the US dollar equivalents for those prices were approximately $1.17, $4.84, and $12.50.

REFERENCES

I. Materials in English

Alexeev, M., C. Gaddy, and J. Leitzel (1992), 'Economics in the former Soviet Union,' *Journal of Economic Perspectives*, **6**, pp. 137-48.

Blaug, M. (1997), *Economic Theory in Retrospect*, 5th ed. Cambridge: Cambridge University Press.

Brue, S. and C. MacPhee (1995), 'From Marx to markets: Reform of the university economics curriculum in Russia,' *Journal of Economic Education*, **26**, pp. 182-94.

Gerschenkorn, A. (1978), 'Samuelson in Soviet Russia: A report,' *Journal of Economic Literature*, **16**, pp. 560-73.

Hansen, W.L. (1991), 'The education and training of economics doctorates: Major findings of the American Economic Association's Commission on Graduate Education in Economics.' *Journal of Economic Literature*, **29**, pp. 1054-87.

Hyman, D.N. (1993). *Modern Microeconomics: Analysis and Applications*, 3rd ed. Homewood, Illinois: Richard D. Irwin.

Katz, M.L. and Rosen, H.S. (1998), *Microeconomics*, 3rd ed. New York: McGraw-Hill Irwin.

Krueger, A.O. et al. (1991), 'Report of the Commission on Graduate Education in Economics,' *Journal of Economic Literature*, **29**, pp. 1033-53.

Lipton, D. and J.D. Sachs (1992), 'Prospects for Russia's economic reforms,' *Brookings Papers on Economic Activity*, **2**, pp. 213-65.

McConnell, C.R. and Brue, S.L. (2002). *Economics*, 15th ed. New York: McGraw-Hill Irwin.
Rushing, F.W. (1994), 'The changing face of economics instruction in Russia,' in W.B. Walstad (ed.), *An International Perspective on Economic Education*, Boston, Massachusetts, USA: Kluwer Academic Publishers, pp. 233-54.
Scherer, F.M. and D. Ross (1990), *Industrial Market Structure and Economic Performance*, 3rd ed. Boston: Houghton Mifflin Company.
Varian, H.R. (1999), *Intermediate Microeconomics: A Modern Approach*, 5th ed. New York: W.W. Norton, Inc.

II. Materials in Russian, Belarusian, or Ukrainian

1. Textbook by BSEU professors:
   Economic Theory: Textbook. 2nd ed./N.I. Bazylev, A.V. Bondar, S.P. Gourko and others.- Minsk: BSEU, 1997.-500 pp.
   Economicheskaya teoriya: Uchebnik. 2-e izd./ N.I. Bazylev, A.V. Bondar, S.P. Gourko...- Minsk: BGEU, 1997.-500 s.
2. Emtsov R.G. and M.Y. Loukin *Microeconomics*: Textbook. 2nd ed.-M.: MSU named by M.V. Lomonosov, 'Delo i Servis', 1999.-320 pp.
   Emtsov R.G. y M.Y. Loukın *Microeconomica*: Uchebnik. 2-e izd.-M.: MGU imeni M.V. Lomonosova, 'Delo i Servis', 1999.-320 s.
3. Agapova T.D. and S.F. Seregina *Macroeconomics*: Textbook. 2nd ed.-M.: MSU named by M.V. Lomonosov, 'Delo i Servis', 1999.-416 pp.
   Agapova T.D. y S.F. Seregina *Macroeconomica*: Uchebnik. 2-e izd.-M.: MGU imeni M.V. Lomonosova, 'Delo i Servis', 1999.-416 s.
4. Miklashevskaya N.A. and A.V. Kholopov *International Economics: Textbook*.-M.: MSU named by M.V. Lomonosov, 'Delo i Servis', 1999.-320 pp.
   Miklashevskaya N.A. y A.V. Kholopov Mezhdunarodnaya Economica: Uchebnik. -M.: MGU imeni M.V. Lomonosova, 'Delo i Servis', 1999.-320 s.
5. Curriculum Guide of Economic Department of MSU in 'Economics.'-M.: Economic Department of MSU, TEIS, 1995.
   Katalog uchebnyh program economicheskogo fakulteta MGU po napravleniyu 'Economica.'-M.: Economicheskii facultet MGU, TEIS, 1995.
6. Curriculum Guide of Economic Department of MSU in 'Economics'. 1998-1999, 1999-2000. M.: Economic Department of MSU, TEIS, 1998.-369 pp.
   Katalog uchebnyh program economicheskogo fakulteta MGU po napravleniyu 'Economica.' 1998-1999, 1999-2000.-M.: Economicheskii facultet MGU, TEIS, 1998.-369 s.
7. Curriculum Guide in Economic Disciplines for the Students of Economic Specialties. Minsk: BSU, 1998.-243 pp.
   Programmy coursov po economicheskim disciplinam dlya studentov economicheskih specialnostei.-Minsk: BGU, 1998.-243 pp.
8. Curriculum for the specialty E 01.01.00 'Economic Theory.' Approved by the Scientific-Methodical Council of the BSU and signed by the rector in 1998.
   Uchebnyi plan spetsialnosti E 01.01.00 'Economicheskaya teoriya.'
9. Curriculum for the specialty E 01.10 'Economics'. Approved by the Scientific-Methodical Council of the BSU and signed by the rector in 1999.
   Uchebnyi plan spetsialnosti E 01.10 'Economica.'
10. Curriculum of the Bachelor Program (Specialty 'Economic Theory') of the Economics Department of Kiev University named by Taras Shevchenko.
    Uchebnyi plan po programme bacalavrov (spetsialnost 'economicheskaya teoriya') economicheskogo fakulteta Kievskogo universiteta imeni Tarasa Shevchenko.
11. Markov, A.R. 'I bakalavrv, I majistry ... [Both Bachelors and Masters...],' *Ekonomika I zhizn*, October 1990, 41, 9.

4. The Effects of Teacher Programs on Student Economic Understanding and Market Attitudes in Transition Economies

William B. Walstad

In the United States, the United Kingdom, Japan, and other western market economies, a major focus of economic education is training classroom teachers in basic economics and the use of instructional materials for teaching the subject. These teachers often have limited economic knowledge and lack effective instructional skills because they completed few economics or economic education courses during their undergraduate education or thereafter. Substantial research has been conducted in the United States over the past 40 years showing that such teacher training and materials use in economics is an important factor in improving economic understanding of high school students, after accounting for other student or school characteristics (Allgood and Walstad, 1999; Becker, Greene and Rosen, 1990; Bosshardt and Watts, 1990). In other western nations with a market economy, studies also report the value of teacher training and instructional materials for improving teaching economics (Lietz and Kotte, 2000; Walstad, 1994). Whether these findings also apply to economic education for secondary schools in nations making transitions to a market economy had not been investigated, at least in studies available in English, until this study was undertaken.

The absence of studies in economic education with student data from the transition economies, especially with results available in English, is not surprising. Only a relatively short time period has elapsed since market-based programs in economic education for teachers have been conducted in the transition economies. Financial and personnel constraints in these nations are even more severe than in the western economies, making it difficult to obtain the resources for such studies. Adding to the complexity of the situation is the need to conduct such studies across several nations so that learning outcomes can be compared in multiple transition economies and under different national circumstances.

The National Council on Economic Education (NCEE) and its national network of some 270 college and university centers for economic education have a long tradition of supporting research and evaluation in economic education. Until the 1990s the focus of that work has been almost exclusively on economic education programs that were offered in the United States. In 1995 the NCEE received major grant funding from the US Department of Education to expand its work and deliver teacher training programs in many nations making a transition to a market economy. This funding also enabled the NCEE to invest significant resources in program assessments in these transition economies, to see whether the teacher training models it regularly uses in the United States are also successful 'in translation,' so to speak, not only in terms of languages, but also in terms of holding up in very different cultural and institutional settings.

This chapter presents the results from a research study on the effects of the NCEE's International Education Exchange Program (IEEP). Pre- and posttest data were collected during the 1996-1997 school year from almost 3,000 high school students in five nations – Lithuania, Latvia, Ukraine, Kyrgyzstan, and Poland. These data included measures of the economic understanding of students and their opinions about markets and the market economy. Additional data were available on the teachers and the characteristics of their classes. The data set provides a rich resource for studying economic education in these nations.

The primary purpose of this study is to investigate whether IEEP and other factors contributed to improved economic understanding of high school students, who will soon become the future workers, voters, and leaders of these nations. A secondary objective was to study what students think about how markets and the market economy works and whether IEEP had an influence on their perceptions. There are two major reasons for conducting this kind of study.[1] First, establishing factors that improve the learning of these students, and what students think about markets, should help other nations making the transition from command to market economies increase the economic literacy of their students, and thus help to sustain the process of economic and educational reforms. Second, the study is one of the first major research projects in economic education conducted in the transition nations. Therefore, the methods, problems, and findings from this research should be a useful example and guide for conducting future studies in these nations. It should help build a research literature on economics instruction in secondary schools in transition economies and also provide new insights on teacher and student studies in economic education that have been conducted in the United States and other western nations.

I. BACKGROUND AND RESEARCH DESIGN

In 1995 and 1996, 204 teachers from Lithuania, Latvia, Ukraine, Kyrgyzstan, and Poland participated in IEEP seminars sponsored by the NCEE. The seminars were designed to increase teacher understanding of basic economics and how a market economy works. The seminars were also designed to improve the skills of the participants in teaching about economics and to provide teachers with instructional materials to use with their students.[2]

Each week-long seminar included about 32 hours of content and pedagogical instruction, plus another four hours for pre- and posttesting, and to complete surveys. The sessions were usually taught in one and one-half hour blocks and typically covered one or more basic economic concepts and ways to teach economics. Lectures, transparencies, handouts, and lesson activities including classroom simulations and small-group discussions and assignments were used to teach the economic concepts to teachers. After completing the seminars, teachers could then use many of the class handouts and lesson materials from the seminars for instruction in their high school courses. See Appendix 4.A for a sample agenda.[3]

Education Development Center, Inc. (EDC) conducted evaluations of these workshops for the NCEE and reported findings in two reports (EDC, 1996; EDC, 1997). An extensive data file was collected on each of these teachers – their personal characteristics, teaching situation, economic knowledge, attitudes towards a market economy, opinions on economic issues, and teaching skills. The EDC analysis showed that each IEEP seminar significantly increased teacher economic understanding of basic economic concepts. For example, the scores of teachers in Lithuania, Latvia, Ukraine, Kyrgyzstan, and Poland increased from 60 to 70 percent correct on the 46-item *Test of Economic Literacy* (Soper and Walstad, 1987). The program also appeared to develop greater appreciation of the workings of a market economy and fostered more positive attitudes towards it. In addition, teachers reported significant improvement in their teaching skills and a greater understanding of how to teach economics using the IEEP materials.[4]

After participating in the seminars, teachers were expected to return to their classrooms and use the IEEP training and materials to improve the economic education of their students. But until this study was conducted, nothing was known about the effects of IEEP training and materials *on students* in the five nations. This study investigates the effects of IEEP training on the economic understanding of high school students who were being taught by IEEP teachers, compared to classes taught by other teachers.

A nonequivalent control group design with pre- and posttesting was used for the study (Cook and Campbell, 1979). This research design is often used because it has the advantage of being flexible for studies conducted in field settings, which was necessary given the characteristics of the five nations in which this research was being done. The design reduces many of the threats to internal and external validity to a study, and often provides interpretable data for addressing a research hypothesis.

The main hypothesis in this study focused on the effects of IEEP training and materials. It was expected that students of IEEP-trained economics teachers who used the IEEP materials (the experimental group) would show a significantly greater increase in understanding of economics than students of economics teachers without any IEEP characteristics (the control group). Although groups were taught economics over the same time period and under similar conditions, the IEEP students were expected to have an advantage in learning economics because of the teacher training for the IEEP teachers and the materials they had available for classroom instruction.

II. EXPERIMENTAL AND CONTROL GROUPS

The selection of teachers to participate in the study began with the universe of teachers who had received IEEP training in 1995 and 1996 seminars (EDC, 1996; EDC, 1997).[5] This group included 40 teachers from Lithuania, 38 from Latvia, 41 from Ukraine, 43 from Kyrgyzstan, and 42 from Poland, for a total of 204 teachers. Teachers in Latvia, Lithuania, Ukraine, and Poland only participated in single week-long seminars. In Kyrgyzstan teachers had participated in two or three one-week seminars because of past work in that nation.[6]

From this initial group, three uniform criteria were established that would significantly reduce the number of IEEP teachers who were eligible to participate in the study. For each nation, EDC used its database to prepare a list of the universe of teachers based on their survey responses to a 'Participant Information Form' that indicated whether a teacher: (1) had participated in the 1995 and 1996 IEEP seminar(s); (2) was currently teaching economics; and (3) was teaching economics in grades nine or ten in their country. Thus, the study focused on *economics instructors* teaching a class on economics at grades nine or ten.[7]

Experimental Group (IEEP)

About 15-20 IEEP teachers per nation were sought to participate in the testing to provide a sufficient number of pre- and posttests from students for the group comparisons. In Lithuania and Poland, the universe of teachers who met the three criteria closely matched the desired sample size, so all IEEP teachers in those nations were asked to participate. Of this group, 15 in Lithuania and 18 in Poland agreed to participate.

In Kyrgyzstan 36 teachers met the criteria. Although all teachers were asked to participate, geographic distances, poor communications facilities, and bad weather finally resulted in the participation of just 19 of the 36 potential participants. In Latvia, only teachers from the Riga area were asked to participate, due to logistical concerns in facilitating the testing. which resulted in only five IEEP teachers participating from that nation.

In Ukraine, the procedure was somewhat different because of the history of past seminars in two locations. Among the Ukrainian teachers trained in IEEP seminars in Lviv in 1996, about 11 met the criteria and agreed to participate. A decision was also made to invite Ukrainian teachers from Kharkiv to participate to supplement the initial Ukrainian group. The Kharkiv teachers had participated in seminars conducted by the NCEE from 1992 to 1994 before the IEEP program began. These seminars were similar in content and method to the IEEP seminars because they were conducted by the same organization administering the IEEP project and taught by some of the same staff as the IEEP seminars. For the purposes of this study, therefore, these Kharkiv teachers were considered IEEP teachers. In this case the EDC's in-country partner (university faculty or public schools officials) secured the participation of teachers who met all three criteria. This work eventually added 12 teachers from the Kharkiv area, making the Ukrainian total 23.

Control Group (No IEEP)

EDC also worked with its network of in-country partners to identify about 15 teachers per nation who met two of the three criteria for the experimental group (teaching economics at grades 9 or 10), but not the third criterion (attended an IEEP seminar). All of the in-country partners from these five nations were able to identify these teachers and secure a control group willing to participate in the study. The control group of 43 teachers included 11 from Lithuania, two from Latvia, 10 from Ukraine, seven from Kyrgyzstan, and 13 from Poland.

The same kinds of constraints affected the participation of these teachers as for the experimental group. In Latvia and Kyrgyzstan selection of teachers was limited by geographic and logistical constraints in the distribution and collection of tests. In Ukraine there were no such geographic constraints, but because the NCEE had been active in the Lviv and Kharkiv areas for several years it was more difficult to find teachers who had not been trained to serve in the control group. There were no such limitations in Lithuania or Poland, although in Lithuania there were teachers in the control group who had not participated in IEEP seminars but who had attended Junior Achievement programs.

The nonequivalent design is often used in this kind of evaluation when random assignment of subjects to treatment groups is not feasible, a situation that affected this study. Nonrandom assignment of teachers to the experimental and control groups raises sample selection concerns, however. There may have been some other characteristics associated with the economics teachers who volunteered for the IEEP seminars, who met the three criteria, and who volunteered for the study, other than the training received or the instructional materials used, that could lead students of IEEP teachers to gain, on average, more economic knowledge during a course than students of economics teachers in the control group. For example, the argument could be made that the IEEP teachers were more motivated or were better teachers initially than control teachers. These initial differences in teacher characteristics, rather than IEEP training, may explain the difference in student scores between the groups.[8]

The selection issue was investigated in this study, but it could never be eliminated as a rival hypothesis. According to EDC the control teachers were willing to participate in the study because of the credibility of EDC's in-country partners. When the in-country partners asked teachers to cooperate, that was sufficient reason and incentive for them to volunteer. Many teachers also thought the research project would be an interesting one to be involved in and were willing to take the time to administer the tests and questionnaires. EDC found no evidence to suggest that the control teachers were in some ways a less motivated or less able group, which would be expected because both teacher groups were composed of volunteers. In the opinion of the EDC manager in charge of data collection, both the IEEP and non-IEEP teachers were 'fully comparable.' Unfortunately, the data on all experimental and control teachers who could have participated in the study was incomplete, so this EDC assessment could not be tested in a sample selection model to account for the nonrandom assignment of teachers to groups.

Teachers

There were 123 teachers (80 IEEP and 43 control) who agreed to participate in the study and who gave a pretest. Of this group, 102 teachers (68 IEEP and 34 No IEEP), or 83 percent of all teachers, also gave a posttest.[9] It is the students of these 102 teachers who are the primary focus for this study. The distribution of these teachers by nation and group is shown in Table 4.1. Most of the 102 teachers (87 percent) also completed a teacher questionnaire. Information on teacher characteristics and the courses they taught will be important for use in regression analysis described later in the chapter. In cases where teacher data are missing the sample size is reduced when the regression analysis uses variables based on the teacher information. The distribution of teachers who completed the questionnaire and whose students completed both pre- and posttests is also shown in Table 4.1.[10]

III.   TESTING AND DATA COLLECTION

EDC used rigorous procedures to ensure uniformity of data collection and test security. The economics test, attitude measure, and background questionnaires were translated by EDC, photocopied, and delivered to participating teachers in separate envelopes. Thirty-five numbered copies of the test instrument were given to each teacher for pretesting. Classroom teachers handled the administrations of the tests and brief student questionnaires. Teachers then returned all numbered tests in signed and sealed envelopes, so a check could be made that all tests were returned. The in-country partners for EDC kept the returned test envelopes under lock and key until they were needed for the posttest. The same test security procedures used for the pretests were also used when the posttests were administered. Answer sheets were packaged separately for all teachers, and were returned by all teachers to EDC in sealed envelopes through the in-country partner, with the test count and teachers' certification signatures on the outside. The same procedures were followed in all nations. According to EDC, there was no reason to suspect cheating or deviations from the uniform testing and data collection procedures.

Table 4.1: Number of teachers by nation and group: pre-post matched sample

	Overall	By Group	
		IEEP	No IEEP
Overall			
Pre- and Post Match	102	68	34
With Teacher Information	89	59	30
Lithuania			
Pre- and Post Match	19	10	9
With Teacher Information	10	4	6
Latvia			
Pre- and Post Match	6	5	1
With Teacher Information	6	5	1
Ukraine			
Pre- and Post Match	30	21	9
With Teacher Information	30	21	9
Kyrgyzstan			
Pre- and Post Match	30	18	3
With Teacher Information	19	16	3
Poland			
Pre- and Post Match	26	14	12
With Teacher Information	24	13	11

The classroom teachers handled the administration of all tests and student questionnaires because of the difficulty and expense of having the in-country partners collect this data.[11] There were uniform, written instructions for all teachers and students that had been translated into the local language. The tests and classroom instructions were distributed at an EDC briefing for teachers in Latvia, Lithuania, and Poland. In Ukraine and Kyrgyzstan the in-country partner distributed the tests and instructions to teachers.

The in-country partners collected all sealed and signed test envelopes and answer sheet envelopes. The answer sheet envelopes were delivered to EDC by the prescribed deadlines. In many cases envelopes were hand-carried back to the United States by an EDC staff member who had other business in the nation where the testing was done. Pretests were administered to students from 15-30 October 1996. Posttests were administered to students from 10-20 March 1997. Thus, the evaluation was conducted over only five of the nine months of the school year.

IV. SAMPLE

Posttest data were obtained from 2,811 students who also took the pretest.[12] There
were 1,941 students in the IEEP group and 870 students in the control group.
Table 4.2 presents selected characteristics of each group. The groups were similar
by gender (58 percent versus 59 percent females) and age (for example, 14-15
years: 27 percent versus 24 percent). The biggest difference was the distribution
of students across the nations. The largest percentage of students in the IEEP
sample came from Ukraine and Kyrgyzstan (63 percent) whereas the largest
percentage of students in the No IEEP sample came from Ukraine and Poland (66
percent). Thus, students in Kyrgyzstan accounted for a larger percentage of the
IEEP group compared with the No IEEP group (29 percent versus 12 percent)
while students in Poland accounted for a smaller percentage of the IEEP group
compared with the No IEEP group (18 percent versus 38 percent). In Lithuania,
Latvia, and Ukraine, the percentage distribution between the two groups was
roughly similar (plus or minus seven percent or less).

Table 4.2: Student characteristics: Five nations sample (N = 2,811 students)

	IEEP Pre/Post (N = 1,941)		No IEEP Pre/Post (N = 870)	
	N	percent	*N*	percent
By Nation				
Lithuania	230	12	161	19
Latvia	139	7	31	4
Ukraine	659	34	248	28
Kyrgyzstan	554	29	103	12
Poland	359	18	327	38
By Gender				
Female	1,120	58	516	59
Male	821	42	354	41
By Age				
14-15	520	27	197	23
16-17	915	47	530	61
Other/Missing	506	26	143	16

Table 4.3 reports data on the teacher characteristics of the Table 4.2 students
in those cases where a teacher completed a questionnaire. The distribution of
teachers in the pre- and posttest sample from each nation was roughly proportional

to the percentage of students in the pre- and posttest sample. The differences between the characteristics of IEEP and No IEEP teachers across breakdowns by gender, age, years of teaching experience, length of course, and content coverage, fell in a modest range (8-13 percent). The IEEP group, however, had a greater percentage that had only been teaching economics for one to two years (56 percent versus 37 percent). The most likely explanation for this difference was that participation in IEEP encouraged more teachers who had not taught economics before to begin teaching it.

Table 4.3: Teacher characteristics: Five nations sample (N = 89 teachers)

| | IEEP Pre/Post (N = 59 teachers) | | No IEEP Pre/Post (N = 30 teachers) | |
	N	percent*	*N*	percent
By Nation				
Lithuania	4	7	6	20
Latvia	5	8	1	3
Ukraine	21	36	9	30
Kyrgyzstan	16	27	3	10
Poland	13	22	11	37
By Gender				
Female	46	78	20	67
Male	13	22	9	30
By Age				
≤ 39	36	62	18	60
> 39	23	39	11	37
By Years Teaching				
1-10	28	47	16	53
≥ 11	31	53	13	44
By Years Teaching Economics				
1-2	33	56	11	37
≥ 3	22	38	17	57
Course Length				
≤ 1 year	26	44	17	57
> 1 year	27	46	11	37
Course Content				
Micro and Macro	49	83	21	70
Micro or Macro	4	7	7	23

*Percentages do not sum to 100 due to rounding or missing data.

V. TEST INSTRUMENT

The *Test of Economic Literacy* (*TEL*) is a nationally normed test of economic understanding for US high school students (Soper and Walstad, 1987). The *TEL* has been successfully used as a valid and reliable measure of high school student economic understanding in other nations. In fact, national norming studies and program evaluations with the *TEL* have been conducted in the United Kingdom, Germany, Austria, Switzerland, Bulgaria, Korea, China, and Australia (Beck and Krumm, 1998; Lietz and Kotte, 2000; Walstad, 1994).[13]

A shortened version of form A of the *TEL* was translated into the national languages used for this study. Only 23 of the 46 *TEL* items were used to give students time to complete the test and answer other survey questions during a typical class period of about 45 minutes. The shortened test still adequately represented each of the four major content areas of the *TEL* as outlined in *A Framework for Teaching the Basic Economic Concepts* (Saunders and Gilliard, 1995). There were six fundamental (26 percent), six microeconomic (26 percent), seven macroeconomic (30 percent), and four international (17 percent) items on the modified *TEL*. The percentages in each category were proportional to that found on the full test, and indicated that the modified version retained a high degree of the content validity found in the full test.

Construct validity is also an important consideration because it shows whether a test is capable of detecting those with more subject matter knowledge. This validity can be established by comparing scores for students with and without economics instruction (or by comparing pre- and posttest scores). A re-analysis of the US norming data using the shorter *TEL* produced a mean score of 9.25 (standard deviation = 4.14) for the 1,082 students without instruction in economics. The mean score for the 3,153 students with economics instruction was 12.30 (standard deviation = 4.18).[14] This 3.05 point difference was statistically significant and suggests that the 23-item version of the *TEL* is still a valid measure. In addition, item data show that US students with economics instruction had a higher percentage correct on each of the 23 items than those without instruction.

Further investigation with the 23-item *TEL* was conducted with the sample of students who participated in this study to determine if it measured differences in economic understanding. Overall, students had a mean pretest score of 12.23 and a mean posttest score of 13.79 points, for an average gain of 1.56 points. This change was statistically significant (*t*-value = 20.04) and represents about a 13 percent improvement in *TEL* scores from the pretest mean. These results provided evidence of the construct validity of this *TEL* for detecting changes in economic understanding for this study. There were also pre- and posttest score differences in the expected direction for almost all of the major subgroups of students, including males and females, each age group (14, 15, 16, and 17), and for four of the five nations.[15]

Although the average change from pre- to posttest was small, it is not uncommon for standardized tests in economics to show an average gain of about this size (adjusted for the fact that only half the test items were used). There are several reasons for this result. First, only a limited number of questions can be included on a test, so it is difficult for a short classroom test to capture fully what students learn from pre- to posttest. Second, although there is supposed to be a reasonable match between the class instruction and test content, there can occasionally be a mismatch between the two because of teacher decisions or some other factors, and this situation can reduce test scores. Third, adjustments are sometimes made with normed-referenced tests to keep test items from being too easy or too hard for students, and thus increasing test reliability. Fourth, guessing by students will tend to increase pretest scores and reduce the potential difference between pre- and posttests. Fifth, limited instructional time can restrict content coverage and test performance. These and other factors will tend to narrow the spread between pre- and posttests in economics.

The accuracy of a test in measuring a construct is also an important property that is often estimated by the internal consistency among test items. Alpha reliability gives an estimate of the average correlation between test scores on all possible split halves of a test. The coefficient ranges from a low of 0, indicating no internal consistency, to a high of 1, indicating perfect consistency among test items. The alpha for the *TEL* was 0.87 when the full test was administered to 4,235 high school US students. A re-analysis of the US data shows that the alpha would have been 0.72 for the 23-item test, a respectable alpha for a test half its original length.[16]

The alpha reliability was estimated at 0.75 for the overall sample in this study. This estimate is slightly higher than the estimate from the US data, and comparable with the reliability found for other national normed tests in economics.[17] A further breakdown of the overall sample showed that the 23-item *TEL* was a reliable measure of economic understanding for students of IEEP teachers or students of control teachers (0.76 and 0.74 respectively) and by nation (0.64 to 0.77). These results show that there was no reason to think that the modified *TEL* was an inappropriate measure of the economic understanding of the experimental or control groups.

VI.   ECONOMIC UNDERSTANDING

Table 4.4 reports the pre- to posttest difference in percent correct for each *TEL* item for the IEEP and No IEEP groups. For 22 of 23 items, the IEEP group showed a statistically significant increase in item means (or percent correct) from pre- to posttest.[18] By contrast, the No IEEP group showed a statistically significant improvement on only 15 items, no significant change on 5 items, and a statistically significant decrease on 3 items. The item analysis indicated that the improvement in economic understanding for the IEEP group was the result of exposure to a wider range of economic content, and not just large gains on a few items. One likely explanation for this outcome was that IEEP teachers were more

knowledgeable about the micro and macro content that should be taught in a high
school economics course, and better prepared and equipped with materials to teach
this content.

For the sake of parsimony, the item analysis for each nation is not reported in
table form in this chapter. Nevertheless, the results for each nation showed a
pattern similar to the overall results. In those nations with greater gains for the
IEEP group than the No IEEP group, there were more items with a statistically
significant increase in item means (or percent correct). In Latvia the ratio was 17
to 4, Ukraine 15 to 7, Kyrgyzstan 18 to 8, and Lithuania 6 to 2. Only in Poland
was the ratio slightly negative for the IEEP group compared to the No IEEP group.

Table 4.4:   TEL item percent correct by group (N = 2,811 students)

Question	IEEP % Correct (N = 1,941)				No IEEP % Correct (N = 870)			
No.	Pre	Post	Post–Pre	t-value*	Pre	Post	Post-Pre	t-value
1 (2)[+]	67	78	11	8.68[a]	64	75	11	5.81[a]
2 (3)	61	68	7	5.74[a]	59	58	- 1	0.56
3 (6)	62	68	6	4.12[a]	54	62	8	4.28[a]
4 (7)	82	88	6	5.18[a]	84	81	- 3	2.20[b]
5 (9)	63	70	7	6.05[a]	65	80	15	8.65[a]
6 (12)	71	84	13	10.70[a]	74	83	9	5.23[a]
7 (13)	53	65	12	9.03[a]	65	65	0	0.29
8 (16)	55	67	12	8.91[a]	55	66	11	5.74[a]
9 (17)	37	50	13	9.15[a]	42	47	5	2.72[a]
10(19)	76	80	4	3.25[a]	80	83	3	1.56
11(21)	74	79	5	3.92[a]	73	77	4	2.47[b]
12(23)	35	44	9	6.77[a]	29	28	- 1	0.74
13(26)	61	72	11	7.78[a]	58	72	14	6.68[a]
14(27)	54	59	5	3.28[a]	51	57	6	2.54[b]
15(29)	31	42	11	7.64[a]	33	49	16	6.72[a]
16(30)	49	58	9	7.01[a]	66	60	- 6	2.68[a]
17(31)	38	48	10	6.31[a]	45	50	5	2.59[a]
18(34)	37	51	14	10.17[a]	46	46	0	0.16
19(37)	45	54	9	6.00[a]	46	52	6	2.82[a]
20(40)	45	46	1	.48	50	44	- 6	2.88[a]
21(41)	49	52	3	2.08[b]	47	52	5	2.68[a]
22(43)	23	25	3	2.17[b]	11	19	8	5.34[a]
23(45)	58	67	9	6.42[a]	61	68	7	3.99[a]

[+]Numbers in parentheses are the original *TEL* form A item number (see Soper and Walstad, 1987).
*Absolute *t*-values.
[a]Significant at the .01 level (two-tailed test).
[b]Significant at the .05 level (two-tailed test).

Comparisons of means on the *TEL* between the IEEP and No IEEP groups were also made based on scores for pretests, posttests, and pre- to posttests. Table 4.5 reports the *t*-test results from each comparison for the overall sample and each national sample. The results for students in the overall sample showed that the IEEP group had a lower pretest score than the No IEEP group. The difference was about a third of a point, but statistically significant. By the posttest, the situation was reversed. The IEEP group scored about a third of a point higher than the No IEEP group, a statistically significant difference. The IEEP group went from a 0.34-point pretest disadvantage to a 0.37-point posttest advantage for an overall gain of 0.71 points.

Table 4.5: Mean TEL comparisons by test and group: Overall and by nations

	N	Pretest Mean	Pretest S. D.	Posttest Mean	Posttest S. D.	Post–Pre
Overall						
IEEP	1,941	12.25	3.65	14.12	4.23	1.87[a]
No IEEP	870	12.59	3.60	13.75	4.11	1.16[a]
Difference		-0.34[b]		0.37[b]		
Lithuania						
IEEP	230	11.09	3.21	11.54	3.80	0.45
No IEEP	161	12.01	3.13	11.73	3.04	-0.27
Difference		-0.92[a]		-0.19		
Latvia						
IEEP	139	12.08	3.03	16.25	3.13	4.17[a]
No IEEP	31	11.19	2.50	12.74	3.18	1.55[a]
Difference		0.89		3.51[a]		
Ukraine						
IEEP	659	13.35	3.29	14.96	4.56	1.61[a]
No IEEP	248	13.82	3.09	14.19	3.99	0.37
Difference		-0.47[b]		0.77[b]		
Kyrgyzstan						
IEEP	554	12.13	4.32	14.32	4.24	2.20[a]
No IEEP	103	12.92	4.48	14.48	3.87	1.55[a]
Difference		-0.79		-0.16		
Poland						
IEEP	359	11.24	3.03	13.11	3.07	1.87[a]
No IEEP	327	11.96	3.71	14.27	4.48	2.31[a]
Difference		-0.72[a]		-1.16[a]		

[a]*t*-value significant at .01 level (two-tailed test).
[b]*t*-value significant at .05 level (two-tailed test).

The pre- to posttest change was 1.87 points for the IEEP group and 1.16 points for the No IEEP group. Both increases were significant, which was expected because both groups were receiving economics instruction, but the change for students with an IEEP-trained teacher using IEEP materials was greater by 0.71 points. If a 1.16 point increase represents the average gain for a student with a regular economics teacher, then it appears that IEEP training and materials had the effect of increasing that gain by 61 percent.

Table 4.5 also reports the *TEL* mean comparisons for the five nations. An inspection of the pre- to posttest results showed a significant increase by IEEP students in four of the five nations – Latvia, Ukraine, Kyrgyzstan, and Poland. In Latvia IEEP students scored 4.17 points higher on the posttest than the pretest, but the No IEEP students scored only 1.55 points higher. In Ukraine the change was 1.61 points for IEEP students versus an insignificant change of 0.37 points for No IEEP students. For Kyrgyzstan the difference was 2.20 points for IEEP compared with 1.55 points for No IEEP, significant at the .01 level. In Lithuania both groups had an insignificant change from pre- to posttest, although the slight difference favored IEEP students (0.45 versus 0.27). Only in Poland was the gain for the IEEP group (1.87 points) less than the gain for the No IEEP group (2.31 points).

The pre – post data indicated that the size and significance of the IEEP effects varies by nation, but overall the program was clearly beneficial. There was stronger evidence in three nations (Latvia, Ukraine, and Kyrgyzstan) and weaker evidence in one nation (Lithuania) that IEEP made a more positive contribution to student economic understanding than No IEEP. In Poland the pre-to-post gains were slightly larger for the No IEEP group, but the difference in gains was not statistically significant (*t*-value = 1.62).

VII. REGRESSION ANALYSIS

A problem with the item analysis or mean comparisons is that they do not control for the influence of other factors that are likely to affect the results. The IEEP and No IEEP groups may have differed in economic understanding because of differences in the characteristics of the two groups on another factor (e.g., age) and not because of a program effect. To control for these other factors, a regression model was specified and estimated using the *TEL* posttest minus the pretest as the dependent variable.[19] The model was similar to other studies evaluating program effects in education (Becker, Greene, and Rosen, 1990).

Variable Rationale

Variables to control for the effects of age and gender were included in the regression because research in economic education in the United States and other nations has shown that these factors may influence student test scores in economics (Walstad, 1994). Other things equal, older students tend to do better than younger students and males tend to score slightly better than females. The equation included a dummy variable to control for gender (1 = MALE) and a variable for AGE (14 to 17 years).[20]

The length of an economics course was also likely to have an effect on student achievement. Data collected from a teacher questionnaire indicated that the length of economics courses varied for students. For about half the students the economics course lasted one year or less, while for the other half the course lasted two years. A dummy variable was included in the model to capture the effect of course LENGTH (1 = two-year course). A case can be made for either a positive or negative effect. On the positive side, those students with a longer course would be expected to score higher because they had more instructional time. On the negative side, some students in the longer course were taking the posttest after covering only half of the course material, and so would be at a disadvantage on some test items. The direction of the effect, however, is most likely to be negative because the test instrument covers a broad range of economic content and thus would disadvantage students taking a two-year course who were in the middle of their economics instruction.

In addition, the teacher data indicated that there were differences in course content. In most cases teachers reported teaching both micro- and macroeconomics in their courses, but in a few cases teachers stated that they taught only micro or only macro. Accordingly, a dummy variable for CONTENT (1 = both micro and macro) was included. It was expected that students of teachers who taught both micro and macro would outperform students taught one or the other topic, because the *TEL* includes questions covering both micro and macro.

The regression analysis also controlled for the effects of national differences. Four dummy variables were included to capture the effects of student scores in Lithuania, Latvia, Ukraine, and Kyrgyzstan. The omitted variable was for Poland, so the nation coefficients reflect the national differences in scores relative to Poland. No a priori expectations were made for national differences because the IEEP seminars were similar in all nations.

Finally, a dummy variable was included to reflect teacher group membership. If students were taught by an IEEP teacher that variable was given a value of one, but if the students had another teacher the variable had a value of zero. It was expected that the IEEP variable would be positive and significant given that the IEEP teacher had additional training in economics and used IEEP materials. The coefficient for this variable was an estimate of the contribution to students of an average IEEP teacher.

Table 4.6 presents the regression results for the students across all five nations. The variable mean and standard deviation are reported in the square brackets beneath the acronym for each variable. The dependent variable is the change from pre- to posttest in student learning in economics as measured by the

TEL. The table reports findings from a sample of 1,746 students for whom there were complete data across all variables.

The regression results show that students with an IEEP teacher received an additional benefit of 1.4 *TEL* points on the 23-item *TEL* relative to students with a No IEEP teacher, after accounting for the effects of other relevant variables. In relative terms, this additional 1.4 points represented an 11 percent increase over the mean pretest score of 12.76 for both the experimental and control groups.

Table 4.6: Regression results for IEEP and control students

Regressors	Dependent Variable = TELCHANGE [2.07; 3.71]	Absolute values of *t* statistics
AGE [15.69; 0.77]	-0.291*	2.25
MALE [47.2%]	0.100	0.57
IEEP [64.2%]	1.417**	7.68
LITHUANIA [10.1%]	-0.559	1.67
LATVIA [6.1%]	0.967*	2.30
UKRAINE [47.2%]	-1.343**	5.77
KYRGYZSTAN [11.5%]	-0.067	0.19
LENGTH [49.1% two-year]	-0.536**	2.80
CONTENT [87.2% micro & macro]	0.726**	2.72
Constant	5.950	
N	1746	
F	17.701**	
$\bar{R}^2$	.079	

Note: Variable means and standard deviations, or percent, are shown in brackets.
**Significant at the .01 level (two-tailed test).
*Significant at the .05 level (two-tailed test).

The instructional effects in different nations varied in terms of statistical significance and the direction of the effect, relative to the baseline comparison group of students from Poland. It is, of course, important to recognize that the samples of students from these countries may not be representative of all students in their five respective countries. Nevertheless, for this study it was important to control for national differences in the five samples. In particular, students in Latvia had significantly higher scores, while a negative difference was found for students in Lithuania and Kyrgyzstan compared to students in Poland, although those differences were not statistically significant. There was a significant difference in scores between students in Ukraine and Poland in favor of students in Poland.

Considering student-specific factors, no significant gender effects were found, which is consistent with prior US research that tends to show that the rate of learning economics is the same for males and females (Becker, Greene, and Rosen, 1990). There was, however, a surprising negative effect for age, which was statistically significant, with younger students outscoring older students. This result is difficult to explain. It may reflect differences of curriculum effects or motivation to do well on the test for students of different ages (older students may not take the test as seriously as younger students because they are about to graduate). It may also be that younger students gained more life experience with markets and the economy, especially in the transition economies, because the time period for the study is a bigger percentage of their life and experience than it is for older students.

The results for the course variables supported one hypothesis, but raised questions about another. The breadth of the course content seemed to have a significant effect on students. As expected, students with teachers who reported teaching both micro and macro showed an increase in posttest scores over students who have teachers covering only one of the two topics. Students in two-year courses scored lower than students in one-year courses. This result is probably due to the short duration of the evaluation (five months), which would give an advantage to those students in a one-year course because they would have covered most of the economics content that would be included on this basic test. Some students in the two-year course might have covered only half of the test content.

VIII. ATTITUDES ABOUT MARKETS

Another goal of the IEEP was to improve teacher attitudes towards a market economy and perceptions of how markets work. The basis for this change partially rests on improved knowledge of economics. As IEEP teachers learned more about how markets and the economy functioned in IEEP seminars they showed somewhat greater support for competitive markets and market reforms (EDC, 1996; EDC, 1997).[21] This change probably occurred because they better understood the benefits of this economic system from the seminars.   It is also reasonable to expect that IEEP teachers would convey their more positive attitudes about markets and the market economy to their students.   The question to be answered in this study, therefore, was whether teacher participation in IEEP seminars had any measurable effect on the market attitudes of students.

In many respects this analysis of the affective domain in economics proved more difficult and less conclusive than the analysis of the cognitive domain. This situation is understandable once the three aspects of attitudes are recognized. First, attitudes are more deep-seated in people's thinking and reflect a somewhat stable way of perceiving the world, and thus are not easily changed.[22] Given this characteristic, it is not realistic to expect much change in students' views of markets and the market economy before and after instruction, especially in the short time frame for this research study. Second, the forces that influence attitudes are not always easy to identify and capture. For example, although economic knowledge should influence economic attitudes, the effects are sometimes uncertain, the economic knowledge takes time to change attitudes, and it may not be known how important other variables are in influencing a student's perspective of markets and the market economy. Third, the methods that teachers can use for influencing student attitudes are less direct than those available for instruction in economics content. Teaching students an economic concept can easily be done through classroom lessons. Altering students' perception of their economic world may take considerable time, especially if their everyday experiences with economics run counter to what they are told in the classroom. Nevertheless, the attempt to measure the effects of IEEP on market attitudes and interpret the findings is instructive for future research studies.

From the outset, the major measurement problem was the fact that there was no existing instrument with known psychometric properties that could easily be modified and translated for use in measuring market attitudes, as was the case with the *TEL* in measuring economic understanding. Consequently, a new attitude measure had to be constructed for assessing this dimension of IEEP on students. The task of developing a valid attitude measure is more difficult than developing a cognitive test because of the problems of defining the attitude construct, sorting out unobservable factors that can influence an attitude, and the fact that attitudes are often hard to change. As a consequence, the reliability estimates for attitude measures are usually lower than those for cognitive tests in economics. These problems are evident in most attitude measurement studies found in economic education (Walstad, 1996).

The time constraints for the study also made it impossible to develop, translate, and field test new attitude items. To short-circuit this process, a market attitude survey was created by using nine attitude items that had already been tested in three published studies with adults (Alston, Kearl and Vaughan, 1992; Boeva and Shironin, 1992; Shiller, Boycko and Korobov, 1991) and with teachers participating in IEEP seminars (EDC, 1996; EDC, 1997).[23] The nine items asked about government intervention in markets, the fairness of market prices for products, business in a market economy, and support for market reforms in transition economies.

The problems with this set of attitude items became apparent in the construct validity analysis in the five nations. Although the survey could detect some change among students, the magnitude of the change was small and simply not meaningful.[24] In addition, the alpha reliability was only 0.34 overall, and it was found to be zero in Lithuania and Poland, making this nine-item survey instrument unsuitable for use as a measure of attitude change. The alternative was to use the analysis to identify just those attitude items that showed reasonable measurement properties. Six of the nine items exhibited statistically significant change from pre- to posttest when they were evaluated with the complete sample of students.

Table 4.7 presents the pretest, posttest, and change in percent correct on these six market attitude items for the IEEP and No IEEP groups. The wording of these item statements is given in Appendix 4.C. What should be noted first is that the perceptions of markets across most of the items are relatively positive, on average (IEEP: 69 percent; No IEEP: 65 percent). The one item (#4) with the lowest score asked, 'Should the government introduce limits on the increase in the price of flowers, even if it might produce a shortage?' The responses here indicate that many teachers in both groups favor government limits on prices, perhaps because they do not see how markets work in this particular case.

Table 4.7: Market attitude item percent pro-market: Five nations by group (N = 2,811)

Question No.	IEEP % Correct (N = 1,941)				No IEEP % Correct (N = 870)			
	Pre	Post	Post-Pre	*t*-value[+]	Pre	Post	Post-Pre	*t*-value
1*	74	80	6	4.20[a]	74	74	0	0.25
2	82	86	4	3.80[a]	80	84	4	2.64[a]
3	70	75	5	3.60[a]	65	70	5	2.97[a]
4	50	56	6	5.03[a]	35	41	6	3.62[a]
5	80	84	4	3.98[a]	73	72	- 1	0.22
6	60	67	7	4.70[a]	62	64	2	0.60

[+]Absolute *t*-values are reported throughout this table.
[a]Significant at the .01 level (two-tailed test).
*Copies of questions are found in Appendix 4.C.

The results also show that the overall increase in support for markets for the IEEP group was attributable to a statistically significant increase in the percent correct from pre- to posttest on *all* six items. For the No IEEP group, a statistically significant and positive change from pre- to posttest was found in just three of the six items. These results suggested that the improvement in market attitudes for the IEEP group was broader than for the No IEEEP group. The mean percentage increase in positive views about the markets for the IEEP group was 5.3, about double that of the 2.7 percent for No IEEP group.

These findings need to be qualified in several respects. First, the magnitude of the difference is still small even if it is statistically significant. That may be because both groups are starting at a relatively high base of support for market outcomes. Second, although there is a substantial difference between the two groups in their attitudinal response, the reasons for the difference are hard to interpret. This analysis also does not control for other factors that might explain the results, as was the case in the analysis of economic understanding. Certainly the more positive results for the IEEP group are promising, but more study is needed to establish confidence in these findings.[25]

IX. CONCLUSIONS

One of the most significant historical events of the twentieth century was the dismantling of the Soviet Union, followed by the difficult and uneven transition from a command economy to a market economy in the nations of eastern and central Europe and parts of central Asia. Economic education is central to the dramatic transformation of these economies because support for market reforms often relies on an understanding of economics and how a market economy works.

In this context, the main research question addressed in this study was whether seminars in basic economics for high school teachers conducted by the National Council on Economic Education (NCEE) through its International Education Exchange Program (IEEP) were effective in improving the economic understanding of high school students of these teachers. To answer these questions, data were collected from a pre- and posttest sample of students in high school economics courses during five months in 1996-1997. The courses were taught by 102 teachers in five transition economies – Lithuania, Latvia, Ukraine, Kyrgyzstan, and Poland.

Economic understanding was measured by a shortened version of the *Test of Economic Literacy* (*TEL*), a nationally normed test developed in the United States that has been shown to be reliable and valid for use in studies with students in many other nations. A careful investigation of the measurement properties of the shortened form of the *TEL* indicated that it was also a reliable and valid measure of economic understanding for use in the five nations included in this study.

The results showed a significant increase in the economic understanding of students with IEEP teachers using IEEP materials relative to students of teachers with neither of these characteristics. The findings were relatively robust. They were found across different types of analysis and sample sizes using a five-nation data set. What the results indicated was that IEEP teacher training in economics contributed to student learning of economics. Although this conclusion has been drawn in research studies of economic education in the United States, this study provides evidence of the training and materials link for improved student achievement in economics in nations making a transition to a market economy.

Several caveats qualify these results and place them in perspective. The first issue is that there may be other explanations that account for the findings. Chief among the rival hypotheses is sample selection. The type of teacher who volunteered for the IEEP seminars may have been qualitatively different from non-IEEP teachers, and thus it may be this difference and not the IEEP program that explains the test score results. It was not possible to investigate the issue with this data set and to determine whether the problem would seriously change the results or whether it was an inconsequential concern.

The second issue is the magnitude of the differences. The week-long NCEE seminars raised the economics test scores of IEEP teachers by about 10 percentage points. The evaluation of student economic learning only lasted five months and found a gain of about six percentage points. These teacher and student gains, while statistically significant, are limited in size and may not seem very impressive, unless the gains are considered in the context of similar programs using similar evaluation measures. It is important to remember that the changes provide only an indication of what is possible if there had been more instruction for teachers and the student evaluation had lasted over a longer time. It is also likely that the very short, standardized test instrument is not complete enough or sufficiently sensitive to capture all that teachers and students are learning from these economic education programs. In some ways it is more useful to compare student performance across all of the individual items on the exam than the percentage gain in the overall test score.

There was also interest about the effect of IEEP on market attitudes, and the results were generally positive or at least suggestive. The comparison of pre- and post responses to six opinion questions indicated that IEEP students became significantly more positive in their views of markets and the market economy, although both groups showed a high level of initial support for markets. This preliminary evidence suggests that IEEP seminars for teachers do make some contribution to improved student positive perception of markets and the market economy. Nevertheless, the attitude change is slight due to the measurement problems and the short time period for the evaluation. It was also not possible to control for other potential factors that might explain the results.

Research on economic education in transition economies is only beginning to be given serious study. More research will be needed to advance our understanding of how to best enhance student learning of economics and how to test the outcomes from economics instruction in each transition nation. This study provides some initial findings and indicates how that work should be conducted, but more investigation is needed to substantiate and extend the findings.

APPENDIX 4.A: Sample agenda: IEEP workshop for secondary
                    teachers

Session and Time	Concepts
1. Pretests and Participant Information (2 hours)	Assessment
2. Opening Activity: Why Do People Trade? (1 1/2 hours)	Trade, incentives, costs, benefits, mutual gains from exchange
3. Introductions, Goals of Seminar and Economic Education, Philosophy of NCEE (1 hour)	Active learning, academic content, economic education
4. Overview of High School Economics in the US (1 1/2 hours)	Fundamental concepts, microeconomics, macroeconomics, international economics
5. Broad Social Goals of an Economy and Comparing Economic Systems (1 1/2 hours)	Economic freedom. efficiency. equity, security, full employment, price stability, growth; traditional, command, market systems
6. The Economic Way of Thinking: Personal Decision-Making (1 1/2 hours)	Allocation, trade-offs, opportunity costs, decision-making
7. The Economic Way of Thinking: Solving Economic Mysteries (1 1/2 hours)	Choices, economizing, incentives, voluntary trade, economic systems
8. Basic Institutions of a Market Economy: Paper Clip Activity (1 1/2 hours)	Private property, self-interest, laissez-faire, competition, free markets.
9. Scarcity and Rising Opportunity Costs: The Geologist's Dilemma (1 1/2 hours)	Scarcity, rising opportunity costs, resources, interdependence, incentives

APPENDIX 4.A: (continued)

10. Supply, Demand, and Equilibrium Price
    (1 1/2 hours)

    Supply, demand, price, markets

11. Changes in Supply and Demand
    (1 1/2 hours)

    Demand, determinants of shifts in demand; supply, determinants of shifts in supply

12. Extensions of Supply and Demand: Price Floors and Price Ceilings
    (1 1/2 hours)

    Markets and prices, supply and demand, shortages and surpluses, rationing

13. Interdependence of Markets
    (1 1/2 hours)

    Markets and prices, supply and demand, interdependence

14. Productivity: The Book Factory
    (1 1/2 hours)

    Productivity, specialization and division of labor, investment in capital goods, human capital

15. Entrepreneurship
    (1 1/2 hours)

    Entrepreneurship, costs of production, total revenue, profit, loss

16. Business Organization and Market Structure
    (1 1/2 hours)

    Proprietorship, partnership, corporation, perfect competition, monopolistic competition, oligopoly, monopoly

17. Imperfect Competition: Widgets and Blasters Simulation
    (1 1/2 hours)

    Competition, incentives, utility, revenues, costs

18. Economic Functions of Government in a Market Economy
    (1 1/2 hours)

    Economic functions of government, public goods, market failures, externalities, stabilization, taxes, nonexclusion, shared consumption, 'free riding'

19. Social Decision-Making: Where to Spend the Money
    (1 1/2 hours)

    Scarcity, decision-making, role of government

APPENDIX 4.A: (continued)

20. Introduction to Macroeconomics   GDP, aggregate supply and demand,
    and Stabilization Policies   business cycles, inflation and
    (1 1/2 hours)   unemployment, fiscal and monetary
                                          policies, multiplier effects

21. Demonstrating the Circular   Circular flow of goods, services,
    Flow: The Econo Game   resources, and money
    (1 1/2 hours)

22. Money, Banking, and Monetary   Interest rates, inflation, monetary
    Policy   policy, money supply
    (1 1/2 hours)

23. Closing Activity   Concepts vary
    (1 1/2 hours)

24. Posttest and Seminar Evaluation   Assessment
    (2 hours)

APPENDIX 4.B: 23-Item *Test of Economic Literacy**

1. The opportunity cost of a new public high school is the:
   A. money cost of hiring teachers for the new school.
   B. cost of constructing the new school at a later date.
   C. change in the annual tax rate to pay for the new school.
   D. other goods and services that must be given up to build the new school.

2. Which of the following choices do all economic systems face? How to:
   A. balance imports and exports.
   B. balance the government's budget.
   C. make the best use of scarce resources.
   D. save money to reduce the national debt.

3. The specialization of labor results in:
   A. increased price inflation.
   B. less output per hour worked.
   C. greater economic interdependence.
   D. more equal distribution of income.

4. Which of the following is the most essential for a market economy?
   A. Effective labor unions.
   B. Good government regulation.
   C. Responsible action by business leaders.
   D. Active competition in the marketplace.

5. Profits are equal to:
   A. sales minus taxes and depreciation.
   B. sales minus wages and salaries.
   C. assets minus liabilities.
   D. revenues minus costs.

6. The functions of money are to serve as a:
   A. unit of account, a medium of exchange, and a store of value.
   B. determinant of investment, consumption, and aggregate demand.
   C. determinant of capital spending, aggregate supply, and exchange.
   D. system for accounting, a means of income redistribution, and a resource allocator.

APPENDIX 4.B: (continued)

7. If your annual money income rises by 50% while prices of the things you buy rise by 100%, then your:
   A. real income has risen.
   B. real income has fallen.
   C. money income has fallen.
   D. real income is not affected.

8. The price of shoes is likely to be increased by:
   A. new machines reducing the cost of shoe production.
   B. more capital investment by producers.
   C. a decrease in the demand for shoes.
   D. a decrease in the supply of shoes.

9. 'Americans are a mixed-up people. Everyone knows that baseball is far less necessary than food and steel. Yet they pay ball players a lot more than farmers and steelworkers.' Why?
   A. The employers of the ball players are monopolists.
   B. Ball players are really entertainers rather than producers.
   C. There are fewer professional ball players than farmers or steelworkers.
   D. Good ball players are more scarce, given the demand for their services.

10. A newspaper reports, 'COFFEE GROWERS' MONOPOLY BROKEN INTO SEVERAL COMPETING FIRMS.' If this is true, we would expect the coffee-growing industry to:
    A. increase output and decrease prices.
    B. decrease output and increase prices.
    C. use more capital goods and hire fewer workers.
    D. use fewer capital goods and hire fewer workers.

11. In a market economy high wages depend mostly on:
    A. minimum wage laws.
    B. actions of government.
    C. high output per worker.
    D. socially responsible business leaders.

12. From an economic point of view, which of the following approaches to pollution control is most efficient?
    A. Abolish the use of toxic chemicals.
    B. Use resources to reduce all pollution damage.
    C. Control pollution as long as the extra benefits exceed the extra costs.
    D. Prohibit economic activities that cause pollution or harm the environment.

APPENDIX 4.B: (continued)

13. Gross Domestic Product is a measure of:
    A. the price level of goods and services sold.
    B. total spending by federal, state, and local governments.
    C. the quantity of goods and services produced by private businesses.
    D. the market value of the nation's output of final goods and services.

14. The limit of an economy's potential output at any time is set by:
    A. the quantity and quality of labor, capital, and natural resources.
    B. business demand for final goods and services.
    C. government regulations and spending.
    D. the amount of money in circulation.

15. If from time to time total spending declines relative to productive capacity, the growth rate of the economy over a long period will be:
    A. lower because some productive resources will not be fully employed.
    B. lower because of a heavier reliance on the raw materials of foreign countries.
    C. higher because inefficient plants, equipment, and labor no longer need be employed.
    D. higher because production will be concentrated on necessary goods rather than luxuries.

Questions 16 and 17 are based on the following graphs.

ECONOMIC CONDITIONS IN PARKLAND

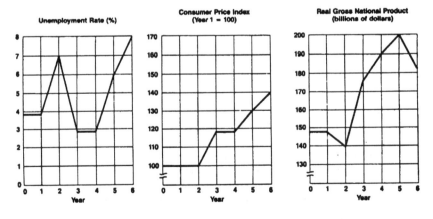

APPENDIX 4.B: (continued)

16. Parkland had both rising unemployment and a high rate of inflation during which period?
    A. Years 1 to 2.
    B. Years 2 to 3.
    C. Years 3 to 4.
    D. Years 4 to 5.

17. Parkland had an increase in output with a relatively low inflation rate during which period?
    A. Years 1 to 2.
    B. Years 2 to 3.
    C. Years 3 to 4.
    D. Years 4 to 5.

18. When commercial banks increase their loans to businesses and consumers, this usually results in:
    A. a decrease in the spending power of consumers and businesses.
    B. an increase in government control over the economy.
    C. an increase in the banks' excess reserves.
    D. an increase in the nation's money supply.

19. One reason the federal government might reduce taxes is to:
    A. slow down the rate of inflation.
    B. slow down a rapid rise in interest rates.
    C. decrease business spending on plant and equipment.
    D. increase consumer spending and stimulate the economy.

20. If Britain has a comparative advantage over France in the production of cars, then:
    A. there are no gains from specialization and trade in cars between Britain and France.
    B. the opportunity cost of producing cars in Britain is higher than in France.
    C. the opportunity cost of producing cars in Britain is lower than in France.
    D. Britain will benefit from a decline in the demand for cars.

21. Which of the following statements about tariffs is true?
    A. Tariffs increase the market for exports.
    B. Tariffs decrease employment in protected industries.
    C. Tariffs benefit some groups at the expense of others.
    D. Tariffs encourage the growth of the most efficient industries.

APPENDIX 4.B: (continued)

22. To correct a balance of trade deficit in the United States, many members of Congress want to increase import tariffs. If this occurs, then we should also expect:
    A. increased U.S. imports and exports.
    B. decreased U.S. imports and exports.
    C. increased U.S. imports and decreased U.S. exports.
    D. decreased U.S. imports and increased U.S. exports.

23. Which of the following best measures a nation's standard of living over time?
    A. Money income per capita.
    B. Real income per capita.
    C. Rate of unemployment.
    D. Rate of inflation.

APPENDIX 4.C: Market attitude questions

1. If the price of coffee on the world market suddenly increased by 30 percent, what do you think is likely to be the blame?
   A. Interventions of some government.
   B. Such things as bad harvest in Brazil or unexpected changes in demand.
   C. Speculators' efforts to raise prices.

2. Who should run businesses?
   A. State ownership is the best way to run a business.
   B. An enterprise is best run by entrepreneurs producing goods people want.
   C. Do not know.

3. On a holiday, when there is a great demand for flowers, their prices usually go up. Is it fair for flower sellers to raise their prices like this?
   A. Yes.
   B. No.

4. Regarding the prices for flowers, should the government introduce limits on the increase in prices of flowers, even if it might produce a shortage of flowers?
   A. Yes.
   B. No.

5. Do you think that people work better if their pay is directly tied to the quantity and quality of their work?
   A. Yes.
   B. No.

6. In the movement from a non-market to a market economy it is important that the ownership of productive resources be privatized at the onset.
   A. Agree.
   B. Disagree.

NOTES

This chapter is based on material originally reported in Walstad (1997). That report was prepared with the support of the National Council on Economic Education through funding provided from the Office of Educational Research and Improvement (OERI) at the US Department of Education. Further analysis using a more limited data set is found in Walstad and Rebeck (2001). I received many helpful comments from Mike Watts in preparing this chapter.

1. These two reasons are in addition to the initial purpose of the study, which was to evaluate the effectiveness of the NCEE's teacher training programs in these nations.
2. The NCEE viewed these teacher programs as 'demonstration seminars.' The NCEE never intended to conduct all of the teacher training seminars in these nations, but sponsored them to give examples of what can be done in each nation. To sustain this seminar work, the NCEE also recruited people who would conduct additional seminars in these nations after they successfully completed one of the NCEE's 'Training of Trainers' workshops. As for the composition of the 204 participants, most were secondary teachers, but there were a few school administrators and university faculty who also attended.
3. The sample agenda was typical of most seminars, but there may have been some variation based on topics of particular interest at some workshop locations, or the preferences of individual instructors.
4. For the cumulative record of evaluation results from teacher testing and surveys in all seminars, see EDC (2000).
5. The descriptions of the experimental and control groups, and testing and data collection procedures, are based on information obtained from Jody Spiro, Evaluation Manager for International Programs at the Education Development Center, Inc. The selection procedure for teacher participation at IEEP workshops varied and did not follow a precise rule. The teachers were chosen for IEEP seminars by the local partners of the NCEE in each nation, who recruited teachers from recommendations from education officials and responses to ads in newspapers. The most important criteria for selecting the volunteer teachers were that they be currently teaching or likely to be teaching economics at the pre-university level. A few school administrators and university faculty were also admitted to the seminars. For a description of the characteristics of teachers attending IEEP seminars see EDC (1996) and EDC (1997).
6. The first Kyrgyzstan seminar was attended by 31 teachers in 1995. Of this group, 22 attended a second seminar in the spring of 1996 along with 12 new teachers. Eighteen of these teachers attended a third seminar in summer of 1996. Teachers in this group, therefore, had the most extensive training in economics and how to teach it.
7. There were about 139 of the 200 participants in the five IEEP seminars who met these criteria (Lithuania: 15; Latvia: 26; Ukraine: 37; Kyrgyzstan: 36; and Poland: 25). Economics is frequently taught in grades nine and ten in these nations, as noted in many of the country studies in later chapters of this volume. In the United States, economics is typically taught in the eleventh or twelfth grades. For a description of economic education in US high schools, see Walstad (2001).
8. As another example, the control and experimental teachers taught at different schools within a nation, so this difference may have affected student scores.
9. The rate of teacher attrition from pretest to posttest in the two groups is roughly similar (IEEP: 14 percent; No IEEP: 21 percent), and not statistically significant in two-tailed tests of population proportions. It is not unusual for some teachers to drop out from a voluntary study because of classroom time constraints, a lack of interest, or some other factor that cannot be easily identified. The 21 dropouts from the 123 teachers were distributed across the nations: Lithuania (7 of 26); Latvia (1 of 7); Ukraine (3 of 33); Kyrgyzstan (6 of 26) and Poland (5 of 31).
10. The percentage of teachers in each group who did not complete a questionnaire is about the same for each group (IEEP: 13 percent; No IEEP: 12 percent). No information was available from EDC on why teachers did not complete a questionnaire.
11. This data collection procedure raises two concerns, but they are not likely to be important. First, the fact that there was no EDC partner on site to administer the test and insure that copies of the test or of some test items were not made while the instruments were under the teachers' control can raise doubts about whether there was cheating or test manipulation by the teachers. This issue is probably a minor one in this study, however, because: (1) teachers had little or no incentive to engage in such unprofessional behavior (this was not high-stakes testing); (2) EDC or in-country partners briefed teachers on the purpose of the research and made it clear that it was not a personal

evaluation of their teaching; and (3) test data are often collected under test 'insecure' conditions in economic education research projects without any apparent problems (e.g., see Saunders, 1991, or Walstad and Rebeck, 2001). Second, IEEP teachers were given the *Test of Economic Literacy* during their training seminar and thus may have used this information to their advantage when they tested their students. This manipulation is also unlikely because: (1) teachers did not know they would be participating in this study until long after their training seminar was over, were authorized to use copies of the *TEL* to study during or after the seminar, and were not likely to remember the test questions; (2) the *TEL* teachers were given as a test had twice the number of items as the version given to students, so they would not know which items would be used for student testing; and (3) teachers had little or no incentive to act in this way.

12. Another sample selection issue for this data set is the nonrandom data loss for students between the pre- and the posttest (Becker and Walstad, 1990). The pretest was administered to 3,745 students: 2,396 IEEP students and 1,349 No IEEP students. Posttest data were also obtained from 2,811 students who took the pretest: 1,941 IEEP students and 870 No IEEP students. The problem for this study was that it was not possible to specify a selection equation to adjust the regression analysis because the set of variables was too limited for explaining why the posttest was not taken. Whether the student took the posttest, however, was in almost all cases decided by the teacher and not the student, unless the student happened to be absent the day the posttest was given. This teacher attrition issue is discussed in a previous endnote. A similar percentage of teachers in each group gave a pretest but did not give a posttest to students. This equivalence suggests that group membership is not likely to affect the decision of the teacher to posttest, and thus inflate the IEEP gains. Also, the average score on the pretest for students of IEEP and No IEEP teachers who did not give a posttest was essentially the same.

13. Since this evaluation was conducted, a third edition of the *TEL* has been prepared (Walstad and Rebeck, 2001). There is a strong connection between the two editions because 40 of the 69 items in the third edition are the same or modified versions of items from the second edition.

14. These calculations were obtained using a formula described in Wood (1988).

15. The only national exception was Lithuania, whose students showed no significant differences from pre- to posttest on the *TEL*. That may be the result of less economics instruction for both student groups in this nation. a problem with the test translations. or some other factor. No specific information is available to explain this outcome.

16. The calculation was derived from a formula in Wood (1988).

17. For example, the reliability for the *Test of Understanding of College Economics* is 0.76 for the macro version and 0.82 for the micro version (Saunders, 1991).

18. The one exception was an item on comparative advantage. This concept was probably not given much emphasis in the seminars (see Appendix 4.A).

19. The regression can also be estimated with the posttest as the dependent variable and the pretest as a regressor. The results from this specification were similar to those using the change score as the dependent variable that are described later in this section.

20. Age may also capture the effects of differences in students' grade levels in their schools. The problem with including a grade variable was that many students did not report their grade, and even for those who did the definition of a grade level was not consistent across nations.

21. One reason for the limited amount of change in teacher attitudes on many market-related items was that their support for markets was high initially before attending the seminars.

22. There is a difference between economic attitudes, which reflect a psychological predisposition to think in a certain way about many topics, and economic opinions, which are more transitory and can easily change as facts or information changes. This study looks at attitudes towards markets and whether they tend to favor or oppose market processes in explaining or determining economic outcomes. For further discussion of this distinction in the research literature, see Walstad (1996, pp. 165-7).

23. The content validity of the survey items was based on their previous use in seminars for IEEP teachers. The pre- to posttest results from the seminars showed that some of the items were able to detect changes in opinions towards markets among teachers (EDC, 1996; EDC, 1997). The successful use of items with teachers suggested that some could be used with students, just as the *TEL* was used with teachers and with students; but that proved not to be the case.

24. Responses that indicated the most support for competitive markets or market reforms were given a value of 1, and other responses received a zero, so the scale ranged from 0 to 9. Students had a pretest mean attitude score of 5.28 and a posttest score of 5.51 points, for a statistically significant gain of only 0.22 points (t-value = 6.93) on the 9-point scale.

25. It might be thought that the solution is to specify a regression equation with the post–pre survey score as the dependent variable and using a set of regressors as found in Table 4.6. The problem with this approach is that six attitude items produce pre and post scores with a very limited range (0-6). This summated measure is highly unreliable given the few items on the survey, and creating a post-minus-pre change score only compounds the reliability and validity problems. Some preliminary work was conducted along those lines with the nine-item survey and produced inconclusive results (see Walstad, 1997). A better approach would be to use probit analysis to analyze the student, teacher, and class factors affecting specific responses to particular survey items. This complicates the analysis, however, because it produces six estimated equations that have to be interpreted rather than one. Such analysis is beyond the current scope of this chapter and will be the focus of another study.

REFERENCES

Allgood, S. and W.B. Walstad (1999), 'The longitudinal effects of economic education on teachers and their studies,' *Journal of Economic Education*, **30** (2), pp. 99-111.

Alston, R.M., J.R. Kearl, and M. Vaughan (1992), 'Is there a consensus among economists in the 1990s?' *American Economic Review*, **82** (2), pp. 203-9.

Beck, K. and V. Krumm (1998), *Wirtschaftskundlicher Bildungs-Test (WBT): Handanweisung*, Gottingen, Germany: Hofrefe-Verlag.

Becker, W., W. Greene, and S. Rosen (1990), 'Research on high school economic education,' *Journal of Economic Education*, **21** (3), pp. 231-45.

Becker, W. and W.B. Walstad (1990), 'Data loss from pretest to posttest as a sample selection problem,' *Review of Economics and Statistics*, **72** (1), pp. 184-8.

Boeva, I. and V. Shironin (1992), 'Russia between state and market: The generations compared,' *Studies in Public Policy* (#205), Glasgow, Scotland: Centre for the Study of Public Policy, University of Strathclyde.

Bosshardt, W. and M. Watts (1990), 'Instructor effects and their determinants in precollege economic education,' *Journal of Economic Education*, **21** (3), pp. 265-76.

Cook, T.D. and D.T. Campbell (1979), *Quasi-Experimentation: Design and Analysis Issues for Field Settings*, Boston: Houghton-Mifflin.

Education Development Center, Inc. (EDC) (1996), *International Economic Education Exchange Program: Program Report*, New York: EDC, International Programs.

Education Development Center, Inc. (EDC) (1997), *Final Program Evaluation: International Economic Education Exchange Program, 1996-1997*, New York: EDC, International Programs.

Education Development Center, Inc. (EDC) (2000), *Program Results: 1995-2000*. New York: EDC, International Programs.

Lietz, P. and D. Kotte (2000), *The Importance of Economic Literacy*, Frankfurt, Germany: Peter Lang.

Saunders, P. (1991), *Test of Understanding of College Economics: Examiner's Manual* (3rd ed.), New York: Joint Council on Economic Education.

Saunders, P. and J. Gilliard (1995), *A Framework for Teaching the Basic Economic Concepts: With Scope and Sequence Guidelines*, New York: National Council on Economic Education.

Shiller, R.J., M. Boycko, and V. Korobov (1991), 'Popular attitudes toward free markets: The Soviet Union and the United States compared,' *American Economic Review*, **81** (3), pp. 385-400.

Soper, J.C. and W.B. Walstad (1987), *Test of Economic Literacy: Examiner's Manual* (2nd ed.), New York: National Council on Economic Education.

Walstad, W.B. (ed.) (1994), *An International Perspective on Economic Education*, Boston, Massachusetts, USA: Kluwer Academic Publishers.

Walstad, W.B. (1996), 'Economic knowledge and the formation of economic opinions and attitudes,' in P. Lunt and A. Furnham (eds), *Economic Socialization: The Economic Beliefs and Behaviour of Young People*, Cheltenham, England and Brookfield, Massachusetts, US: Edward Elgar, pp. 162-82.

Walstad, W.B. (1997), *The Effects of the International Economic Education Exchange Program on Student Economic Understanding and Market Attitudes: A Research Report*, Lincoln, Nebraska: National Center for Research in Economic Education.

Walstad, W.B. (2001), 'Economic education in US high schools,' *Journal of Economic Perspectives*, **15** (3), pp. 195-210.

Walstad, W.B. and K. Rebeck (2001), *Test of Economic Literacy: Examiner's Manual* (3rd ed.), New York: National Council on Economic Education.

Wood, R. (1988), 'Item analysis,' in J.P. Keeves (ed.), *Educational Research, Methodology, and Measurement: An International Handbook*, Oxford, England: Pergamon, pp. 376-84.

5. Economic Education as the Missing Link in Georgian Policy Reform

Craig R. MacPhee

The economies of the Soviet Union were sick before the demise of communism and took a turn for the worse after the USSR split into 15 separate republics. The patients fell into depression accompanied by greater unemployment, inflation, poverty and their complementary social ills. Western advisors prescribed PILLS: Privatization; Investment; Liberalization; Legislation (to establish the rule of law); and Stablilization.

The dosage of PILLS has been the subject of controversy, as summarized by Stiglitz (1999). Shock therapy requires large doses of PILLS over a short time and gradualism would involve low doses over an extended period. Nevertheless, western economists generally agree that PILLS are necessary for the restoration of economic growth and future prosperity.

Unfortunately, the patients do not share the western doctors' confidence in PILLS. Soviet propaganda, transmitted through the media and schools, glorified the productivity of Soviet workers and factories, the security of life isolated from the West, and 'free' government services including electricity and health care. Capitalism was criticized for its high crime rates, monopolistic exploitation, and macroeconomic instability. The propaganda was repeated so often that it took on the status of truth, at least among large segments of the population. Contradictions, such as high standards of living in western nations, could always be attributed to capitalistic imperialism, exploitative foreign trade, and investment practices that impoverished the rest of the world.

Even if the average Soviet citizen did not believe all the propaganda, survival in a Marxist totalitarian regime required adopting a Soviet mindset: A system of laws was not necessary; just follow the orders of those in authority. To influence and benefit from the orders that were given, do the bosses a favor. Don't make independent decisions; leave it to the higher authorities. Avoid making recommendations, giving specific answers, and taking responsibility; that could lead to Siberia or worse. It was better to do nothing, to act like everyone else, and to speak with vagueness and ambiguity. There were no private property rights, so people helped themselves to public property. Successful party officials advanced by sponsoring big new construction projects; never mind the operation, maintenance, and repair of the existing capital stock.

Because production goals were usually quantitative, no one bothered about quality. Because prices were set, there was no interest in monetary policy.

Because virtually all inputs and output were allocated by the government, no one was concerned about taxes, expenditures, and fiscal deficits. Because external trade was mostly prohibited, there were no worries about trade deficits or tariff revenue. Because the important decisions were made in Moscow, government officials in the republics neglected policy-making. Because so many policy decisions were arbitrary and opaque, the public was cynical about the behavior of government officials. Because the republics resented Moscow, local government officials and state enterprise managers were more intent on limiting exports to other republics than on fulfilling Moscow's five-year plans.

Those attitudes make PILLS alone inadequate for reform in the former Soviet Union, because as Fischer (1999) has noted, successful transition requires a broad consensus supporting implementation of reforms. Although attitudes can be changed through economic education, that itself requires substantial work, and reformers have been slow to appreciate the role of economic education in transitional economies.

In fact, one can make a case that advising on economic policy has a substantial economic education component whether it takes place at home or abroad. As the reminiscences of former members of the Council of Economic Advisers in the United States suggest, advising on economic policy can be thought of as 'opportunities to teach economics' (Feldstein, 1992). At least one collection of CEA memoranda has even been cited as material that would enrich the teaching of macroeconomics (Gramlich, 1993). There are some important distinctions, however, between domestic advising of the CEA variety and foreign advising on reform in transitional economies.

American presidents choose their economic advisors whereas governments in transitional and developing countries usually receive advisors assigned to them by the International Monetary Fund (IMF), World Bank, or US Agency for International Development (USAID) as part of a package of financial and technical assistance. To quote Samuelson (1962, p. 17) in the case of an American president or high official, '...note that he who picks his own doctor from an array of competing doctors is in a real sense his own doctor. The Prince often gets to hear what he wants to hear.' On the other hand, the finance minister, central bank president, or president in a transition economy are confronted by advisors who give them bitter pills to swallow: cut government expenditures and deficits, stop monetizing deficits with inflationary increases in the money supply, open your borders to imports, and so on.

The public role of the top economic advisors in the US has been limited. According to Weidenbaum (1988), 'some of the most successful [CEA] chairmen kept the lowest profiles, avoiding formal speeches and press conferences.' In contrast, foreign advisors who once worked mainly behind the scenes have engaged in more public economic education activity in order to build and sustain support for reform.

Broad-based efforts to support reform initiatives through education programs have been organized with increased frequency in recent years. Visiting professor appointments in universities, fellowships for students, and other academic and cultural exchange programs with western institutions have been funded for many years. Advising programs for government officials have also included educational seminars and training through simulation exercises and tutorials. A new emphasis is on public education through the media: training for journalists; coordinated press conferences and interviews; publication of reports and information (GEPLAC, 1998); call-in radio programs; and advertising on television.

This chapter gives some illustrations of these educational efforts and concludes with a discussion of the necessary conditions for their effectiveness. The illustrations are presented in the context of some hard lessons taught by recent economic events in Georgia. This portrayal of broad-based economic education in Georgia is based on my experiences while working at the Caucasus Center of the University of Maryland's Center for Institutional Reform and the Informal Sector (IRIS) in 1998-99 and at the KPMG Consulting Barents Group Fiscal Reform Project in 1999 and 2000-01. These projects were two of about 40 supported in Georgia by the USAID. In addition, the European Union program of Technical Assistance for the Commonwealth of Independent States (TACIS), the embassies of the United States, Germany, Japan, China, and the United Kingdom, as well as the European Bank for Reconstruction and Development (EBRD), the IMF, and the World Bank were all part of the technical and humanitarian assistance community in Georgia. Threats to Georgia's territorial integrity also prompted assistance from the US Army, Coast Guard, and Border Patrol. Below I refer to this foreign aid community simply as the donors.

I.   LESSON 1: OPEN ECONOMIES ARE SUBJECT TO EXTERNAL SHOCKS

After independence, Georgia was cut off from rubles previously supplied by the Russian central bank in payment for Georgian goods and services, as well as inter-bank and inter-governmental transfers. In 1993, the government of Georgia ignored warnings from the World Bank and IMF (1995-98) and began printing currency coupons so fast that prices rose by 7,488 percent in 1993 and another 6,474 percent in 1994. After the introduction of a new currency, the lari, in 1997, however, responsible monetary policy eventually eliminated inflation and preserved a stable dollar/lari exchange rate of $0.75 through early 1998.

The Russian Crisis of 1998

Public confidence in the lari was shattered by the Russian financial crisis of August, 1998. The lari plummeted to $0.50 during the first weekend in September and Georgian newspapers were soon full of stories variously blaming the devaluation on Georgia's dependence on trade with Russia, on the incompetence of Georgian government officials, on unscrupulous foreign exchange retailers, and on manipulation by a banking oligopoly. The Georgian media reflected Soviet attitudes against international trade, against pro-market reformers in government, and against exploitation by financial capitalists.

The nation's central bank, the National Bank of Georgia (NBG), quickly raised interest rates on inter-bank credit (the equivalent of the American federal funds rate) from 22 percent to 38 percent, intervened in the small foreign exchange market by selling $15 million, and announced its intentions to stabilize the exchange rate on television. The lari rose back to $0.74 within days, but media coverage of this episode demonstrated the need for more widespread and reliable economic education in Georgia.

The IRIS center in Georgia responded with a report examining the economic links between Russia and Georgia (MacPhee, 1998a). This report pointed out that Russia accounted for only one-fourth of Georgian exports and that these amounted to only one percent of Georgia's GDP, hardly a vehicle to wreak havoc on the Georgian economy. Georgian imports from Russia were mainly natural gas, electricity, grains, and machinery, items with price elasticities low enough to lower Georgia's import spending in the aftermath of the ruble devaluation. The main difficulty created by the Russian crisis was one that had not been mentioned in the press. Many Georgians earned income in other parts of the former Soviet Union, converted this income into dollars, and made dollar remittances (unilateral transfers to Georgia) which accounted for an unknown but probably substantial share of Georgia's GDP. The Russian recession would lower those remittances, reduce the spending based on the remittances, and slow the Georgian economy. The decline in demand for the lari could therefore be explained by expectations of recession in Georgia, rather than by evil doings in the foreign exchange markets.

Nevertheless, the NBG used the crisis as an excuse to shut down 343 of the 465 currency exchange booths that operated in Tbilisi, the capital city which houses almost one-third of the Georgian population. The NBG's move would obviously increase the market power of the remaining booths, which were associated with a few dominant banks. This anti-competitive action was opposed by some donors, however, and most exchange booths were allowed to reopen. But then bank lobbyists successfully pressed the government for stricter licensing regulations of the exchange booths (e.g., requiring bullet-proof glass), which would have increased the costs of operating booths and thus driven some of the small booths out of business. Fortunately for the sake of competition, the government has failed to enforce these regulations.

The Russian Crisis of 2000

Despite all the problems in Russia in 2000, it was a large nation that could provide better opportunities for many entrepreneurial Georgians than they could find in their small and isolated homeland. Access to Russia was easy because the Bishkek Agreement of 1992 allowed citizens of the Commonwealth of Independent States (CIS) to move among member countries without visas. On 30 August 2000, however, Russian Foreign Minister Igor Ivanov announced that Russia would withdraw from the Bishkek Agreement and negotiate visa regimes with other CIS member states on a bilateral basis. In fact, Georgia seemed to have been singled out as the one CIS member state of concern because of its open northern border with Chechnya. Russia said it was ready to impose visa requirements on Georgian citizens by 5 December, provoking press reports of catastrophe for the Georgian economy.

Some Russian officials claimed that 900,000 Georgians were working in Russia and a member of the Georgian parliament predicted that the Russian visa restrictions would cut annual remittances from Russia to Georgia by $3 billion. Seeking to quell any panic, the NBG issued a report stating that only 130-150 thousand Georgians in Russia were making remittances and that the annual amount was only $150-180 million. The Bank also noted that the adverse effects of visa restrictions would be mitigated by the repatriation of assets, including human capital.

Obviously there was considerable uncertainty about the size of the remittances from Russia, and the wide range of predictions about the consequences of the new Russian visa regime created serious problems and concerns for government ministries and foreign donors and lenders. Would Georgia fall into a depression or remain stable? Would the demand for the lari fall as in 1998? The answers to these questions depended not just on economic analysis, but also on economic facts that had been measured imprecisely, if at all. But the discipline of economics has developed ways of thinking about problems even without complete information, and this second Russian crisis provided an opportunity to illustrate this way of thinking (MacPhee, 2000a).

The USAID Fiscal Reform Project first searched out the most reliable information on migration. The State Department of Statistics received no funding to conduct a census in 2000, but it did report bits and pieces of information with widely varying relevance. This information was compared and cross-checked for consistency, producing an estimate of 430 thousand Georgians working in Russia – less than half the number claimed by Russia but about three times the NBG estimate.

Second, indirect evidence could be used to infer the amounts remitted from Russia. Clearly, the parliament member's estimate of $3 billion was far too high, because Georgian GDP only amounted to $2.3 billion (IMF, 2000). The NBG had reported that commercial bank account and wire transfers ranged from $60 to $80 million in recent years. Transfer expenses, fear of bank failure, the ease with which tax authorities attached bank accounts, and an age-old tradition of secretiveness, however, probably induced people to carry most cash remittances on their person. NBG data show that Georgians keep less than a fifth of their lari on deposit in banks, supplying some support for an assumption – another element of the economic way of thinking. If Georgians were behaving in the same way with respect to their use of banks for domestic deposits and for dollar remittances from

Russia, then total remittances would be about five times the amount transferred through banks, or $300 to $400 million annually.

The $400 million in remittances was a relatively large amount for the small Georgian economy, about one-sixth of GDP. If all Georgians were forced out of Russia that would probably trigger a substantial recession. But the economic way of thinking also involves considering alternatives and long-run responses. The Russians gave Georgians plenty of time to respond to the threat of visa restrictions. Obvious evasion tactics included false marriages to Russians and bribery of Russian officials. The Russian government also said that it would not enforce visa restrictions on the secessionist regions of Abkhazia and South Ossetia, thereby creating more opportunities for Georgian citizens to enter Russia through those regions. Finally, many Georgian citizens already carry Russian passports and may continue to enter Russia freely. Thus, consideration of economic alternatives suggested that only a small fraction of Georgians would be forced to come home, and that the likely decline in remittances would yield at most a small recession.

II. LESSON 2: AUTOMATIC ADJUSTMENT MECHANISMS WORK

Between its introduction in 1995 and September, 1998, the lari had only depreciated nine percent against the dollar; but this was due to the IMF's willingness to finance relatively small balance of payments deficits. The NBG had spent $172 million defending the lari in 1997, but it had not had to intervene at all in 1998 until the September crisis. By the end of October, 1998, the lari fell briefly to $0.67, the NBG had only $100 million left in reserves, and the IMF was threatening to cut off stabilization funds because the Georgian government had not collected as much tax revenue as it had agreed to collect. This situation provoked wild commentary from government officials and from the media that the lari would go into free-fall and the Georgian economy would collapse. Once again, the ignorance of market equilibrating mechanisms was manifest.

The IRIS center in Tbilisi responded with another report that examined the various components of Georgia's international payments and calculated that the balance of payments deficit was doubling in size (MacPhee, 1998b). A simple elasticities approach was used to estimate that the dollar value of the lari would fall 40 percent if no stabilization funds were received from external sources. This devaluation would be substantial, but as the report noted, not out of line with the recent experience of other transition economies. And 40 percent was hardly a free-fall. The report did not eliminate sensationalism in the media, but the lari did fall about 40 percent. It fluctuated around that low level for most of 1999 before stabilizing at about $0.50 throughout 2000.

Georgian economic stability in the aftermath of the large devaluation surprised many locals as well as donors. They worried about continued government budget deficits and trade deficits (6.7 percent and 18.8 percent of

GDP, respectively) in 1999 (IMF). They asked whether the Georgian economy would be destabilized by these deficits. Clearly, there was a need for an economic explanation that short-run macroeconomic equilibrium does not require every sectoral balance to be zero.

Economic advisors needed to give tutorials on the simple leakage-injection approach to equilibrium income determination. The equilibrium condition ($I + G + X = S + T + M$) could be rewritten to show that $M - X = (G - T) + (I - S)$. Thus, it was quite easy to have a trade deficit ($M > X$) and budget deficit ($G > T$) in short-run equilibrium. The problem lay in the long-run effects of the financing of these deficits. The budget deficit needed to be eliminated not to avert an immediate crisis, but to build public confidence, increase saving and investment, and thereby foster economic growth.

III.   LESSON 3: INSTABILITY HINDERS GROWTH

The report on the devaluation of the lari (MacPhee, 1998b) also explained the effects of the devaluation on inflation, on the burden of Georgia's large foreign debt, and perhaps most importantly on Georgia's fledgling financial sector. In the absence of stock and bond markets, banks were the main source of funding for local business investment. (A stock exchange did not open until mid-2000.) After independence, many defunct state enterprises formed bank subsidiaries, and there were as many as 229 banks in 1995 with less combined capital than one mid-sized US bank. Most of these so-called banks had made loans to insiders who promptly fled with the money, so their assets were often worthless. Moreover, the government had frozen deposits during the hyperinflation of 1994, certainly not a policy to inspire confidence in potential depositors. Consequently, Georgians kept their monetary wealth in dollars hidden under floorboards, and the banks were largely unable to perform their role of financial intermediation. Bankruptcy and consolidation, encouraged by NBG enforcement of minimum capital requirements and other regulations, reduced the number of banks to 47 by 1998. Only 22 banks were considered viable, and they accounted for almost all the deposits and current lending in Georgia.

The concentration in banking made this sector a natural target for the media and the politicians who decried low interest rates on deposits (averaging about 14 percent during the first half of 1998), high interest rates on loans (about 37 percent), and supposed manipulation of the exchange rates. The devaluation report (MacPhee, 1998b) attempted to explain, however, that devaluation actually weakened the banks even more. They were required to hold lari reserves, which lost relative value, and nervous depositors were making withdrawals. Thus, the abysmally low level of bank lending would fall even lower in an economy that desperately needed more investment.

Risk and inflationary expectations were keeping loan interest rates high and also explained the large spread between deposit and loan rates. The links among the exchange rate, inflationary expectations, and the government's failure to collect taxes also needed emphasis. In the absence of a bond market and IMF funds, the NBG would be under pressure to monetize the deficit, actions that the public remembered as leading to the hyperinflation of 1994. Inflationary expectations increased the demand for dollars and kept downward pressure on the value of the lari.

These principles of economics were presented to about 40 journalists who attended a three-day workshop sponsored by the World Bank in December, 1998 (MacPhee, 1998c). The workshop also covered trade liberalization and the implications of World Trade Organization (WTO) accession for Georgia, privatization in the energy sector, private lending activities of the International Finance Corporation and of subsidized western banks, as well as sessions devoted to journalism issues.

The discussion of media issues turned out to be revealing as conflicts surfaced between the new private journalists (mostly young) and the state-run broadcasters and publishers (mostly older). When a producer of a state radio news series described some of her public information programs on reform, she was derided by the younger journalists who criticized her hypocrisy as a former communist, the tedium of her program, which the youths claimed had low ratings, and her biased reporting on reforms, which the cynical youths regarded as ineffectual. This criticism of the slow pace of reforms presented an opportunity for discussion of the economic concepts of long-run growth and short-run instability, with emphasis on the centuries it took for the market system in western Europe to develop. Even if no institutional changes were required, Barro and Sala-i-Martin (1991) have found that differences in per capita incomes between regions tend to be reduced by only about two percent per year. The Southern states after their defeat in the Civil War have grown faster than the rest of the US, but after more than one hundred years, personal income in the South is still a little below the US average.

To counter widespread cynicism and to build support for economic reform, USAID expanded its support for public education in 2000. News conferences, public seminars, interviews, conferences, short-courses, and site visits were arranged to cover most elements of the reform process. Every educational event involved economics.

Public education was necessary to implement many reforms. For example, a non-profit, nongovernmental organization helped one million farmers obtain legal, transferable titles to their privatized land; but in order to accomplish this the media had to explain the concepts of property rights and to publicize the availability of legal assistance. Another USAID contractor established a Georgian stock exchange, but people then had to be given information about capital markets, the role of the new Securities and Exchange Commission, shareholder rights, and management obligations. Publicity of the lending activities of several banking joint ventures subsidized by USAID and provided with loanable funds by the International Finance Corporation included lessons on money markets and on the effects of investment on the local economy. Economic theories of production and cost were covered by short-courses for managers and accountants. Organized media coverage of reform activities such as these occurred on a daily basis.

IV. LESSON 4: DEFICIT MONETIZATION LEADS TO CURRENCY DEPRECIATION

In the aftermath of the 1998 Russian crises and Georgian devaluation, the need for journalists to learn about the harmful effects of fiscal deficits was evident. In response, the World Bank sponsored a second three-day workshop. The European Union also sponsored a semester-long course in Tbilisi. In addition, the Academy for Educational Development used USAID funds to send eight journalists to California State University at Chico for courses including macroeconomics and microeconomics. Weekly seminars for journalists were also held during the spring of 1999 by the Fiscal Reform Project. Economic advisors from USAID, the Fiscal Reform Project, and the US Treasury also offered a three-week course on macroeconomics to 35 future government officials in the Master's program of the new Georgia Institute of Public Administration, a program supported by the National Association of Public Administrators and the University of Georgia. Reporting on the importance of fiscal reform improved and the media expressed more skepticism toward government officials who blamed their failure to collect more tax revenue on the bad weather and the Russian crisis. A public opinion survey indicated that the public was getting the message (GORBI, 1999). About 92 percent believed that corruption was an impediment to collecting taxes and 82 percent said that they would pay their taxes if everyone else did. Seventy-two percent felt that tax rates were too high, however, and most thought that revenues were going to pensioners and the police rather than to their highest priorities: education and health care. Despite increased public awareness of the causes and consequences of deficits, the rate of tax collections actually fell in late 1998 even though nominal growth in GDP continued.

On 4 December, 1998, the NBG gave up its defense of the lari and, as noted above, the currency's value fell about 40 percent. This unleashed a torrent of wild statements in the media, reflecting either economic ignorance or demagoguery. The press reported immediate price increases of 60 percent, stirring up fears of a new round of runaway inflation. The volatility of the lari's exchange value, which bobbed up and down between $0.47 and $0.63 a dozen times in the first two months of floating, also contributed to uncertainty. Of course, the press was full of stories blaming the ups and downs on conspiracies among banks, exchange dealers, and corrupt government officials. A jump in kerosene prices was attributed to a cartel controlled by Nugzar Shevardnadze, the President's nephew, instead of the onset of cold weather and a decrease in electricity supply. (In fact, the ease of smuggling prevented any cartel from being effective.)

The time was right for another exercise in economic education for the general public. In December of 1998, American economic advisors went on a radio call-in show and in February, 1999, the IRIS center issued another report explaining the reasons for currency volatility and the links between inflation, devaluation, and the fiscal deficit (MacPhee, 1999a).   One did not need conspiracies to explain volatility.   The exchange market for lari was very thin and it was driven by expectations that changed with each bit of bad or good news from Russia or the IMF.   People held more dollars than lari, but they would change into lari for transactions such as holiday shopping, thereby causing temporary appreciation. Monetary policy tightened after the September crisis, but government spending financed by the NBG led to a 22 percent increase in the lari money supply in December, 1998. The report concluded that 'Nothing would bolster the lari like a big increase in tax collections.'

Both the February report and a subsequent IRIS study (MacPhee, 1999b) disputed the runaway inflation claims. The IRIS staff carried out an independent survey of the most important items in the Georgian CPI and found that the CPI was fairly accurate. In the first two months after the devaluation the CPI rose only 15 percent. The media reports of 60 percent inflation were bogus.

V. LESSON 5: POTENTIAL REVENUE = (TAX BASE) × (TAX RATE)

Shortly after issuance of the February IRIS report (MacPhee, 1999a), the US announced a narrower emphasis for technical assistance efforts with concentration on just a few areas, perhaps the most important being tax revenue. The fiscal deficit had only fallen from 314 million lari in 1997 to 310 million lari in 1998 (6.5 percent of GDP), so not much progress had been made in improving budgetary discipline. Moreover, the government had to 'finance' 64 million lari of this deficit by accumulating arrears, or in other words by failing to pay its obligations (mainly to its employees and pensioners).

The large deficits stemmed in part from a failure of the government to collect all of the revenue that it planned in the budget. In 1998 the central government planned on revenue of 762 million lari but collected only 622 million, giving Georgia one of the lowest revenue/GDP ratios among transition economies (Tanzi and Tsibouris, 2000).   All of the transition economies have had problems collecting revenue, largely from lack of experience. During the Soviet period the government relied almost exclusively on just three taxes (enterprise, turnover, and payroll) that were collected simply by tapping the state bank accounts of state enterprises.

To focus on the problem of revenue shortfalls, the US ambassador visited with the Georgian president to gain his assurance of cooperation. After that, the Fiscal Reform Project became a much more aggressive program. Most of the fiscal reform activities involved retraining tax inspectors, reorganizing the tax department, and overseeing the implementation of new policies such as excise tax stamps.

Donors had been asking the Georgian government to increase tax collections for a long time. Higher revenue was favored by the IMF, the World Bank, USAID, the Georgian parliament, and the Georgian president. But there had never been any systematic effort to estimate the size of the tax bases that would determine how much revenue could be raised. This meant that no realistic targets could be established in order to assess the performance of the Ministry of Revenue. Consequently, there was a need to educate the responsible government officials on the methods that economists would use to estimate the size of the tax bases.

In 1999 advisors from the US Treasury, the IMF, and the Fiscal Reform Project met with officials of the State Department of Statistics, the Macroeconomic Forecasting Department of the Ministry of Finance, the Parliament Budget Office, members of the Parliament Budget Committee, and the Ministry of Economy. The main problem in estimating potential tax revenue turned out to be the lack of reliable statistics on the economy. The Statistics Department and most ministries were full of Soviet-era *apparatchiks* (bureaucrats) even though the leaders were young and some had US training in economics. The *apparatchiks* were used to sitting back and accepting often erroneous and usually unaudited reports from state enterprises, which they would then aggregate in order to issue their quarterly statistical review for the republic.

In fact, the Statistics Department staff were not doing what we normally think of as economic statistics. They had little awareness of sampling techniques or statistical inference, and were slow to grasp and adopt these ideas. When advisors demonstrated to them how the travel component of the current account could be estimated with a short telephone survey of 20 active hotels in Tbilisi (MacPhee, 1998d), the staff responded by developing a 10-page questionnaire for one thousand (mostly defunct) hotels in Georgia. They also proposed a law requiring hotels to complete and file the extensive survey every month. At this point the advisors conducted a short lesson on cost-benefit analysis, which unfortunately did not halt the bureaucratic momentum behind the comprehensive questionnaire.

Despite years of intermittent training by IMF and European advisors, the national income accounts and trade statistics are still unreliable. The World Bank, however, funded the recruitment of some former statistics professors to work in the Statistics Department on a fairly reliable household survey. Thus, there was reasonably accurate information on consumption that could be pieced together with some of the more reliable production data, using the international trade identity: consumption = production − exports + imports. Economic advisors in the Fiscal Reform Project demonstrated how the Georgian agencies could estimate the tax bases for customs duties and excises on cigarettes, gasoline, and alcohol, as well as the value-added tax (VAT) (MacPhee, 1999a, d, e, h, i, j). Eventually Georgian officials agreed to form an inter-agency working group that would employ these methods to introduce more realism into the Georgian revenue targets.

Most of the potential revenue estimates were astounding. The foregone revenue from cigarettes alone would have covered 40 percent of the total government budget deficit. The tax collection rate on petroleum products was only 44 percent and collection of VAT was only 48 percent of potential. Clearly there was much room for improvement at the Ministry of Revenue.

VI.   LESSON 6: ACTUAL REVENUE = (COLLECTION RATE) × (POTENTIAL REVENUE)

The estimation of potential revenue and establishment of realistic targets for the Ministry of Revenue addressed only one part of the fiscal problem in Georgia. Unrealistic budgets were another piece of the fiscal puzzle. After some initial consolidation of the government in the first years of independence in the early 1990s, government expenditures began rising in both real and nominal terms. They rose from 19 percent of GDP in 1995 to 23 percent in 1998 (IMF, 2000).

The pressure to increase expenditures in the face of limited means to finance deficits led the Ministry of Finance to project unrealistic increases in budget revenue: 28 percent in 1998 and 65 percent in 1999. In fact, total revenue increased only 10 percent in 1998 and 11 percent in 1999. Obviously there was a need for some lessons in budget revenue forecasting, but the forecasts had to be based on more than anticipated increases in the tax base. There also needed to be annual estimates of how much the Ministry of Revenue would improve its rate of collecting taxes (MacPhee, 1999 f, g).

On the subject of forecasting economic growth, the previous educational efforts of a series of short-term advisors from the US Treasury, the IMF, and the World Bank had gone astray. Forecasting seminars had been offered to Ministry of Finance staff and computer hardware and software had been provided. Afterward the staff spent their time constructing models by data mining from unreliable time series covering no more than four years. Then they would issue their over-optimistic revenue forecasts without disclosing anything about the model. The links between the economic projections and revenue forecasts were also not described. The central government budget for 1999, for instance, forecast 10 percent real growth and six percent inflation, but forecast a total state budget revenue increase of 26 percent (Ministry of Finance, 1999). In fact, real growth turned out to be only three percent, inflation was 11 percent, and state revenue grew only five percent (Ministry of Finance, 2000).

The Fiscal Reform Project approached the problem of unrealistic budget revenue projections from two angles. First, US-trained Georgian staff worked with the forecasting staff in the Ministry of Finance to document their model, to review the unreliable data and, in the process, to suggest improvements. The advisors also explained the importance of careful interpretation of forecasts in light of their inevitable inaccuracies. The staff of the Ministry of Finance reacted favorably to this approach and began to include more specific commentary about the economy and measurement problems in their documents.

The Ministry of Finance forecasts became more conservative in the 2000 budget. Real growth was projected to be five percent, inflation eight percent, and consolidated government budget revenue growth 15 percent. As it turned out, however, these forecasts were not conservative enough. The Georgian economy ended up stagnating in 2000 and total tax revenue rose only six percent, barely keeping up with inflation. Because government expenditures were budgeted to rise 40 percent, the Ministry of Finance could not finance the resulting deficit and had to ask the Parliament to revise the budget in mid-2000.

In the second approach to the revenue projection problem, advisors from the Fiscal Reform Project and the US Treasury tried to bring the Ministry of Finance and the Ministry of Revenue into closer cooperation in projecting improvements in rates of tax collection. The estimates of potential revenue were adjusted for forecasted economic growth and were then used as the ultimate goal for the Ministry of Revenue. Reasonable steps toward meeting that goal would then be established over a series of years. In essence, tax collection targets would be raised each year until the Ministry of Revenue finally met its long-term goal. The series of targets would be revised each year in light of new forecasts of economic growth.

The idea of a long-term progression of revenue targets was first proposed in mid-1999 (MacPhee, 1999i), but it still had not been implemented in early 2001. This episode in itself is a lesson in public choice economics. The proposal faces great resistance from the Ministry of Finance, which wants the freedom to make revenue projections that will cover planned expenditures and put the pressure on the Ministry of Revenue to collect sufficient taxes.

VII. LESSON 7: TAXPAYERS DEMAND TRANSPARENCY IN GOVERNMENT

The unsuccessful attempts to raise revenue could be attributed in part to widespread public cynicism about government. As noted earlier, public opinion surveys demonstrated that the vast majority of Georgians thought that government revenue mainly benefited corrupt officials instead of the public priorities such as health care and education.

Public cynicism was reinforced by a lack of transparency in the budget process. During the Soviet period the budget had been a state secret and the budget process was shrouded from outside scrutiny. Although the parliament began to debate and ultimately ratify budgets after the fall of communism, complete transparency still has not been achieved. The budget approved by parliament was a stack of tables full of detailed, unexplained budget line numbers and monetary amounts categorized by function rather than by government agency. No minister or parliamentarian, let alone journalist, could decipher government priorities from this mass of information. Clearly there was a need for economic education in the expenditure area of public finance.

The Fiscal Reform Project tried to increase budget transparency through two demonstration projects in which Georgian staff were trained in some basic principles of public finance and ministries were shown how their budgets could be usefully summarized and evaluated. One project presented the Georgian fiscal situation in a 40-page 'Budget in Brief' (Ministry of Finance, 1998, 1999, 2000). The Budget in Brief began with a review of the macroeconomic environment and the forecasts on which the budget was based. Then it presented the overall budget before going into explanations of each major component on both the revenue and expenditure sides. This was very basic material, but something that had never been done before in Georgia.

The second project attempting to increase transparency was a budget-line review of public expenditures. Georgia experienced many of the same fiscal problems as other developing and transition economies. Linkages among policies, plans, and budgets were weak. Expenditure control was so poor that there was seldom a close connection between budgets and actual spending. Government agencies could not count on a reliable flow of funds and there was inadequate reporting on specific expenditures and the outcomes of spending. An expenditure review would examine these problems in each agency and serve as a guide for improving future budgets and expenditure control.

Because reporting was so sporadic and inconsistent, the Fiscal Reform Project advised the Ministry of Finance to add forms to the annual budget requests. Each budgetary unit would report its expenditures by budget line for the previous two years as well as the current year. Of course, in this type of economy there are three different ways of measuring each expenditure: (1) the amount planned to be spent; (2) the amount of spending commitments made; and (3) the amount actually paid in cash. Each unit was asked to explain differences among the three measures of expenditures, reasons for large changes, purposes and outcomes of various expenditures, priorities, revenue sources, and legislative mandates if any. Again, this was a very basic informational rather than conceptual exercise, but never before had it been undertaken in Georgia. It will be interesting to see if expenditure reviews are continued by the Georgians after the current Fiscal Reform Project winds up in the summer of 2001.

VIII.   LESSON 8: TELEVISED INSTRUCTION ON ECONOMIC PRINCIPLES SUPPORT REFORM

In order to encourage taxpayer compliance and the re-election of reformers, the USAID funded an extensive public education campaign. No specific candidates or political parties were endorsed; instead, a series of public-service messages appeared on television in the spring of 1999. The television messages were scripted and produced by Georgians and, like commercials, they were short and superficial. Nevertheless, each of the messages reflected a principle of economics, although not all were the principles that we commonly emphasize in US classrooms.

Here are the ten lessons that the television messages attempted to communicate:

1. People must make choices.
2. People have to be adaptable because economic growth requires change, illustrated visually by a steam locomotive being transformed into a bullet train and by a VW Beetle being transformed into a racecar.
3. Growth will benefit future generations, reinforced by a scene of the Pilgrim ships giving way to the lunar landing.
4. The US market system is worthy of emulation, demonstrated by scenes of the Manhattan skyline.
5. People have to cooperate and work together in the new system in order to accomplish their goals, illustrated by armies of workers building the pyramids in Egypt and by two cartoon spacemen working cooperatively on an alien planet.
6. Reform is a long process but it has a lot of momentum and there is no going backward, symbolized once again by the locomotive transformed into bullet train.
7. World markets are competitive and competitors have to move fast, again demonstrated by the transformed VW racing around a speedway.
8. The main purpose of taxation is to finance public goods, illustrated with pictures of Georgia's natural scenery and wildlife, historical monuments, roadways, and schoolchildren.
9. Tax evasion hurts all of us by denying public goods to ourselves.
10. There are penalties for failure to pay taxes, illustrated by a scene of tax inspectors confiscating cases of unstamped cigarettes and alcohol.

These were basic messages, some might even say platitudes, but public opinion surveys had revealed widespread public ignorance about the reform process. The television messages addressed the fundamental ideas that markets are a form of cooperation and that government has a legitimate role in a market economy.

Whether the messages accomplished their goal, however, is an open question. The pro-reform coalition in parliament managed to maintain its majority in elections at the end of October, 1999 and the President was elected to a second term in April, 2000. Tax collections rose throughout the first half of 1999, but fell again in the autumn and aside from a December spike remained at low levels through the first half of 2000. The IMF again withheld stabilization funds and insisted on fiscal improvements, which the Georgians made in the second half of 2000. State budget expenditures were cut and state tax revenues were increased so that the deficit was reduced by about 10 percent from its 1999 level. A new set of IMF conditions were met and the IMF Executive Board provisionally approved

$150 million in credit for Georgia to be disbursed subject to further conditions over the 2001-03 period.

IX. CONCLUSION

Although this narrative is confined to broad-based efforts for economic education in only one of the 15 republics of the former Soviet Union, there is a similar need for more economic education in most other transition economies. After a decade of reform, there is still widespread belief in the outmoded Soviet ideas of isolationism, government control, and capitalistic exploitation and instability. These ideas impede the process of reform by providing a rationale for government policies that are inefficient, fiscally and monetarily irresponsible, anti-competitive, and inflationary. These ideas also foster corruption among poorly paid government officials and cynicism among citizens.

Donors have gradually become aware of the barriers to reform erected by the old ways of thinking. This awareness has motivated the recent emphasis on economic education through advising government officials, training journalists, and providing accurate economic information to the general public. These economic education efforts have faced their own share of difficulties: mistakes in translation; lack of continuity; overly sophisticated concepts; and poor coordination among the various organizations providing technical assistance.

When advice to a government involves some difficult economic lessons, the prince sometimes does not listen to what he does not want to hear. Over the last several years in Georgia the donors have not succeeded in educating the Ministry of Finance about the need to reduce expenditures given projected revenues and deficits. Fiscal austerity, however, has not always been welcome advice in the US either (De Long, 1996; Stein, 1996), so one should probably not attribute this lack of success to any peculiar characteristics of Georgian officials or their advisors. De Long (1996) quotes one former member of the CEA as saying, 'in this business, .250 is still a very, very good batting average.'

Recent experience in places like Georgia carries some lessons for those involved in the unique economic education process of foreign advising. Economic educators in transition economies should place more emphasis on the basic ideas of scarcity, choices, the short-run, the long-run, and trade-offs. They should stress the importance of accurate measurement of economic variables. They should give repeated explanations of the sources of change and the equilibrating mechanisms in market economies. They should clarify the roles of competition, property rights, and stable government policies. Finally, they should remind local citizens and donors that the reform process is a long one. The evolution of the market system in western Europe did not take place overnight, and we should not have unrealistic expectations that the present economic reforms will take less than a generation to begin showing positive results.

NOTE

This chapter updates and extends my article in the Winter 2001 issue of the *Journal of Economic Education*. Marah Ovakimian deserves credit for superb translation.

REFERENCES

Barro, R. and X. Sala-i-Martin (1991), 'Convergence across states and regions,' *Brookings Papers on Economic Activity*, **1**, 107-82.

De Long, J.B. (1996), 'Keynesianism, Pennsylvania Avenue style: Some economic consequences of the Employment Act of 1946,' *Journal of Economic Perspectives*, Summer, **10**, pp. 41-53.

Feldstein, M. (1992), 'The Council of Economic Advisers and economic advising in the United States,' *Economic Journal*, September **102**, pp. 1223-34.

Fischer, S. (1999), 'The financial crisis in emerging markets: Lessons for eastern Europe and Asia,' Speech to the East West Institute. New York.

GEPLAC (Georgian-European Policy and Legal Advice Centre) (1998), 'Georgian economic trends (3),' Tbilisi: TACIS (Technical Assistance for the Commonwealth of Independent States from the European Union).

GORBI (Georgia Opinion Research and Business Information) (1999), 'Public Opinion Survey Report for USAID,' June 11.

Gramlich, E. (1993), 'Review of memos to the president: A guide through macroeconomics for the busy policymaker,' *Journal of Economic Literature*, September **31**, pp. 1453-54.

International Monetary Fund (1995-2000), 'Georgia: Recent economic developments.' IMF Staff Country Reports No. 95/112 (November), 96/116 (November), 97/36 (May), June 12, 1998, and 00/68 (May). Washington, DC.

MacPhee, C.R. (1998a), 'Georgia and the fall of the ruble,' Tbilisi: IRIS Caucasus Center, September 7.

MacPhee, C.R. (1998b), 'Devaluation of the lari and its effects,' Tbilisi: IRIS Caucasus Center, October.

MacPhee, C.R. (1998c), 'Credits for travel in the Georgian balance of payments,' Tbilisi: IRIS Caucasus Center, December 1.

MacPhee, C.R. (1998d), 'Q&A on the lari and the Georgian economy,' Tbilisi: IRIS Caucasus Center, December 5.

MacPhee, C.R. (1999a), 'Cigarettes and deficits in Georgia,' Tbilisi: IRIS Caucasus Center, February 4.

MacPhee, C.R. (1999b), 'The lari roller-coaster and the Georgian economy,' Tbilisi: IRIS Caucasus Center, February 17.

MacPhee, C.R. (1999c), 'Inflation in the aftermath of the Georgian devaluation,' Tbilisi: IRIS Caucasus Center, March 5.

MacPhee, C.R. (1999d), 'Where have all the flours gone?,' Tbilisi: IRIS Caucasus Center, March 15.

MacPhee, C.R. (1999e), 'The consistency of Georgian statistics on ethyl spirits and derivative beverages,' Tbilisi: IRIS Caucasus Center, March 19.

MacPhee, C.R. (1999f), 'General principles for the macroeconomic component of the basic directions document for the budget in 2000,' Tbilisi: Barents Group Fiscal Reform Project, May 10.

MacPhee, C.R. (1999g), 'Basic directions document for the 2000 budget: Macroeconomic environment,' Tbilisi: Barents Group Fiscal Reform Project, May 19.

MacPhee, C.R. (1999h), 'Potential government revenue from gasoline in Georgia,' Tbilisi: Barents Group Fiscal Reform Project, June 9.

MacPhee, C.R. (1999i), 'Forecasts of Georgian value-added tax revenue,' Tbilisi: Barents Group Fiscal Reform Project, June 10.

MacPhee, C.R. (1999j), 'Potential Georgian government revenue from petroleum products,' Tbilisi: Barents Group Fiscal Reform Project, June 23.

MacPhee, C.R. (2000a), 'The impact of Russian visa restrictions on the Georgian economy and postscript on the impact of Russian visa restrictions.' Tbilisi: Barents Group Fiscal Reform Project, November 24 and December 4.

Ministry of Finance (1998, 1999, 2000), 'Budget in brief,' Tbilisi: Government of Georgia and USAID Barents Fiscal Reform Project.

Samuelson, Paul A. (1962), 'Economics and the history of ideas,' *American Economic Review*, **52** (1), 1-18.

Stein, H. (1996), 'A successful accident: recollections and speculations about the CEA,' *Journal of Economic Perspectives*, Summer, **10**, pp. 3-21.

Stiglitz, J. (1999), 'Whither reform? Ten years of the transition,' Annual Bank Conference on Development Economics, Washington, DC.: World Bank.

Tanzi, V. and G. Tsibouris (2000), 'Fiscal reform over ten years of transition.' International Monetary Fund Working Paper WP/00/113.

Weidenbaum, M. (1988), 'The role of the Council of Economic Advisers,' *Journal of Economic Education*, Summer, **19**, pp. 237-44.

PART TWO

Country Reports on Reforming Economic
Education

6. Economics Instruction in Belarus

Alexander Kovzik, Anatoli Kovalenko, Mikhail Chepikov, and Michael Watts

The Republic of Belarus borders Russia, Ukraine, Lithuania, Latvia, and Poland. It declared its independence on 27 July 1990, and took its first step towards the establishment of a democratic system of government through the adoption of a new constitution on 15 March 1994. That much of its history during the transition period is generally in line with other European nations that were part of the former Soviet Union. From that point on, however, the Belarusian experience is unique.

In 1995, President Alexander Lukashenko moved the country back toward his version of market socialism. His powers to direct the economy were greatly expanded in a national referendum that modified the constitution in November of 1996. Since then he has reimposed administrative controls over prices (including foreign exchange rates) and subjected private businesses to numerous regulations and controls – some imposed retroactively – including frequent and rigorous inspections, and prohibitions of many previously legal practices.

Politically, Belarus not only maintains formal economic and political connections with Russia, but has occasionally discussed the possibility of a formal reunion. Generally, the structure and pace of its economic reforms is much closer to what has occurred in Russia than the reforms implemented by its neighbors to the West and North, due largely to what has been called its 'self-isolation' from US and European market economies. All of this has, predictably, limited western investment in the country. Two poor harvests in 1998 and 1999 made the situation even worse, as have persistent trade deficits. GDP per capita fell from an estimated $3,500 in 1993 to $2,180 in 1998. The population fell from 10.4 million in 1993 to just under 10 million in 2000 (World Bank, 2000).

The educational system in Belarus also continues to reflect a strong influence from Russian practices, philosophy, and ideology. It is a very large system – at the beginning of the 1998-99 school year it included 4,500 pre-school institutions, 4,783 elementary and secondary schools, 249 vocational schools, 151 state special secondary schools, 57 state and private[1] higher educational institutions, and over 100 skill improvement and retraining institutions. Over 2.1 million students and about 200,000 teachers attended or worked in these schools, excluding the retraining institutes. Overall, education employs about 400,000 workers, representing about 10 percent of total employment in the Republic (UNESCO, 2000).

I. ECONOMICS IN THE COMPULSORY CURRICULUM

General education is delivered in three stages: primary education (four years, grades 1-4), basic education (five years, grades 5-9), and general secondary education (two years, grades 10 and 11). As in most former republics of the Soviet Union, the quality of precollege education in Belarus is generally high and meets or exceeds international standards in many areas, especially math and natural sciences. However, it has three notable weaknesses that were also inherited from the Soviet era. These problems play a crucial role in current efforts to develop and deliver economic education in the nation's schools.

First, students are overloaded with required courses and homework. All students in a school district take the same courses, and almost all districts in the nation offer courses in the same basic disciplines, including mathematics, chemistry, biology, physics, geography, history, literature (mostly Russian and Belarusian), foreign languages, and a few other disciplines. Usually the total number of disciplines taught in a school system is between 24 and 27. Almost all of the disciplines are compulsory, and every teacher treats his or her subject as a major requirement in the curriculum. High school students who are interested in humanities and plan to major in fields such as literature, history, or economics after graduation have to study chemistry, biology, and physics as if they planned to be future chemists, physicists, or biologists. This course overload is a holdover from the cold war period, when every Soviet student had to be well prepared in these 'strategic' subjects.

Second, secondary humanities and social sciences courses, including economics, are still treated as an important part of the state ideological system. Many textbooks are still based on Marxist-Leninist methodology, in spite of the fact that officially students are to receive instruction on 'humanistic values.' This ideological bias is not surprising in a country that continues to celebrate 7 November – the anniversary of the 'Great October Socialist Revolution' – as a major holiday, and where the president decides which textbooks on Belarusian history are right or wrong.

Third, economics was never a separate discipline in the general secondary schools during the Soviet era. Some elements of economics from the Marxist perspective were, however, included in humanities courses on Man and Society, world history, the history of Belarus, and geography. Today, economics is still not a compulsory subject in the secondary schools. In grades 10-11, however, students study such topics as production, the national standard of living, property rights, the distribution of income. the market and its role in the development of society. monopoly, competition, and the role of the government in the Man and Society course.

Some positive changes occurred in the early 1990s, due to a high demand from the emerging market economy for economists and lawyers. Private colleges and universities offering just two majors, business and law, grew like mushrooms.

These changes led to a rising demand for basic economic education from high school students who planned to enter these colleges and universities.

In 1992-93 the Ministry of Education allowed general secondary schools to offer special economics and businesses classes, and adopted the following list of approved course titles for those classes: introduction to economics, principles of entrepreneurship, basic secretarial training, economic geography of the world, economic geography of Belarus, mathematics, and informatics (information systems). By 1996, 135 of these classes with a total enrollment of 6,505 students were registered by elementary and secondary schools across the nation – a significant but relatively small start, compared to the national total of nearly 5,000 schools at these grade levels. Looking at the distribution of those student enrollments, 156 students were in grades 1-4, 3,013 in grades 5-9, and 3,336 in grades 10-11 (Plotnitskii et al., 1997, p. 6).[2]

Under the 1992-93 Ministry plan, general secondary schools were also allowed to offer economic subjects (principles of entrepreneurship and introduction to economics) as elective courses. By the end of 1996 there were 370 of these classes in grades 8-11, enrolling 8,425 students.

In 1998 the Ministry of Education adopted an elective course with 136 hours of instruction (68 hours in grades 8-9 and 68 hours in grades 10-11), titled Introduction to Economics. This program was revised in 2000, retitled as Principles of Economics and Entrepreneurship and scaled back to 102 hours of instruction. Schools are allowed to increase or decrease these hours, which means teachers now have some flexibility in developing and using their own course outline and materials. These changes, however, must be approved by the regional teachers' retraining institutes that offer courses and training programs that educators are required to periodically complete to keep their jobs as teachers or administrators.

One broader initiative was initially proposed in 1996 when, in cooperation and with financial support from the Belarus Soros Foundation (BSF), the Ministry of Education started to develop state standards in high school economics. Unfortunately, shortly thereafter the Belarusian national government banned the Soros Foundation due to political and ideological disagreements with the president of the BSF and with George Soros himself. Without the organizational and financial support of the BSF, national economic standards have still not been developed.

In another initiative launched in 1996, staff members from the Ministry of Education, a group of professors from Belarus State University (BSU) and Belarus State Economic University (BSEU), and members of some non-government associations, developed ideas for a new concept of economic education in the nation's elementary and secondary schools. The main goal was to incorporate economics instruction in the curriculum at all three levels of the elementary and secondary schools. It was claimed that this new approach would provide students with more economic knowledge at an earlier age, be based on international standards, and help students understand the real economy[3] (Plotnitskii et al., 1997).

The proponents of this approach argued for the adoption of four key principles for economic education at the precollege level. It should: (1) become an essential part of secondary education; (2) prepare all students to work and live in the newly emerging market environment (not just a priority for special groups of students, such as those who attend special schools, gymnasiums, or lyceums); (3) begin in the primary schools and continue in the second and third levels of general secondary education; and (4) be both complex and realistic, with classwork supported by extracurricular activities that provide students real life experience in the fields of production and business.

It was further argued that these principles could be realized by introducing economic terms and topics in the syllabuses of the other compulsory social studies subjects. This objective could also be achieved by offering optional classes on economics, which students could choose in accordance with their interests, and by including special classes on economics and economics courses as a required part of the curriculum for students in grades 1-11 or 8-11.

The planning group then suggested the following goals and content breakdowns for economic education in the four stages of Belarusian elementary and secondary schooling. In preschool the main objective is to give children a basic understanding about people's roles in the economy as workers and consumers, and to introduce basic economic terminology connected with life experiences. For example, at this stage children would be introduced to such concepts as a person, worker, consumer, wants, money, personal budgets, and saving.

In elementary schools (grades 1-3), students are introduced to the basic concept of each person's role in his or her family and society, and shown how certain economic concepts can be applied in real life using real-world examples. Here children become familiar with such concepts as a family and its wants, the different types of jobs performed within families, the relationship between work and the fulfillment of a family's wants, what society is, and why citizens are responsible for the economic welfare of their society. They also learn what firms and enterprises are, and what types of enterprises exist.

The principal objective for grades 4-9 is to prepare students to make careful and deliberate economic decisions. Students learn the basic principles of what economics systems are, how they operate, and how the Belarusian economic system and the domestic economy function. They begin to see and use economic analysis, and gain some understanding of entrepreneurship and the basics of operating a business.

The secondary level (grades 10-11) is the final stage of forming students' understanding of economics and the economy. Students study complex problems related to the development of various social and economic processes in society. In other words, at this stage a pre-professional competence of the students is to be achieved, which prepares a student to function in society or in some cases to pursue professional levels of training in economics and business.

This proposed structure represented a giant step forward from the existing forms of economic education in Belarus. Many features of the plan are based on curriculum ideas that are often proposed, although not always achieved, in the United States. That is not surprising because some of those involved in developing the concept proposal were familiar with US standards and practices in the field of economic education, and had been participants in several international seminars and conferences.

The program has not yet been officially adopted in Belarus, however, for several reasons. Perhaps the two major obstacles are the lack of funds in the state budget to launch such a major project, and the political resistance of many Belarusian government officials to adopting market reforms. At present, only some schools in the country are trying to implement some principles of the overall concept, in collaboration and with sponsorship from the economics departments at universities in their regions. As long as the complete program is not adopted, each teacher is able to decide what questions, topics, and concepts are to be included in the curriculum, and what questions are not important. That much flexibility is not always a good thing. particularly given the peculiar history of teaching economics in Belarus and the other republics that were part of the Soviet Union.

II. VOLUNTARY AND ELECTIVE PROGRAMS IN ECONOMICS

As things stand today there is not likely to be widespread and routine inclusion of economics in the nation's school curriculum in the near future. Instead, the main avenue for introducing economics in the secondary schools is through optional courses and programs. Currently there are two basic approaches for that kind of coursework, extracurricular classes and classes of 'labor education.'

Extracurricular Classes

Students can sign up for extracurricular classes in economics in the same way they do for sports, dancing, music, etc. These programs in economics are popular among high school students, but there are important limits to their scope and reach. First, there must be a teacher in the school who is willing and able to teach the elective economics class, and often that does not happen because pedagogical universities in Belarus do not prepare secondary school teachers of economics. Also, the salary of Belarusian teachers is extremely low. In September of 2000 the average monthly salary in education was 44,000 Belarusian rubles, which was equal to $40. The relative wage for teachers was 53.4 percent of the average industrial wage. Moreover, to get these wages teachers had to work on average 31 percent overtime (Skuratovitch, 2000). That leaves teachers very little time or energy to prepare special courses for extracurricular activities.

There were several attempts to organize extracurricular economics classes on a commercial basis (meaning that students would pay several dollars a month for the classes). This format would create some financial incentives for teachers, but the Ministry of Education usually opposed these arrangements. And actually, almost all commercial activity in the country meets with considerable resistance from state officials.

The most successful example of extracurricular economic education is the Youth School of Business, *Velesitchi*, which was established in 1990 and sponsored by the Belarusian Union of Entrepreneurs and Employers. During the past 11 years nearly 1,500 students in grades 10-11, from Minsk and surrounding regions, graduated from the school. With strong financial and organizational support from the Union the school offered a wide range of classes, including Principles of a Market Economy, Introduction to Entrepreneurship, Principles of Management and Marketing, Financial Management of the Enterprise, Principles of Accounting, and an Introduction to International Business. The school has received extensive publicity in the educational media because of its innovate approach to economic and business education.

Another successful educational organization, the Youth Entrepreneurship Support and Development Center,[4] organized in 1996 by 17 teachers, offers similar programs teaching economic concepts and other kinds of business courses. The Department of Education of the Minsk Executive City Committee finances some of their programs, but grants and charitable donations sponsor most of the activities. The Center not only organizes classes for students, but also provides seminars for teachers on active methods of teaching and conducts a student competition called 'Stairway to Success.' It also organizes student teams to participate in a US-based stock market game and competition.

Labor Education

The second approach to offering optional courses on economics in general secondary education is quite new, emerging only over the past two to three years in classes called 'labor education.' These classes have been an essential part of the general curriculum since the Soviet era, but including economics concepts and coursework in these programs represents a radical departure from past practice. In these programs, students spend two to four hours a week in what are called educational-manufacturing guilds. These programs are similar to US programs in vocational education, and students receive training in basic skills for such crafts as carpentry, mechanics, and tailoring. Today the Ministry also allows these hours to be used for instruction in such disciplines as computer science, business, foreign languages, economics, and law. Each school has some flexibility to decide how to use this time, which creates a good opportunity to introduce economics in the curriculum. Once again, however, the main obstacle is that not every school has teachers who are trained in economics, and know how to include it in labor education courses.

One specialized program that works in this area was started in 1998 when the nongovernmental Institute of Parliamentarism and Entrepreneurship created a department of precollege education. The faculty members of this department teach courses on business English, basic economics, introduction to entrepreneurship, and introductory business, finance, and accounting. The audience for these courses is secondary school students from nine Minsk schools, using hours in the curriculum that were previously used for professional training. Currently this department offers 22 classes to 576 students.

III.   TEACHER TRAINING IN ECONOMICS

A major obstacle to developing and expanding economic education in secondary schools is the lack of teachers who are prepared to teach economics. That problem is particularly severe in Belarus because universities and pedagogical institutes do not train future secondary school teachers of economics. There is only one department in the country, the Department of Economics at Belarus State University, which trains future educators. But this program does not address the problem of training secondary or elementary teachers because it is intended that graduates of this department will work at universities and colleges. At most there are 30 graduates a year from this program, which basically meets the demand for university economics instructors but certainly not the demand for economics instructors at the precollege level.

Teacher retraining institutes that updated content and pedagogy training for secondary instructors both during the Soviet period and today are not able to offer programs in economics due to their own lack of specialists in this field. That is not surprising because all retraining institutes are operated by the Ministry of Education and are supposed to deal with subjects that are included in the curriculum. Thus, there are retraining programs in history, biology, chemistry, and other major subjects, but it is administratively impossible to initiate a new retraining program until the institutes receive permission and funding from the Ministry. In 1999-2000 there were discussions in top educational circles on the question of who could potentially teach economics courses if the subject is included in the secondary curriculum as a compulsory discipline. Theoretically teachers of history, geography, information systems, or mathematics could provide the instruction. Most likely it would be geography teachers, which means that students of the geography departments of pedagogical universities should take economics as a second major. The question then becomes who at the retraining institutes will retrain the current (and future) geography teachers? This vicious circle must be broken if economics is adopted as a compulsory discipline.

Several years ago the National Institute of Education (NIE) in Minsk started a master's program for secondary school teachers who were teaching economic theory and who wanted to improve their knowledge of economics. From 1997-2001 there were 53 graduates of this program. But all education programs at public universities and institutes in Belarus are under the control of the Ministry of Education, and in 2001 the NIE program in economics was cancelled, apparently because the Ministry decided it was not important as long as economics was not added to the curriculum as a compulsory discipline.

Fortunately this gap in the state retraining system has been partly filled by nongovernmental initiatives. There are two major institutions that deal with secondary economics instruction in Belarus: Junior Achievement and the Belarusian Economics Association.

IV. JUNIOR ACHIEVEMENT IN BELARUS

In 1991-92, 16 Belarusian teachers interested in economic education took part in retraining seminars in Moscow that were organized by Junior Achievement (JA). In 1994, 11 graduates of that program established the Belarusian headquarters for Junior Achievement. In August of that year the Belarusian Ministry of Justice registered the organization and the Ministry of Education offered its support to the newly established organization.

The educational goals for JA are to organize retraining programs for school teachers in JA programs, and to translate, adapt, and update JA teaching materials developed in the United States for Belarus. From the outset the leaders of this program were interested in introducing economic education at all grade levels, following the JA model in the United States. The retraining program included three basic segments: Elementary School (grades 0-6), Project Business (grades 7-9), and Applied Economics (grades 10-11).

The JA retraining programs for teachers are structured in five stages. Stage 1 is a five-day training seminar, with participants receiving a temporary certificate to begin teaching a JA economics class. Stage 2 is a two-day pedagogical conference, after which permanent certificates are awarded. Stage 3 is a series of monthly retraining seminars, focusing on a different topic each month. Stage 4 is a five-day training program for trainers who then train other teachers of JA programs. Stage 5 training is provided by specialists in economics, management, and marketing – these are typically sessions for all JA teachers conducted by professors from BSEU and some other institutions.

With this limited instruction in economics teachers start offering JA courses in their schools, which are annually registered by JA. Since 1991, JA reports that 447 teachers have attended training sessions and 975 classes have been offered in Belarusian schools, enrolling a total of 26,478 students. In recent years JA in Belarus has sharply reduced its activities, mainly due to a lack of funding. Several attempts have been made to invite teachers to training programs on a tuition basis, but those attempts have failed because teachers in Belarus simply do not have money to pay for courses.

Economic 'Olympiads'

JA Headquarters did initiate the first student competition in economics in Belarus. Their first 'Forum' took place in 1994 with 16 teams from Belarus, one from Lithuania, and one from Russia. The second Forum attracted 32 teams from all six regions of Belarus. JA helped the Ministry of Education organize the first national Olympiad in economics in 1996, in cooperation with BSEU. The winners of the Olympiad were admitted to BSEU without taking the customary admission exams.

In December 1997 the Ministry issued an official document to specify the rules for national Olympiads in economics and management. Since then Olympiads have taken place every year. The official recognition for these contests demonstrates that economics has begun to play an important role in Belarusian secondary education. That recognition is really quite remarkable, as previously Olympiads only took place in compulsory subjects.

The main goals of the economics Olympiads are to increase students' knowledge of economics and help students choose their future professions; identify the most talented secondary school students and interest them in enrolling in special economics classes and pursuing careers in economics; involve more scientists, students, Ph.D. students, and professors in the development of a higher level of economic education for the secondary level; and to more closely integrate secondary and higher education.

The Olympiads are organized in four stages: school, city, region, and national. The final stage includes competitions in principles of economics, marketing, accounting, computer modeling in economics and management, and business projects of school companies.

The winners of the Olympiads continue to receive special privileges in entering BSEU. Belarus State University also offered an Olympiad in 2000, following the official rules established by the Ministry but featuring a different structure. The first round of this state competition was conducted on an individual basis. An economics problem was published in a newspaper, which secondary school students could answer by correspondence. There were 362 responses coming from all over Belarus, although nearly half came from Minsk. Then the second and third rounds were held on the premises of the economics department of BSU. Of 70 participants in the third round, 10 were recognized as winners and awarded full tuition waivers to study in the BSU economics department.

V. THE BELARUSIAN ECONOMICS ASSOCIATION

The other national organization that conducts teacher training programs in Belarus – and currently the only group offering a comprehensive series of teacher training programs in economics – is the Belarusian Economics Association (BEA). This group grew out of several different international retraining programs and continues to cooperate with several international programs and organizations.

The Economic Development Institute (EDI) of the World Bank launched its retraining program to provide instruction on basic principles and institutions in a market economy for government officials from the economic ministries of the former Soviet Union. Teams of professors from these nations were invited to Washington DC to attend sessions offered by economists at the World Bank and the International Monetary Fund, providing intensive instruction on teaching micro- and macroeconomics. Retraining centers at the EDI offices in these countries were created in 1993. From 1993-97, the Belarus EDI center organized 20 three-week intensive retraining seminars in microeconomics, macroeconomics, and the major macroeconomic policy areas for approximately 600 participants from the key economic ministries.

In 1994 the Belarusian Economics Association (BEA) was formed as a nongovernmental, nonprofit organization, following the EDI model and philosophy. The founders of BEA were Belarusian economists, managers, and professors of economics.[5] The main purpose of the Association is the promotion of a liberal market economy in Belarus. The Association intends to take part in the creation of an information environment that will permit easier and better decision-making by officials, businesspeople, and consumers. The principal areas of Association activities are offering and supporting high quality continuing education and retraining programs for government officials, university professors, high school teachers, and students. Today there are approximately 200 members of the BEA.

VI. THE NATIONAL COUNCIL ON ECONOMIC EDUCATION AND JOINT PROGRAMS WITH BEA

The US National Council on Economic Education (NCEE) has conducted training programs for teachers and teacher trainers throughout eastern and central Europe and the former Soviet Union since 1992. Its first 'demonstration workshop' for teachers in Belarus was conducted in Minsk in January 1995.

In spring 1995 the Belarus Soros Foundation organized a joint meeting of JA and the BEA to determine who could help them offer a retraining program for school teachers. The initial suggestion was to hold an NCEE-type workshop and have JA incorporate NCEE materials into their retraining program. The BEA representatives argued that was premature for two reasons: first, JA did not have instructors who were familiar with the NCEE's materials; and more important, they lacked instructors who were familiar with the market economy and western economics.

As noted earlier, the JA basic training program is very short, and covers a relatively small number of topics, limited to the coverage in the JA materials. The most valuable aspects of the JA program in Belarus was that, through their activities, they advertised economic courses among school teachers, helped teachers organize economics courses at the secondary level, and kept a record of where those courses were taught, with the names of instructors and numbers of students enrolled. But frankly, what economics was actually taught in those classes, given the limited training and materials provided to teachers, is open to some question. Certainly some JA instructors have been found to have serious gaps in their training and understanding of basic economic principles. Given the high general standards of education in Belarusian schools, among both teachers and students, secondary teachers should go through an intensive retraining program in university economics to prepare them to teach good economics courses. They also require training in non-lecture, active-learning strategies such as games, simulations, and role playing.

The BEA offered to create a retraining system for up to 200 secondary teachers and professors who taught in secondary schools on a part-time basis. In these programs, participants covered the principles of microeconomics and macroeconomics using the standard curriculum of any major American university. The program was offered in two phases: three two- or three-week workshops in basic economics in phase one, and in phase two three eight-day workshops on methods of teaching economics in secondary schools, featuring NCEE materials.

The Belarus Soros Foundation provided a three-year grant to the BEA to launch the program. These programs were offered in cooperation with JA, which helped to identify almost half of the participants – most of whom were already registered as teaching economics classes. While preparations for these programs were being made all of the BEA and JA instructors for these programs took part in the NCEE's Training of Trainers Program in 1996-97.

By the middle of 1997, 22 workshops on basic economics had been conducted for approximately 200 participants, completing the first phase of the program. Overall, approximately half of the participants in these programs taught at general secondary schools, about a fourth were secondary teachers in special schools or programs, and the remaining fourth were university professors who also taught secondary classes.

The second (pedagogy) phase was about to begin in 1997, using NCEE materials. The Belarus Soros Foundation was expelled at that time, however, which meant that this retraining program was interrupted for two years. During those two years several additional BEA professors attended the NCEE Training of Trainers seminars, bringing the total number of trainers to 28 during the period 1996-2001.

BEA conducted its own training of trainers program (jointly organized and partly funded by the NCEE) using NCEE materials and syllabuses for 39 participants from Belarus in 1999-2000. In 2001 it conducted a series of two workshops for 30 secondary school teachers, taught by the best graduates of the BEA program. BEA has also hosted seven of the NCEE's workshops for international participants, including 'Training of Trainers' and 'Elementary Economic Education' programs for participants from over 20 nations, which are taught in Russian and English.

Through these training programs BEA and its cooperating organizations have been able to achieve five outcomes: 1) influence the economics curriculum in Belarusian universities and secondary schools; 2) raise the level of economic understanding of hundreds of instructors at these schools; 3) replace old, Soviet-style textbooks and instructional materials with teaching materials developed by the NCEE and other US organizations; 4) demonstrate to instructors how to modify western materials to include Belarusian examples and institutions; and 5) convince teachers to share these materials and new instructional approaches with their colleagues. The 'multiplier effect' of working with teachers who will also train their colleagues is actually the key idea behind all of the BEA and NCEE programs. The long-term goal of these programs is to establish local centers for economic education in all regions of the country.

VII. CONCLUSIONS

Any assessment of economic education reforms in Belarus over the past decade must be made in light of the political and ideological climate in Belarus. Although President Lukashenko has adopted some of the public rhetoric of market reforms, he continues to employ Soviet methods of managing the economy. While he claims that it is possible to build a system of market socialism his policies put far more emphasis on socialism than on markets.

Politically Lukashenko is even more hostile to reforms. In fact, his official slogan is 'The West is evil.' He acts on that slogan, and as a result market reforms in Belarus have been very slow. Similarly, reforms of economic education in Belarus have been slowed by the lack of support from government agencies and policy makers, and at times by outright hostility (most notably the expulsion of the Belarusian Soros Foundation).

The Ministry of Education's major achievement in economic education reforms and innovations is probably its role in supporting student Olympiads. Unfortunately, whenever the Ministry explores initiatives in economic education, it usually affiliates with old-line, Soviet-style professors of political economy. These professors are not only out of date in terms of their economic theory, their pedagogy is also based on standard Soviet practice. Most have never used active methods of teaching in their own classrooms.

Fortunately for the individual teachers and organizations that want to promote market-based economic education, the main language of instruction in Belarus schools is Russian. That allows teachers to use textbooks and other teaching materials published in Russia to promote economic education reforms in that nation. The ministry thus far has not objected to that because, as the President is fond of saying, 'Russia is good.'

Through programs that were conducted by the BEA and NCEE, and often with the active support of various JA staff members as well, it has been possible over the past five years to get better instructional materials in the hands of almost all Belarusian teachers who are currently teaching secondary economics courses or units. This outcome is another example of the multiplier effect at work, because many of these teachers have still not had direct training in using the materials. But almost all of the teachers are in contact with at least one or more colleagues who have received the training and the materials.

There is a clear need for continuing support from international organizations in reforming economic instruction in Belarus, given the legal restrictions imposed on organizations that would otherwise fund more such programs in the nation, and the limited support available in this area from the Ministry of Education. The demand for such programs may well skyrocket when changes eventually occur in the political climate and/or the decision is made to make economics a compulsory subject in the secondary school curriculum. But without continuing support from the United States and other nations these reforms can not yet sustain themselves in Belarus.

Joint programs with US faculty have been especially beneficial for introducing new content and materials and for creating links between teachers in Belarus and US professors. This has been enormously important in breaking down negative stereotypes about the West and market economics – especially as it is practiced in the United States – which were strongly cultivated by many Belarusian education agencies and public officials.

The last decade of economic education initiatives in Belarus has been unique in many respects, but in other ways quite representative of events in the other former Soviet republics. The limited pace and sometimes outright hostility towards market reforms and reformers has certainly created special challenges. Nevertheless, strong support from faculty members at the leading university in the nation, and cooperation involving BEA, the NCEE, JA, and Soros Foundation offices, has resulted in an extremely high and comprehensive level of training programs that have been delivered to a large number of teachers. For exactly the same reasons, the future of economic education in Belarus is bright in some respects but extremely uncertain in others.

It is clear that the effects of what has been accomplished so far will be enduring, as hundreds of teachers and thousands of students are involved in courses that could not have been offered in any school in Belarus just a decade ago. That in itself is reason for hope and considerable pride of accomplishment.

NOTES

1. The official term used in government reports is 'nonstate' schools.
2. The chief of the group that wrote this report, M. Plotnitskii, is a vice-rector of BSEU. A. Uloga is responsible for the secondary economic education at the Ministry of Education. V. Starikov is the head of Junior Achievement in Belarus. S. Shcherbakova and A. Koval'chouk are also from JA, and were participants in the NCEE Trainer of Trainers program in 1996-97.
3. For a review of the US research literature on the effects of K-12 'infusion' approaches vs. separate high school courses on economics, see Walstad (1992) and Watts (1991).

4. The two principal organizers were N. Shappo and E. Nesterchouk, both participants in the NCEE Trainer of Trainers program that is described in a later section.
5. Alexander Kovzik has served as the President of the BEA since its formation. Anatoli Kovalenko is an Executive Director of the BEA, and Mikhael Chepikov is the BEA's General Accountant.

REFERENCES

Plotnitskii, M.I., N.M. Il'in, A.A. Uloga, I.V. Novikova, V.Y. Starikov, S.G. Shcherbakova, S.P. Koval'chouk, Z.V. Grinyuk, A.N. Egorov, A.K. Korol'chouk, M.F. Grishchenko, G.G. Venis, V.V. Vlasov, L.E. Loseva, N.A. Smol'skaya, and A.V. Popova (1997), *Concept Paper on a Plan of Study in Economic Education for Young Students*, Minsk: Ministry of Education of Belarus.

Skuratovitch, K. (2000), 'F in Pedagogy,' *Belorusskii Rynok*, #49 (429), December 11-17, p. 7.

United Nations Educational, Scientific and Cultural Organization (UNESCO), International Bureau of Education (2000), 'The system of education in the Republic of Belarus: Basic indicators and tendencies of development.'

Walstad, W.B. (1992), 'Economics instruction in high schools,' *Journal of Economic Literature*, **30**(4), pp. 2019-51.

Watts, M. (1991), 'Research on DEEP: The First 25 Years,' in J.C. Soper and W.B. Walstad (eds), *Effective Economic Education in the Schools*, New York: National Education Association/Joint Council on Economic Education, pp. 81-98.

World Bank (2000), *World Development Indicators 2000*, CD-Rom.

7. Economic Education Reform in Bulgaria

Barbara J. Phipps, George Vredeveld, and Antoanetta Voikova

Throughout the 1990s, Bulgaria, like the rest of eastern Europe and the former Soviet Union, faced the challenging task of designing and implementing a democratic society embodying the freedom of the individual in a market economy. The initial changes were abrupt, creating confusion and destabilization of the familiar economic, social, and political framework. Since then the process of transition has traveled a rocky road. Public support for economic reforms has wavered. At first it was strong, but then citizens of Bulgaria became disillusioned by the economic instability of the transition. After sharp economic decline and high inflation, Bulgarians again sought accelerated privatization and economic transformation. Support for reform has been reflected in democratic elections that have produced several governments, alternating between those headed by the Socialist party and the Union of Democratic Forces (UDF) (a coalition of smaller, more reform-oriented parties). Currently there is a new government led by the former Bulgarian king. Although the process of transition lacks continuity, it seems to be moving toward more privatization and a more stable economic environment.

This chapter provides a case study of Bulgaria's attempts to reform primary, secondary, and higher education in teaching market economics. After a brief background on Bulgaria, the educational system Bulgaria inherited from the Soviet era is briefly described. Then educational reforms over the decade of transition are discussed, with particular emphasis on how economic education at all levels of schooling has been affected. Finally, the obstacles and challenges Bulgaria has faced in teaching market economics are considered, and current economic education activities, curriculums, and teacher training programs are described.

I. BACKGROUND

Bulgaria, a country of approximately 7.8 million people in an area slightly larger than Tennessee, has a literacy rate of 98 percent of people 15 years of age and older. At present, 4.3 percent of Bulgarian GDP is devoted to education. Education begins at age six and is compulsory up to 16 years of age. Elementary school includes grades 1-4; middle or pre-secondary school encompasses grades 5-

8; and high school includes grades 9-12. Curriculum requirements consist of a specified number of classes in various subjects.

The first eight grades prepare students for entrance examinations to high school and channel students into one of three different tracks: 1) a general education program with the option of sitting for university entrance examinations, 2) a vocational program with no option to take the university entrance examination, and 3) a variety of pre-university technical programs, including schools of economics.[1]   The general schools (including grades 1-8) enrolled 887,000 in 2000, the vocational schools enrolled 132,000, and the technical schools enrolled 51,000 for a total enrollment of 1,070,000 in all public schools. There were 86,270 teachers of grades 1-12 in the public school system, some of whom worked part time (National Statistical Institute, 2000).   Of these 1,200 taught economics courses at the high school level.

II. EDUCATION UNDER SOCIALISM

The Bulgarian Communist Party (Party) used education to shape students into good communist citizens, loyal to the State and Party. The result was an education system that put a premium on rote learning and conformity to socialist ideals, while penalizing individual, creative, and critical thinking.   The Ministry of Education had full responsibility for all executive decisions concerning education and implemented policy according to Party dictates. This control went so far as directing how textbooks were to be written and appointing their authors (Bulgarian Communist Party, 1976).

Economic Education

When it became obvious as early as the 1950s that socialism was not producing the 'ideal' state of equality and prosperity, new demands were placed on education. In particular, the need to compete in international markets increased the importance of economic education with a special focus on the 'new economic mechanism,' which at least in theory provided more discretion to managers (Bulgarian Communist Party, 1965). This new focus also affected the structure and management of education. More power and discretion in decision-making were granted to school management boards and local administrative education councils.   Schools were authorized to offer more flexible curricula with some electives and vocational options. These democratic goals were in conflict with the main tenets of the Party, however.   Continuing insistence on communist ideological supremacy prevented the schools from promoting innovative and analytical thinking (Vredeveld and Ispirodonova, 1994).

Economics was taught as a basic course at the high school level and as part of an extensive curriculum at the specialized economics schools. All high school students were required to take an eleventh-grade course entitled 'Basics of

Marxism-Leninism' that dealt with three basic topics: dialectical materialism, political economy, and scientific communism. This course was designed to provide students with a 'reliable and scientific' way of looking at economic and social phenomena, and covered the philosophy, economics, and history of communist theory and practice.

Other economics courses, in addition to the Marxism-Leninism course, were taught in the specialized economics schools. In keeping with the Party's emphasis on management and the implementation of various experimental economic plans, courses at these schools featured a managerial and applied emphasis in such areas as the theory of statistics and statistical applications to commerce, marketing, word and data processing, and stenography, as well as economics (Bulgarian Communist Party, 1976). The economics course covered fundamentals of the market system, but this instruction was largely a critique of the capitalist system, focusing on the contradictions and deficiencies of market economics and its inherently exploitative nature.

Economic education in Bulgaria was often interdisciplinary. For example, 'economic' topics were also taught in history and geography courses. This approach corresponded fully with Party dogma that the Marxist-Leninist 'dialectic' interpretation of the development of civilization should permeate the entire curriculum, and especially the social sciences. These interdisciplinary social science courses were, therefore, taught from the fifth to eleventh grades in all schools to complement each other and reinforce students' socialist outlook on socioeconomic issues (Vredeveld and Ispirodonova, 1994).

III.   EDUCATION REFORMS DURING TRANSITION

Educational reform closely followed political reform after 1989. In 1990, just after the fall of the Communist Party, the Socialist Party's Ministry of Education produced a plan to encourage ideological pluralism in public education as a first step toward encouraging free-thinking and the democratization of education.

In 1991, a different Ministry of Education[2] (under the government headed by the Union of Democratic Forces) expanded the previous initiative by adopting a plan to create a new system of humanistic, ideology-free values, which would culturally and spiritually integrate Bulgaria with contemporary civilization. The plan called for more freedom of choice in coursework, and for textbooks and teaching free of any Marxist-Leninist bias. The Ministry also declared that it intended to give more discretion to teachers and administrators in determining teaching styles and to allow private and public schools to compete for students. While it is significant that the Ministry conceptually recognized the importance of market mechanisms and competition in the sphere of education, in practice the new plan remained highly centralized with the Ministry still determining policy and curriculum.

Reform efforts began again after the return to power of the UDF government in 1997. By 1999 the Bulgarian Parliament had enacted a new statutory framework for education in Bulgaria based chiefly on two laws, the *Educational Degree, General Educational Standards, and Curriculum Requirements Act* and the *Professional Education and Training Act*. The stated intent of these laws was to enhance accessibility, quality, and effectiveness for both general and vocational education. Both acts also sought to decentralize education by offering more control to regional and local authorities, and were designed to meet European Union standards for the quality of education (Voikova, 2000).

Under the *Educational Degree, General Educational Standards, and Curriculum Requirements Act* broad objectives were set for secondary general education including 'active study methods for teaching and learning,' compulsory matriculation examinations, and a national exit assessment system. New content standards under this act mandated expansion of foreign language instruction in early grades, integration of information technologies into the curriculum, and the development of civic, economic, and democratic knowledge (Ministry of Education and Science, 2000).

The *Professional Education and Training Act* regulates vocational and technical schools, including Bulgaria's specialized schools of economics and finance. Like the law for general education, it seeks to decentralize school administration and curricula and promotes cooperation between the schools and other sectors of the community. Based upon these two 1999 laws, each school may choose the subjects it teaches, as long as it provides a certain number of contact hours in each of the eight broad curricular areas set forth in the state *Educational Standards*.[3] Courses at all levels are classified as compulsory, elective-compulsory, and elective, and the degree of freedom in the curriculum increases with the educational level of the school. Specifically, compulsory courses comprise more than 80 percent of all classes for grades 1-8 and between 45 and 80 percent at the high school level.

Although decentralization of administration and curriculum is a stated goal in both of the laws passed in 1999, the Ministry continues to retain tight control over the compulsory courses. It specifies what subjects are required and the course syllabi for these subjects. No teacher or administrator is allowed to make any changes whatsoever in these elements (Voikova, 2000). For elective courses there is more, although not complete, freedom.

Economic Education

Under the new curriculum, standards for economic knowledge have been developed and approved by the Ministry of Education for grades 1-8 and coursework in economics and geography is specified in grades 5-8. Teams of educators have drawn up a teaching strategy guidebook showing how different economic concepts can be introduced and used in the general education subjects. For example, in fifth and sixth grade mathematics, the guidebook recommends:

- taxes be integrated into multiplying and dividing natural numbers
- foreign exchange rates and income be integrated into comparing fractions and multiplying and dividing fractional numbers
- supply, demand, equilibrium, and price changes be integrated into operations with positive and negative numbers
- demand and supply, gross domestic product, and elasticity of demand be integrated into graphic presentation of data, diagrams, bar charts, and graphs (Voikova, 2000).

The new curriculum also defines objectives for specified economics courses. For example, after the completion of the course 'Introduction to Economics' in the eighth or ninth grade, the student should know and be able to understand and analyze the basic concepts and rules of micro- and macroeconomics, such as:

- the laws of demand, supply, and competition that are in operation in a market economy
- the elements of GDP, including its measurement, components, and distribution
- the essence of inflation and unemployment and their effect on GDP and the quality of life
- the factors of economic growth and their manifestation in the Bulgarian economy (Voikova, 2000).

The new laws further require that all twelfth-grade students in the non-economic vocational high schools must take a year-long economics course that meets at least three times per week.

Requirements that market-based economics be taught at the elementary and secondary levels dictate that teachers be educated in some way to become competent teachers of the subject. This might be accomplished through undergraduate education in economics, preservice education courses, or by some form of continuing (inservice) teacher training.

IV.   THE UNDERGRADUATE ECONOMICS MAJOR

Following the examples set by leading Soviet universities, post-secondary economic education in Bulgaria during the socialist period was designed to provide specialists for the command economy. Those majoring in economics studied in one of three economics institutes, each specializing in different fields: an institute in Sofia focused on international economic relations and political economy, an institute in Varna trained students in international tourism and commodity sciences, and an institute in Svishtov specialized in finance, banking, and insurance. At all other institutes and at Sofia University-St. Kliment Ohridski (Sofia University), economics instruction was limited to one or two courses in political economy or the economics of industry, taught in the first two years (Koeva and Yakimova, 1998).

The transformation of university-level economics has followed changes in the political and economic systems. Today, the three economics institutes (now called economics universities) still offer major areas of study based on specific economic sectors, similar to those offered prior to the transition, with the Sofia institute (University of National and World Economics) also offering a degree program in economics and pedagogy. A new university founded in 1991 in Blagoevgrad, the American University in Bulgaria, offers a traditional US liberal arts program with a major in economics that is parallel to economics majors at US universities.

Since 1991 the premier university in Bulgaria, Sofia University, has offered a full range of economics courses. Between 1950 and 1991, faculty members in the department of philosophy taught courses in political economy at Sofia University. Now there is a department of economics and business administration, and approximately 1,500 students study in these four- and five-year programs.

The four-year program leads to the baccalaureate degree, and the fifth year of 720 contact hours completes the Masters of Economics degree. For the baccalaureate degree, approximately 30 percent of the compulsory courses are economics courses, similar to courses taught in US institutions. The remaining course requirements are distributed across four other areas: 25 percent in business and law courses, 20 percent in foreign language courses, 20 percent in mathematics and statistics, and five percent in computer skills courses. Students applying to enter the economics program must pass an English competency exam. Economics courses with descriptions that parallel standard US undergraduate economics courses include introductory macro- and microeconomics, money and banking, intermediate micro- and macroeconomics, international trade and finance, public finance, and labor. Courses that reflect carryover from the socialist era, such as political economy, appear to be relegated to the elective offerings. Other courses reflecting topical concerns about the transition or other economic and business issues, such as 'Protectionism and Competition in the Balkans' and 'The Japanese Model of Management,' also appear among the electives.

The dilemma of retraining former political economists is solved to a large extent at Sofia University by the use of foreign instructors, including extensive collaboration with two German universities whose staff members offer several courses each year. US Fulbright and Civic Education Project Foundation scholars, and other visiting western-trained scholars, also are used frequently.

Despite the progress that has been made, several problems still exist in Bulgaria's post-secondary economic education. One persistent problem is the lack of good textbooks. Professional translations of western textbooks are uncommon, due in part to the limited profitability of translations into a narrowly spoken language such as Bulgarian. Although this is also a problem in other subjects, market-based economics texts may present a unique problem because of the relative newness of the subject in the country. Domestically authored texts, reflecting standard micro- and macroeconomic theory and the Bulgarian transitional experience, remain nearly non-existent at the university level. Although this problem has been partially sidestepped by the English language requirements at Sofia University and the American University in Bulgaria, the other economics institutions typically do not require their students to be fluent in English. One American textbook, *Economics*, 3rd ed., by David C. Colander, McGraw-Hill Irwin, 1998, was translated into Bulgarian and is used as a text in some Sofia University introductory economics classes. Another textbook, *The Economic Way of Thinking* by Paul Heyne, Macmillan College Publishing Company, 1994, has been translated and is used for inservice teacher education.

While Sofia University and the American University in Bulgaria now offer new undergraduate economics curricula, reforms at the other economics universities have often not extended beyond the introductory principles courses (Koeva and Yakimova, 1998). This is attributed in large part to the industry-oriented structure of the programs at these institutions. With majors that concentrate on production, management, and marketing within specific industries, such as agriculture, tourism, and transportation, these programs might be better characterized as business, rather than economics, degree programs. As a result, there seems to be a feeling that these courses do not have to be taught using a modern, theoretical framework for economics. Even if that view were to be accepted, it presents a problem for economic education reform efforts because some of these universities also offer training for students who intend to become high school teachers of economics.

V. TEACHER EDUCATION AND TRAINING

Preservice Teacher Training

Undergraduates who seek to become teachers in general subjects such as literature, math, science, and foreign languages are trained at the Bulgarian pedagogical universities. In addition to courses in content areas, they are required to take courses in methodology, pedagogy, and psychology. Upon graduation they receive a teaching certificate that is valid for the rest of their lives. Typically, teacher education is very traditional and not reflective of modern, learner-centered approaches to instruction. These universities are free to determine their pedagogical curriculum and courses, but in order to be granted a valid teaching certificate a student must have covered a certain set of courses in the discipline in which he or she specializes (Voikova, 2000).

Prospective teachers of economics and other technical subjects take required courses in their subject area at comprehensive universities, but coursework on educational theory or methodology is optional. In many cases high school economics teachers take no preservice courses in education, although it is noteworthy, as indicated above, that the University of National and World Economics in Sofia does offer a degree program in economics and pedagogy.

Inservice Teacher Education

Bulgarian teachers often decide to enroll in further training programs to obtain a higher certification that leads to a higher salary. Teachers may pursue this additional education at Bulgaria's special institutes for further training of teachers or at other institutions of higher education. The institutes for further training are part of the national university system and cooperate closely with the Ministry of Education. Their courses usually focus on methodology and pedagogy and do not currently provide training in economics or economic education.

Over the past decade many teachers also have opted to take seminars and courses offered by educational organizations from the European Union and the United States. In many cases these courses and seminars are approved by the Ministry and thus qualify for credit toward promotions. The economic education programs offered by some of these international organizations are described below.

VI. ECONOMIC EDUCATION PROGRAMS OFFERED BY WESTERN ORGANIZATIONS

University of Cincinnati and University of Delaware Program (UCUD)

The UCUD program was the first outside effort during the transition period to develop an infrastructure for teaching economics in Bulgarian elementary and secondary schools. Faculty members from the University of Cincinnati and the University of Delaware started this program in 1990. The Ministry of Education recruited teachers for two-week teacher training seminars based on the Ministry's priorities for implementing new economics coursework and programs in the schools. A total of 183 teachers, mainly from vocational and technical schools, were enrolled in six seminars over a period of five years. The UCUD program also drafted a curriculum for elementary and secondary grades, sought to organize regional offices of economic education (similar to US centers for economic education) to support economic education throughout the country, and supported a proposal to establish the Foundation for Economics and Business Education in Bulgaria. After providing initial indications of support for this Foundation, the Ministry of Education later opposed it – perhaps out of fear of losing control of the economic education effort – and refused to work with the UCUD program if it continued its association with the Foundation. When funding expired for the UCUD program in 1995, it was discontinued.

Foundation for Teaching Economics (FTE)

The FTE expanded its teacher-training program to include Bulgaria in 1992. These one-week seminars use US university professors to present basic economic concepts with a focus on helping secondary school teachers understand and more effectively teach economic principles in their classrooms. The seminars also introduce Bulgarian teachers to leadership activities and innovative, interactive teaching methods. Through August 2001 FTE had conducted eight summer seminars in cooperation with the Ministry of Education and the American University in Bulgaria. More than 300 educators have enrolled in these seminars.

Bulgarian-Austrian Project on Economics and Management

This project emphasizes a practical, business and economics curriculum. It is conducted at Bulgaria's five technical high schools that specialize in economics and finance. About 51,000 students (12 percent of Bulgarian high school students) attend technical high schools, and nearly 22 percent of those students are enrolled in the economics and finance schools. Students at these high schools are prepared for business careers and university study.

In 2000 the Bulgarian-Austrian project involved 300 students and their teachers in the five high schools. The project addresses needs for a new economics curriculum, training programs in new vocations, and a new spirit and approach toward work. Teachers work in teams to integrate the curriculum across disciplines and students work in teams to organize and manage companies in an educational simulation. Goals of the simulation experiences include promoting independent individual work in a competitive environment, learning new forms of communication, and preparing for future careers. The study of market economics and two foreign languages are important components of the program. A Center for Simulation Companies, staffed by Austrian educators, provides teacher assistance and training to encourage, support, and coordinate the work of the 68 existing simulation companies, and intends to establish new companies in the five economics and finance high schools (Voikova, 2000).

National Council on Economic Education (NCEE)

Based in the United States, the NCEE has assisted teachers at Bulgarian vocational economics high schools since 1996. The NCEE's 'Training of Trainers Program' brings together educators from former Soviet-bloc countries for four week-long courses in basic economic theory and a wide variety of teaching methods. The faculty members in these programs are professors of economics or education at US universities. By the end of the 1999-2000 academic year the NCEE had trained 19 Bulgarian educators in the Training of Trainers Program. In turn, these educators conducted seminars for 142 teachers, 64 percent of whom taught at the economics and finance high schools and 27 percent at the other vocational high schools.

The NCEE also has offered economics seminars in Bulgaria for elementary teachers, a series of seminars for secondary teachers, and seminars jointly instructed by teams of Bulgarian alumni of the Training of Trainers Program and US faculty. In December 1999 the Bulgarian Council on Economic Education was registered with the Bulgarian government as a nongovernmental organization. This new organization receives organizational assistance from NCEE consultants and shows promise in providing sustained support for economic education.

Junior Achievement Bulgaria (JAB)

In 1996 an office of Junior Achievement International was established in Bulgaria. According to the organization's website, 10 US Peace Corps volunteers piloted the first Junior Achievement programs in Bulgaria in response to a 'feasibility study finding a great need for economic education in Bulgarian schools' (Junior Achievement Bulgaria, 2000). In July 1998 the Ministry of Education recognized JAB programs and authorized them to be offered as elective classes in the high school curriculum. JAB indicates that their high school program is offered in 70 high schools in 35 cities, with 100 participating teachers and an estimated 2,000 students during the 1999-2000 academic year. It estimates that since the program's beginning in 1997 more than 4,000 high school students have participated.

Funding for JAB programs comes primarily from international companies located in Bulgaria.[4] Although JAB focuses on student programs it is conducting some teacher training, primarily in programs on how to utilize JA materials in the general comprehensive high schools.

VII. OBSERVATIONS AND CONCLUSIONS

The educational changes that Bulgaria has attempted during the 1990s have been dramatic and have significantly affected the teaching of economics. In many cases the ambitious goals of these reforms were not attained, but there have been some notable successes. As early as 1990 the Ministry of Education was determined to eliminate socialist ideology from its schools and especially from the teaching of economics. One difficulty cited in an earlier report (Vredeveld and Ispirodonova, 1994) was a weak commitment of teachers to the curricular reforms necessary to teach principles of economics without a socialist bias. After ten years of transition and the attrition of many older teachers, the problem of ideological bias has waned significantly.

Economics teaching continues to be plagued by at least three problems that negatively impact elementary and secondary education throughout Bulgaria. The first is that local schools lack the freedom to make decisions on important curricular and administrative issues. The second is the teaching pay structure, which makes it harder for schools to find and keep good teachers. The third is the absence of comprehensive pedagogical training as a requirement to enter the economics teaching profession.

Successive Ministries of Education have articulated the goals of expanding the freedom of the schools to determine their own curriculums and to decentralize the administration of the schools. But these goals have not been easy to achieve, and it remains to be seen whether the support of these goals by the government and the two education acts of 1999 will significantly reduce the Ministry of Education's control of the schools. By 2001 freedom to set the curriculum existed only for the non-compulsory elements, which comprised from 20 to 55 percent of courses. This lack of local control may be less of a barrier to teaching economics now than previously, given the recent formulation of standards and specific requirements for the teaching of economics by the Ministry.

Bulgaria faces severe financial and personnel problems that affect its ability to achieve educational reforms. Low wages offer few incentives for teachers to stay in education. Fewer young people are becoming teachers, and many younger teachers leave the field when they are able to secure other employment in the private sector. In September 2000 the average monthly wage for the nation was 241 leva ($115 US), while for teachers it was 190 leva ($90 US).[5] Consequently, financial hardships often dictate that teachers find additional sources of income. Many tutor students outside regular school hours. Others work part time for other employers or develop their own small businesses. Even teenage students sense a serious problem with this situation. While they mostly embrace the notion of individual economic responsibility, they see as unfair a system in which their well-educated teachers receive low salaries.[6]

The problem of developing teachers who are adequately trained in the content and methods to teach the full range of economic concepts has become even more difficult as universities often offer specialized economics curricula and have been slow to adopt new content. There also are important questions related to teacher training in pedagogical methods. Bulgarian teachers are familiar with a didactic, formal method of presentation, and seem to be trained in these methods during their preservice education. Basic ideas of questioning (inquiry), critical thinking, and other student-centered, interactive methods are, so far, part of the 'new way of thinking' that only international organizations have encouraged Bulgarian educators to adopt and implement in their classrooms. There are important on-going efforts from organizations in the European Union and the United States that have provided teacher economic education programs in Bulgaria, although mostly for teachers in the specialized economics high schools.

Teacher training in the new economics curriculum is also provided for and funded by the Ministry of Education. The willingness of the Ministry of Education to work with outside partners is a positive step toward providing much-needed teacher training in economics. The recent efforts of the NCEE to provide technical assistance in the start up of the Bulgarian Council on Economic Education may help to build an internally sustainable teacher training nongovernmental organization. In addition, the two 1999 education laws have, in essence, officially recognized a place for market economics in the curriculum, and provide a framework for further curricular reform. While these efforts are encouraging, teaching the basic principles of economics is not yet fully institutionalized. That will only occur when many more teachers are trained and changes are fully embraced at the local, regional, and national levels for all categories of schools.

Most of the teachers exposed to new methods of teaching have responded positively, but key questions remain. Unless the new pedagogies become part of future teachers' initial college training and preparation, will most teachers ever use them effectively? Even if some teachers do, can the new teaching methods endure in a system dominated by traditional courses and teaching methods? Will the changes introduced by international organizations receive long-term support from the Ministry and the schools so that these changes become institutionalized?

Taken together, these questions indicate the need for a systemic approach to economic education in Bulgaria, at elementary, secondary, and higher education levels. Current reforms must continue, and even accelerate, and it is critical that they extend into undergraduate teacher preparation. Without system-wide requirements for basic teacher education, it may not be possible to incorporate modern learning theories and pedagogy on a sustained and widespread basis.

NOTES

1. Other programs in the four-year schools include mathematics, chemistry and physics, music, arts, languages, and sports, as well as mechanical engineering, electronics, radio and television, electrical engineering, construction technologies, and industrial chemistry in the technical schools.
2. This Ministry was part of the government organized by the Socialist Party, the successor to the Communist Party. Over the years the Ministry of Education has taken on different responsibilities and different names. For example, since 1990 the Ministry has been named the Ministry of Public Education; the Ministry of Education and Science; and the Ministry of Education, Science and Culture. This chapter uses the generic name, Ministry of Education, to refer to the government body responsible for administering policy on elementary and secondary (grades 1-12) public education.
3. The eight curricular areas include Bulgarian language and literature; foreign languages; math, informatics, and information technologies; civics; natural sciences and ecology; arts; lifestyle and technologies; and physical culture and sports.
4. For example. VIDIMA AD (American Standard Company) of Sevlievo sponsored JAB's pilot middle school program by purchasing educational materials and paying for teachers to teach the course to middle school students in the corporation's language center. The Bulgarian International Business Association and Sheraton Hotel-Balkan Sofia sponsored JAB's Student Day/Award Ceremony. Other firms are sponsoring JAB's participation in the Hewlett-Packard Global Business Challenge.
5. For example, *www.news.bg stories* on 14/9/00 and 8/11/99 describe union demands for higher teacher salaries. Stories on 16/3/00, 10/9/99, and 22/4/99 document teacher strikes or demonstrations in various localities, in retaliation for not being paid for one or more months or for the failure to implement scheduled wage increases.
6. Based on interviews of 60 high school students conducted by Barbara Phipps and Nadia Filipova in Spring 2000.

REFERENCES

Bulgarian Communist Party (1965), *The Bulgarian Communist Party in resolutions and decisions, 1956-1962*, **Vol. V**, (*Bulgarskata komunisticheska partiya v resolyutsii i resheniya*), Sofia.

Bulgarian Communist Party (1976), *Eleventh Congress of the Bulgarian Communist Party*, March 1976 (*Edinadeseti kongres na Bulgarskata komunisticheska partiya*), Sofia.

Colander, D.C. (2001), *Economics*, 4th ed. New York: McGraw-Hill.

Faculty of Economics and Business Administration, Sofia University (2000), 'St. Kliment Ohridski,' Sofia: Presses Universitaires 'St. Kliment Ohridski.'

Heyne, P. (2000), *The Economic Way of Thinking*, 9th ed. Upper Saddle, New Jersey: Prentice-Hall.

Junior Achievement Bulgaria (2000), Website: *http://www.jaintl.org/*.

Koeva, S. and I. Yakimova (1998), 'Transforming economics teaching in Bulgaria,' *Journal of Economic Education*, **29**(1), pp. 88-92.

Ministry of Education and Science, Bulgaria (2000), 'Priorities of the government with regard to the education system,' Website: *http://www.minedu.government.bg*.

Ministry of Public Education (1990), 'Development of education 1988-1990: National report of the People's Republic of Bulgaria.'

National Statistical Institute (2000), National Statistics Reference Book, Sofia, Bulgaria.

Shishkin, P. (1999), 'Growing divisions,' *The Wall Street Journal Europe's Central European Economic Review*, **VII** (December 1999), pp. 14-5.

Voikova, A. (2000), 'Economic education in Bulgaria: Present state and prospects,' working paper.

Vredeveld, G.M. and D.M. Ispirodonova (1994), 'Economic education and transition in eastern Europe,' in W.B. Walstad, (ed.), *An International Perspective on Economic Education*, Boston, Massachusetts, USA: Kluwer Academic Publishers, pp. 255-72.

8.   Economic Education in Kyrgyzstan

James Grunloh and Nataliya Aksenenko

Kyrgyzstan became an independent nation in August of 1991, following the dissolution of the USSR. This small landlocked central Asian country of less than five million people was one of the poorest and most traditional societies of the Soviet Republics. Its people were still strongly influenced by clans, and many of the elderly could still recall the nomadic lifestyle of the majority of Kyrgyz people before the forced collectivization of the 1930s. The newly independent nation had neither a well-developed economic infrastructure nor a set of political traditions on which to build a new society and an industrialized market economy.

The early years of transition in Kyrgyzstan were similar to those in many of the other former Soviet republics. Ethnic differences were once again openly expressed, and the status of religion and the role of the Russian language in the nation's schools and legal and political institutions became hotly debated topics. The first real signs of moving to a market-oriented economic system were provisions in the 1993 constitution dealing with the transfer and ownership of property, but the country had little experience with the actual operation of a market system. In fact, the attitude toward market mechanisms in this tradition-based economy was skeptical at best. Some elders in the rural, mountainous areas of southern Kyrgyzstan talked of relying on the minority population of Uzbeks to do their 'trading,' clearly disdaining this type of activity.

Despite these obstacles, as the importance of economic literacy became clear during the early period of market reform, the Ministry of Education[1] required a course titled Introduction to Economics to be offered to all students in the nation's secondary schools beginning in 1992. There were, however, virtually no market-oriented textbooks for students, and far too few trained economics teachers to teach the course in the 1,950 Kyrgyz primary and secondary schools attended by over a million students. Therefore, this new course and other initial efforts to teach about the workings of a market system immediately ran into serious problems.

Since 1992, the Ministry of Education and various domestic and international nongovernmental organizations and foundations have introduced a variety of programs to help make market-based economic education an integral part of the education curriculum. The Soros Foundation of Kyrgyzstan partnered with the US National Council on Economic Education to begin developing a cadre of well-trained economics teachers with access to effective teaching materials. Junior Achievement of Kyrgyzstan conducted teacher training and introduced its Applied

Economics program in many Kyrgyz high schools. In 1999, a Kyrgyzstan Council on Economic Education with a network of four regional centers for economic education was created to continue the work initiated by the Soros Foundation in teacher training and materials development. In 2000, the Kyrgyz Association of Economics Teachers was created to provide additional training opportunities for teachers and to create economic education programs for students. Taken together, these initiatives have developed an infrastructure that is now working to bring effective market-based economic education courses and other activities to many schools of Kyrgyzstan. The challenges facing this effort are still formidable, however, in this tradition-oriented country with such a turbulent history.

In this chapter we briefly review the nation's historical and cultural heritage and its effects on the current economic transformation. We then describe the initiatives of each of the key organizations that are striving to make market-based economics available to students in Kyrgyzstan.

I. THE HISTORICAL AND CULTURAL BACKGROUND[2]

Most Kyrgyz people followed a nomadic lifestyle until the Soviet-forced collectivization of the 1930s. For the most part they herded sheep, horses, and yaks up and down the mountains as the seasons changed. They lived in yurts, a wool cylindrical tent that could be quickly taken apart and carried by camels or horses. Native Kyrgyz continue to identify themselves by their membership in one of three major clan groupings, which are based in different geographical regions. The 'sol' clans are located in the northern and western parts of the country. The 'ong' clan groupings, called the Adygine, are concentrated in the southern part of the country. The remaining group, the Ichkilik, actually includes many clans that are located in the mountainous east, south, and southwest. Kyrgyz people are very aware of clan membership and use it to seek social, political, and economic advantage. Some Kyrgyz men still wear headgear that identifies their clan membership and position in the clan, and clan membership continues to be a very important factor in national and regional elections.

Given this background, educational reforms to promote market-based economic reform in Kyrgyzstan entail much more than distributing factual information about the operation of markets. The cultural traditions that place great importance on family ties and clan associations present major challenges to the acceptance of an economic system based on individual freedom, personal responsibility and initiative, and profit maximization. For example, managing a business that includes many family members may make personal relationships with employees more important than determining how to maximize profits or minimize losses.

The region that is present day Kyrgyzstan was taken over and made a part of the USSR in 1924 and granted the status of an autonomous republic in 1936. The nomadic lifestyle and clan orientation was also a significant barrier for the Soviets to overcome in their efforts to move people into towns and cities, or onto state-owned collective farms. There was significant resistance to industrial employment and many Kyrgyz continued to move seasonally with their herds. Nevertheless, by the middle of the twentieth century the Kyrgyz Republic was well integrated into the Soviet system of central planning. Its main role in that system was as a supplier of minerals, including gold, antimony, and mercury. It also provided meats, leather, sugar, wine, tobacco, wool, and cotton cloth. The country hosted a major military airbase for the training of Soviet pilots, a torpedo-assembly plant on the shore of Lake Issyk-Kul, and radio-assembly and other electronic plants for the Soviet defense establishment.

With independence in 1991, the demand for defense goods, one of the country's primary industrial exports, decreased sharply; but the country remained highly dependent on energy imports. Privatization of state assets became a national priority in 1992 with the adoption of the *Privatization and Denationalization Law* and the creation of the State Property Fund. By 1994 nearly all services, 82 percent of assets in trade enterprises, 40 percent of industrial assets, and 68 percent of construction assets were privatized. But other essential features of a market system were not present. There was no legal framework or government regulation for the exchange of capital, and no credit system in place. Inefficient state-owned enterprises were essentially bankrupt although they continued to operate with government subsidies, reducing efficiency in the economy.

By 1996 up to 30 percent of the nation's real GDP of $7.8 billion ($1,722 per capita, both measured in 1995 US dollars)[3] was generated by the underground economy. Tax revenues were not sufficient to finance government expenditures and the resulting government budget deficits encouraged excessive money creation, which led to inflation that reached 1,400 percent in 1993. Inefficient barter transactions began to replace cash transactions and unemployment rose sharply. Corruption became pervasive. Kyrgyzstan's GDP declined by 52 percent by the middle of the decade – one of the more severe declines in industrial output among the former Soviet Republics. It was estimated that more than one-third of the people lived below the poverty line by the mid-1990s. After experiencing these economic difficulties support for market reforms began to wane, as in many other parts of the former USSR.

Despite the unique challenges it faced, Kyrgyzstan was one of the most aggressive of the former Soviet republics in adopting significant structural reforms. In 1994 the International Monetary Fund ranked Kyrgyzstan fourth among the former Soviet republics (behind the three Baltic States) in the pace of economic reform. Economic and political events at the time of independence provide the best explanation for this position. In the spring of 1990, ethnic tensions between Uzbeks and Kyrgyz erupted in a series of bloody riots in the city of Osh near the Uzbek border, with over 300 people killed. That led to a series of large student demonstrations at the headquarters of the Communist Party in the capital city (then located in Bishkek), and eventually to the formation of a loose alliance of activists who called themselves the Democratic Movement of Kyrgyzstan. This new group, which quickly attracted wide public support, immediately called for the resignation of the communist leadership.

As a result of this public unrest, the President of the Parliament, Absamat Masaliyev, lost his position. After several unsuccessful attempts to elect other long-time Communist Party leaders, the Supreme Soviet unexpectedly named Askar Akayev, a 46-year-old physicist, as the new President of Kyrgyzstan. Akayev was the first president of a former Soviet republic who had not previously held a high party position. During the following year, the Supreme Soviet formally declared national sovereignty and sought to establish Kyrgyz as the nation's official language. A declaration of independence was adopted on 30 August 1991. President Akayev moved quickly to throw the Communist Party out of the government, and two months later he ran unopposed to become the first popularly elected president of Kyrgyzstan.

Despite the euphoria associated with independence and free elections the country's economic situation continued to be very vulnerable, with ethnic tensions exacerbating the economic problems facing the new government. Early in his term President Akayev recognized that he had to take strong and immediate action to keep the economy moving and to establish a firm basis for the new democratic government. In addition to creating a free news media and fostering an active political opposition, the government embarked on an ambitious plan to privatize enterprises and to adopt other market reforms. By 1994 an estimated 65 percent of industrial output came from non-state enterprises.

The new president initially received broad support for his reform agenda, with the strongest support coming from young, urban, and highly educated people. Northern clans supported the President's reforms more than the agrarian southern clans. This early support for market reforms also led to support for reforms in the country's schools and to the 1992 *National Curriculum Plan* that included the requirement for the secondary course called Introduction to Economics.

II. EDUCATION IN KYRGYZSTAN

General Education in the Soviet and Transition Periods[4]

The structure of education in Kyrgyzstan today has its roots in the model used throughout the former Soviet Union. Under that system students followed a rigid curriculum established by the national Ministry of Education. At age five students enrolled in preschool and kindergarten, and then in primary schools for four years (forms 1-4) where basic skills were emphasized. Students then moved into a standardized basic secondary education program (forms 5-9). In their tenth and eleventh years of schooling, students enrolled either in professional education, technical education, or third-stage secondary education programs. Some students continued on into higher education programs leading to bachelor or master's degrees, or to higher-level professional education programs. Various postgraduate programs award doctoral degrees.

The 1993 national constitution guaranteed free access to education at all state institutions. There are now over a million pupils attending 1,540 secondary schools and 416 kindergarten and pre-schools in Kyrgyzstan. In 1999 there were 42,000 students in professional education programs, 49,000 in vocational-technical programs, and 58,000 in institutions of higher education.

But like most other sectors of the economy, education faces severe resource problems. The Ministry of Education reports that buildings at 40 percent of the nation's secondary schools are more than 50 years old and in extremely unsatisfactory or even dangerous condition. In more than a third of these schools students attend in two or three shifts. More than 60 percent of the textbooks and teacher's guides used in the schools are considered obsolete. The government has tried to improve conditions in existing schools and to build new schools using general revenues and by seeking support from international agencies and foundations (Imanaliev, 2000).

Language difficulties in Kyrgyz schools present an additional challenge. The number of schools in which the primary language of education is Russian has decreased dramatically, and is now less than 10 percent compared to a decade earlier when all instruction was required to be in Russian. Instruction in institutions of higher education is still conducted primarily in Russian, which presents a serious barrier to many students who want to pursue a higher education (Imanaliev, 2000).

The biggest problem facing elementary and secondary schools is the lack of trained teachers. Many qualified teachers have left education because wages are low and often paid late, seeking more attractive positions in other parts of the economy. In 1992 alone, 8,000 of the country's 65,000 teachers resigned because of low salaries and also because many teachers were being asked to teach double shifts (Library of Congress, 1996). A 2000 United Nations report described the shortage of teachers in the secondary schools as 'acute.' The same report noted that in Kyrgyzstan the teaching profession has been generally viewed as not requiring creative thinking and offering limited opportunities for promotion. Many current teachers are actually retirees from other professions, brought in to cope with the shortage of certified teachers. There are especially severe shortages of teachers of English, history, and geography, but the greatest shortage is in economics. One reason for that is because, although economics was included in the national curriculum in 1992, in 1999 there were still no universities offering programs to train economics teachers (United Nations, 2000, pp. 51-2).

Government initiatives to reform the Soviet-era education system began with a 1992 *Law on Education* that established a new Ministry of Education as the central administrative body of the national system of schools. The law maintained the Soviet guarantee of free basic education at state institutions for all citizens and made education compulsory through grade nine. The Ministry was given complete responsibility for administering the country's primary and secondary schools, including textbook selection, curriculum development, teacher training and retraining, and assessment. Chynara Zhakypova, a progressive politician and strong proponent of democratic changes in education and market-based economic reforms, headed the new Ministry. The reform program was launched by conducting a competition for the development of new textbooks and teachers' manuals. Substantial structural and curriculum changes were initiated, including the requirement for an introductory class on western-style economics for all students in grades nine through eleven, taught at least one hour per week. The new curriculum also included a requirement that all students study at least one of three foreign languages (English, German, or French). But for the first time schools were also allowed to offer elective courses, and instructional innovation was encouraged.

Many of the problems facing secondary schools in Kyrgyzstan also plague its 30 public and 15 private institutions of higher education. According to the United Nations' *Human Development Report* (2000, p. 52), some 159,000 students are currently attending these institutions even though there are an insufficient number of professors and lecturers, poor facilities, and an inadequate number of quality textbooks and other instructional materials. There have been some recent attempts to improve higher education, and several particularly weak institutions have been closed. New institutions have been opened around the country and currently almost 50 percent of students are attending institutions outside of the former capital city of Bishkek, up from only 20 percent in the early 1990s. Many institutions now offer a more diverse curriculum and are using materials and educational methods adopted from the educational systems in Russia, Turkey, France, and the United States. Many of these institutions have also adopted western-style bachelor's and master's degree programs, replacing the old Soviet five-year system. Many students are seeking advanced degrees in areas that are not in high demand in Kyrgyzstan but are in demand in other countries (United Nations, 2000, p. 53).

Of the 45 universities and colleges now operating, 15 offer opportunities for specialized study in economics, and all are required to include basic economics as a compulsory course in their core requirements for general education. The Ministry is working with the universities and colleges to standardize the required basic economics course and encouraging those institutions to diversify their specialized professional and degree programs in economics. The Ministry is also encouraging universities and colleges to develop distance education courses and programs in economics. Unfortunately, none of the private or public universities and colleges offers programs designed to prepare teachers to teach economics in secondary schools (Miroshnichenko, 2001).

Education Initiatives of the Soros Foundation: The Pilot Schools Program[5]

The Soros Foundation-Kyrgyzstan was established in 1993 as a nongovernmental organization with the mission of creating conditions necessary for building an open society. This work included the transformation of public institutions and promoting democratic political reforms. In 1995 the Ministry of Education signed an agreement pledging to support the education programs and initiatives of the Foundation. This action was part of a concerted action by the Ministry to attract support for physical improvements and up-to-date textbooks in the schools, reflecting the serious funding constraints facing the Kyrgyz government. The Foundation's initial efforts to promote effective economic education in the schools came in 1995 under the Foundation's 'Education for an Open Society' and 'Economics Reform' programs. The basic strategy of these programs was to initiate new ideas and approaches to education through the establishment of a Pilot Schools program in all regions of the country. To attract educators who were interested in educational reform and open to change, in 1995 the Foundation announced a competition for innovative projects for the secondary schools of the country. The Foundation selected the 50 schools that it felt showed the greatest promise for creative and successful initiatives in school reform. The 50 schools agreed that they would not be associated with political parties, and they agreed to share their experiences and ideas regarding the transformation of education with other schools in their region. In return, the Foundation agreed that all of its education programs, which were very well funded compared to other education programs in the nation, would be initiated through this network of pilot schools.

Programs were developed to introduce modern methods of teaching to the staff of the pilot schools, to establish close connections with parents of students in the schools, and to encourage students' cognitive development and creative initiatives. An association of the directors of the pilot schools was created as an independent, nongovernmental organization, with the goal of spreading new ideas to secondary schools that were not part of the program. The principals of the pilot schools participated in a series of leadership development seminars. The Soros Foundation also initiated a competition to encourage the writing of new textbooks and the translation and adaptation of textbooks from other countries for use in Kyrgyzstan.

The Foundation immediately gave a high priority to economic education initiatives in the pilot schools. Although the introductory course in economics had been mandated by the Ministry of Education in 1992, in fact very little economics was being taught. There was a lack of textbooks, methodological literature, teaching manuals, and most of all teachers who were trained to teach the course. In practice, therefore, teachers of history, geography, and literature were asked to teach the new economics classes, usually without textbooks or other teaching materials. Given these problems, the Soros Foundation engaged the US National Council on Economic Education (NCEE) to offer a series of training workshops for teachers and administrators in its Pilot Schools program.

The Foundation supplemented these workshops with other activities. Students and teachers seeking to upgrade their knowledge of economics received support to attend seminars and study abroad programs. The Foundation devoted substantial resources to obtaining, translating, and distributing economics textbooks, and university economists were provided with modern textbooks and other professional and instructional materials. Each of the 50 pilot schools as well as 70 other Kyrgyz schools with teachers who had participated in Soros-sponsored economic education workshops received 30 copies of four secondary textbooks, as well as ancillary materials for these books. The four textbooks are:

- *Economics for Students*, by V. Avtonomova and E. Goldstan. This is a short textbook that describes basic principles of market economics.
- *Economics Without Secrets*, by Igor Lipsitz. This text describes the basic concepts of modern economic theory and provides a short review of the history of economic thought.
- *Economics*, by Igor Lipsitz. This two-volume set provides a more comprehensive basic course in economic theory and the basics of market activity. It also includes information about the development of economic institutions and about important people in economic history.
- *Remarkable Adventures in the Land of Economics*, by Igor Lipsitz. This book is written for middle school students (aged 10-13), explaining basic concepts of economics including prices, wages, trade, exchange rates, competition, and inflation.

In 1997 the Soros Foundation sponsored the first Economics Olympiad for students in the pilot schools. In the first round students competed by correspondence, answering 50 multiple-choice questions. Students with the highest scores went on to regional competitions where they answered 30 questions and solved five problems. Regional winners were invited to a national competition where they took exams in microeconomics and macroeconomics and competed in an economics and management computer simulation. In April 1999 the three winners of the 1998 Kyrgyzstan National Olympiad competed as a team in the International Economics Olympiad in Moscow, finishing third. In the first five years of the Soros Foundation's sponsorship of the national Economics Olympiad over 2,000 students participated.

The National Council on Economic Education

In December of 1995 in Bishkek, with financial and programmatic support from the Soros Foundation, the NCEE offered the first in a series of three week-long workshops for 47 teachers from the Soros pilot schools.[6] This first workshop was designed to introduce teachers to basic economic concepts and the operation of a market system, and to various active-learning teaching methods. Participants played a market game to see how prices are established by the interaction of buyers and sellers. Other simulations and activities demonstrated the importance of private property, specialization, the role of entrepreneurs, and the gains from trade in a market system. Some classes were lectures on the relationships underlying demand and supply, opportunity costs in the short run and long run, and the circular flow of income in a market economy.

Most of the same group of teachers and administrators returned to Bishkek in March of 1996 for the second workshop in the series, which covered additional topics or revisited topics covered in the first workshop in greater depth, but followed the same general format and used the same variety of teaching methods. This workshop was partially funded by a grant awarded to the NCEE by the Office of Educational Research and Improvement at the US Department of Education. At the end of this program participants applied what they had learned in a macroeconomic computer simulation that illustrates problems of inflation and unemployment and the role of monetary and fiscal policies.

The third workshop in the series was conducted for the same group of teachers and administrators in August 1996 at Lake Issyk-Kul. The sessions at this workshop were pitched at an even higher level of conceptual rigor, with more extensive 'real world' data and current economic problems and policy proposals. There were also some formal sessions devoted exclusively to the basic theory and principles of effective pedagogy, not just applications or demonstrations.

More sessions in this third workshop were designed around public policy themes because evaluations of earlier workshops offered in other former Soviet countries suggested that many teachers found it difficult to accept some ideas, conclusions, and even parts of the basic framework of mainstream economics. This problem arose largely because of the teachers' backgrounds in central planning systems and their basic unfamiliarity with the important but relatively limited role of government in a market economy. In Kyrgyzstan the problem was compounded by the fact that a significant number of the teachers in the program came from rural, tradition-dominated villages.

To address these issues topics in the third workshop included a revisiting of the market game to illustrate the effects of imperfect competition, and a classroom market experiment demonstrating the efficiency of competitive markets and the loss of efficiency associated with price controls and other government policies that interfere with the price mechanism. Later sessions focused on the relationship between firm size and the costs of production, imperfectly competitive market structures, the application of cost-benefit analysis to government decisions, principles of effective taxation, investment in human capital, factors influencing the distribution of income and wealth, alternative strategies for privatization, financial markets and institutions, international trade and trade barriers, and the determinants of economic growth.

Since 1997, 26 lecturers, professors, and secondary school teachers from Kyrgyzstan have completed the NCEE's Training of Trainers Seminars that are designed to create a strong national core of teacher trainers in economics who can offer programs to prepare teachers to teach economics in secondary schools. The program consists of a series of four one-week seminars, emphasizing both economic content and the principles of effective pedagogy. In each of the four seminars some sessions are devoted specifically to pedagogical topics, and most economic concepts are presented using lesson plans from NCEE publications for secondary teachers, supplemented with current data or materials for university courses and instructors. In each seminar participants are asked to create applications or examples of instructional materials and activities appropriate for use with students in their home countries. They also design workshop agendas for use in their home institutions. At the end of each seminar participants receive a complete set of translated instructional materials to use in workshops they offer for teachers in their home countries.

Another 14 teachers from Kyrgyzstan have attended an NCEE multinational workshop on teaching economics in elementary grades, emphasizing the developmental or K-12 infusion approach to teaching economics content. Once again, all of the participants received a translated set of instructional materials to use in replicating this program for teachers in their home regions.

Centers for Economic Education[7]

The Kyrgyz graduates of the NCEE Training of Trainers program immediately began offering workshops for teachers. In 1997 the graduates played key roles in founding and staffing economic education Centers in four cities and regions (Bishkek, Mayluu-Suu, Karakaol, and Kyzyl-Kiya). The Centers are registered as private nongovernmental organizations, not affiliated with universities or other public agencies. They are usually staffed by the teachers/consultants who participated in the original series of three NCEE teacher workshops in Kyrgyzstan. With funding from the Soros Foundation each Center was supplied with office equipment and a basic library of economic education materials. The Centers began by offering regional three-day workshops for secondary teachers from both in and outside the Soros pilot school network. In 1996 and 1997 two workshops were held in each of six regions in southern and northern Kyrgyzstan, each based on NCEE programs in terms of general content coverage and pedagogical methods, and even the instructional materials that were used. This first series of programs was attended by 240 teachers, which means that there is now at least one economics teacher with some training and a set of NCEE teaching materials in 100 of the 1,539 secondary schools of Kyrgyzstan.

In 1998 the Centers began offering three-week workshops for middle school teachers, with 136 teachers completing these seminars by 2000. In 1999 a group of trainers and consultants from the Kyrgyz Centers participated in a NCEE seminar on teaching economics to elementary school children. Following that seminar these trainers and consultants developed a comprehensive program for teaching economics to Kyrgyz students in grades 5-7. A workshop to introduce the program was conducted in December 1999, and other teachers around the country have received help directly from the Centers in developing their economics programs for those grade levels. As a result of these programs almost a quarter of the nation's secondary schools are now offering economics as part of the curriculum in grades 5-7.

All of the Centers have offered one-day programs to introduce economics programs and the services of the Council and its four Centers to school principals and employees of Boards of Education and the Ministry of Education. In 1999-2000, 120 people attended these programs.

The Kyrgyzstan Council on Economic Education[8]

Following the common practice of Soros Foundations in other former Soviet countries, the Soros Foundation of Kyrgyzstan has begun to spin off its direct involvement in the day-to-day administration and sponsorship of economic education programs. To do this, in 1999 the Foundation supported the formation of an independent nongovernmental organization called the National Council on Economic Education of Kyrgyzstan. This new organization will continue to be supported by the Foundation for an indefinite period of time, but the plan is for the organization to become totally independent and self-supporting as soon as possible. Like the NCEE in the United States, the Kyrgyzstan Council will serve as a national umbrella organization, working in cooperation with its network of Centers for Economic Education. The expressed purpose of the Council is to seek support for the promotion and development of economic education classes in all of the secondary schools of Kyrgyzstan, and for the continued support of programs to develop a cadre of well-trained teachers of economics for these schools. The Council also seeks to support the development of economic standards for the nation's schools, the development of new educational and curriculum materials for students and teachers, and other programs such as student competitions.

To date, the primary focus of the Council's efforts has been the ongoing series of teacher training seminars and workshops for secondary teachers. The need for these programs can only be described as urgent, because there is still no national curriculum or set of economics standards to guide teachers in designing required or elective economics classes, and there are no other programs available in Kyrgyzstan for the systematic training of economics teachers. The teacher-training seminars are currently offered through each of the four Centers in three one-week periods with 120 total hours of class time. About 110 teachers participated in these workshops in 1999-2000. The curriculum is based on the NCEE *Voluntary Content Standards* (National Council on Economic Education, 1997) and the 'Modern Economics' program of the International Center for Economic and Business Education in Moscow.

The Council has developed model study programs and lesson plans at three grade levels to improve and standardize the economics classes taught in the schools. The coordinator of the Mayluu-Suu Center and a local secondary teacher developed a comprehensive program for teaching economics in grades 5-7. This plan includes suggestions for 102 hours of economics instruction, which represents one class per week over three school years. The coordinator of the Bishkek Center and an economics teacher in a Bishkek lyceum developed a similar program for grades 9-12 at general education schools. A teacher at the Svetoch school in Bishkek and the Bishkek Center coordinator have also developed a more advanced course for the study of economic theory in schools that choose to teach economics two periods a week over a three-year period (204 hours). All three of these curriculum plans were tested in classrooms in various schools in the country and have now been submitted to the Ministry of Education for approval as a standardized study program in economics.

The regional Centers also offer opportunities for teachers to meet and discuss issues related to economics and to economic education. For example, the Karakaol Center in the Issyk-Kul Region hosts a meeting of an Economics Club of teachers on a monthly basis, with about a dozen teachers regularly attending. The Mayluu-Suu and Kyzyl-Kiya Centers offer open consulting sessions for teachers once a week.

Staff members at the Kyrgyzstan Council and the Centers have undertaken the task of developing new national textbooks and other study aids for use in secondary economics classes. The impetus for this project comes from the fact that many schools, especially Kyrgyz language schools, are still using old political economy manuals from the Soviet period, or texts in management or marketing. The Council has just completed the development of a Kyrgyz language book of economics exercises and tests. This new text includes student exercises on 14 major economics topics including supply and demand, money, inflation, and the basics of international trade. The book includes sample calendar plans (syllabuses) for teaching economics, instructions for monitoring student progress through the use of the book's exercises, and lists of important economic terms and formulas.

The staff of the Council and teachers associated with the Centers are continuing the program of translating and adapting economic education materials developed in the United States and Russia. They are also publishing and distributing copies of at least four issues of a newsletter each year, titled *Lessons in Economics*, to disseminate information about economic education to schools with teachers who have participated in Council or Center programs. This project is supported by the NCEE through a grant from the US Department of Education. The Kyrgyzstan Council also prepared three videotapes to introduce the use of active learning approaches in teaching economics.

With support from the Soros Foundation, the Kyrgyzstan Council has also begun offering a biannual Children's Economic School program for gifted tenth-grade students. Graduates of the NCEE's Training of Trainers program teach this intensive (128 hours) program for students who are selected on a competitive basis. Students who complete this program receive a certificate that entitles them to serve as teaching assistants to secondary economics teachers and to run optional or extracurricular classes on economics for students in their schools. More than

100 students participated in this program in the 1999-2000 school year, and a similar number was anticipated for 2000-01.

Junior Achievement Kyrgyzstan[9]

Junior Achievement (JA) was officially registered by the Ministry of Justice and first began offering programs in Kyrgyzstan in August of 1995. According to information provided by the organization, more than 500 teachers have participated in their training programs and seminars and teach about 25,000 students annually. JA reports that as of Spring, 2001, there are 98 volunteers – mostly secondary teachers – working for the organization in the classroom.

The centerpiece of the JA program is their Applied Economics program for secondary students. These US-developed materials were translated into Kyrgyz in 1999 and are now being taught in both Russian and Kyrgyz. The Applied Economics textbook has been approved by the Ministry of Education as a supplementary resource for teaching economics in grades 1-11. As part of this program groups of students in a school organize and operate their own companies during the school year. Beginning in 1999 JA began conducting national competitions in which these school companies present their business plan to a panel of judges. Ten teams took part in the 1999 competition and 15 teams participated in 2000.

In each year since 1997 JA-Kyrgyzstan has supported Olympiads in Applied Economics in the Bishkek and Chuysky regions. The winners in these competitions are automatically accepted as students at the Bishkek Academy of Finance and Economics, which serves as a local sponsor for the event.

The Association of Economics Teachers of Kyrgyzstan

The newest entrant into the economic education movement of Kyrgyzstan was organized in August 2000. The purpose of this association is to create national standards of economics for students at all grade levels, offer economic education training programs for teachers, and develop economic education teaching materials and reference books. The organization lists a number of additional services it hopes to provide for member teachers, including providing consulting assistance; conducting economic camps, Olympiads, and other competitions; and providing independent assessment of economics materials and programs.

The organization states that its membership already exceeds 100 teachers in the Bishkek and Chu regions, and that it is now recruiting members from other regions of the country. The Association has received in-kind support from the Bishkek Academy of Finance and Economics.

Ministry of Education

The Ministry of Education also played a significant role in the transformation of economic education in Kyrgyzstan. In addition to the basic economics class, the Ministry also requires schools to offer courses on the Basics of Marketing (in the tenth grade) and Financial Accounting (in the eleventh grade). Recognizing that these courses require additional training for teachers, in 1993 the Ministry created a Department of Management and Economic Education in the Kyrgyz Institute of Education. The express purpose of this Department was to provide retraining for secondary school teachers to prepare them to teach economics and business classes. Unfortunately, the Department was closed less than three years later due to financial difficulties. While it was functioning the Department provided retraining for about 100 geography and history teachers. Since 1995 there have been no economic education training programs for teachers available in the universities or at education institutes.

The Ministry has encouraged the development of teacher training programs in economics offered by the Soros Foundation-Kyrgyzstan, the Kyrgyzstan Council on Economic Education, and Junior Achievement. It has also encouraged schools to experiment with innovative approaches to teaching economics. As a result, while most schools are offering economics as a stand-alone course, other schools are attempting to teach the subject using the infusion approach, in such classes as chemistry, physics, and biology. The Ministry also supports extracurricular economic education activities offered through the Republican Center for Children, in which students join such organizations as the Management Club, the Marketing Club, and the Banking Club.

The Ministry estimates that today there are about 500 teachers in Kyrgyzstan who have completed significant additional training and are qualified to teach economics in secondary schools. Given that there are some 2,000 secondary schools in the country, it is obvious that a majority of the schools do not have a qualified teacher of economics (Miroshnichenko, 2001).

III.   CONCLUSIONS AND OUTLOOK

Those who worked to create and implement programs to bring effective economic education to the schools of Kyrgyzstan faced a daunting task in the early 1990s. But the people of this small country had big dreams of a better life when the country rejected the tightly controlled economic system that had dominated their lives through most of the twentieth century. In spite of the fact that Kyrgyzstan had been one of the most tradition-bound republics in the former Soviet Union, especially in rural areas, Kyrgyzstan moved more quickly than most of the former Soviet republics to privatize property and introduce other market reforms. Unfortunately, as in most of the transition countries, national output and income levels initially fell sharply; and runaway inflation from 1993-95 dashed the hopes of those who had expected immediate improvements in national standards of living. The transition period proved to be long and difficult, and a growing proportion of the population started questioning the decision to adopt democratic and market-oriented reforms.

In 1995 when economic conditions reached their lowest level, the Soros Foundation began to devote major resources to the development of a market-based economic education program for the country's schools. Their strategy was to introduce educational reforms in 50 secondary schools participating in a Pilot Schools project. In return for substantial assistance, and with the blessing of the Ministry of Education, each of these schools agreed to adopt the reforms included in the Soros programs – in economics as well as in other subjects. The schools also agreed to implement pedagogical methods being used in western countries, and to share what they learned with other schools in their communities and regions.

Combined with the teacher training programs of the NCEE, the pilot schools project is providing an efficient mechanism for introducing broad-based economic education programs in Kyrgyz schools. More than 500 teachers have participated in training programs for at least a full week, offered by graduates of the NCEE Training of Trainers program or by teachers who participated in other NCEE programs. Hundreds more administrators and teachers have participated in shorter, one-to-three-day workshops. The new Kyrgyzstan Council on Economic Education and its four Centers, along with the Association of Economics Teachers, now provide a solid in-country infrastructure to expand the reach of economic education.

In spite of these achievements, there are significant challenges that need to be addressed. Over half of the schools in the nation still do not have a qualified teacher of economics on their staff, and many rural schools are still using old (that is, Marxian) textbooks. Moreover, the economics program at many other schools consists mainly of marketing or business management courses.

It is unfortunate that the major universities and teacher training institutions of the country have participated so very little in the movement to bring economic education to the nation's secondary schools. It is of special concern that there are currently no public educational institutions in the country offering programs to train economics teachers.

The Ministry of Education has provided strong verbal support for the economic education movement, but it has not been able to devote significant resources to the effort. Ministry officials have indicated that they will work with the Kyrgyzstan Council in the development of economics standards as well as associated teaching materials.

Perhaps the biggest question to be answered about the near-term future of economic education in Kyrgyzstan is whether groups such as the Kyrgyzstan Council on Economic Education will be able to obtain resources to continue the programs that are now being offered once the Soros Foundation fully removes itself from these activities. There is clearly still much to be done. For example, the country needs to complete the development of economics standards or a national curriculum to guide schools in establishing their economic education programs. New methodological manuals and Kyrgyz language textbooks are desperately needed by teachers and schools. And perhaps most important, there are still more than 1000 schools without a trained economics teacher.

NOTES

1. The Ministry of Education of Kyrgyzstan has undergone several reorganizations in the 1990s and has, at various times, been named the Ministry of Education, the Ministry of Education and Culture, or the Ministry of Education, Science, and Culture. In this chapter we always refer to the Ministry of Education.
2. Except as noted, this section is based on the 1996 Library of Congress report on Kyrgyzstan.
3. These purchasing power parity GDP values are from calculations by CountryWatch.com based on data from the US CIA Factbook, the IMF *World Outlook*, the US Census Bureau *International Data Base*, and the UN *Statistical Yearbook*.
4. The information in this section on school structure and enrollments is taken from the 2000 Ministry for Education, Science, and Culture report on 'The System of Education of Kyrgyzstan.'
5. This section is based on a series of Annual Reports and other documents provided by the Soros Foundation-Kyrgyzstan for the period 1995-99.
6. The next five paragraphs are based on program reports provided by the National Council on Economic Education (1995-96).
7. The following four paragraphs are based on program reports submitted to the Soros Fund-Kyrgyzstan in 1997-98 and to the Kyrgyzstan Council on Economic Education in 1999. These reports are summarized in the annual reports of the Soros Foundation-Kyrgyzstan and in the 1999-2000 annual report of the Kyrgyzstan Council on Economic Education.
8. This section is based on the 1999-2000 annual report of the Kyrgyzstan Council on Economic Education and Aksenenko (2001).
9. This section is based on information provided by Junior Achievement-Kyrgyzstan.

REFERENCES

Aksenenko, N. (2001), 'Status of economic education in Kyrgyzstan,' working paper.
Avtonomov, S. and E. Goldstan (1995), *Economics for Secondary Students*, by Moscow: ECONOV.
Country Watch.com – Kyrgyzstan Information: Economy 2001,*wysiwyg://10/http://www.countrywatch.com/files/094/cw_topic.asp?Vcountry=094&TP=ECO*.
Imanaliev, M. (2000), Presentation at the CDF Workshop on the National Poverty Alleviation Program.
Kyrgyzstan Council on Economic Education (1999-2001), *Annual Reports*, Bishkek.
Library of Congress, Federal Research Division (1996), Country Studies: Area Handbook Series; Krygyzstan, G. Curtis, ed. *http://memory.loc.gov/frd/cs/cshome.html.*
Lipsitz, I. (1994), *Economics Without Secrets*, Moscow: VITA-PRESS.
Lipsitz, I. (1994), *Remarkable Adventures in the Land of Economics*, Moscow: VITA-PRESS.
Lipsitz, I. (1996), *Economics*, Moscow: VITA-PRESS.
Ministry for Education, Science, and Culture of the Kyrgyz Republic (2000), 'System of Education of Kyrgyzstan at Present.'
Miroshnichenko, L. (2001), 'The condition of economic education in the Republic of Kyrgyzstan,' working paper.
National Council on Economic Education (1995-96), 'Program reports for teacher workshops in Kyrgyzstan,' New York.
National Council on Economic Education (1997), *Voluntary National Content Standards in Economics*, New York.

Soros Foundation-Kyrgyzstan (1995-99), *Annual reports for the Economic Reform Program and the Education for an Open Society Program.*

United Nations Development Program in Kyrgyzstan. *National Human Development Report (2000),* *http://www.undp.kg/english/publications/nhdr2000/.*

9. Economic Education in Latvia: Yesterday, Today, and Tomorrow

Veronika Bikse and Steven L. Cobb

The *Declaration of the Renewal of Latvia as an Independent Republic* on 4 May 1990 ended 50 years of Latvian incorporation into the Soviet Union. During that half-century, the nation's skilled workforce and a relatively well-developed infrastructure contributed to one of the highest national standards of living in the Soviet Union, although Latvian consumers and industries suffered from periodic shortages of goods and supplies and other problems typical of command economies.

The transition to a market economy was marked by a sudden and unexpectedly large decline in output; by 1993 GDP was half of the 1990 level. GDP began to rise again after 1995, but had only reached 60 percent of the 1990 level by 2000 (*Statistical Yearbook of Latvia,* 2000). The decline in GDP was exacerbated by falling purchasing power, rising unemployment and inflation, and various other social problems.

The transition to a market economy placed a greater emphasis on people's education and their ability to apply knowledge in the labor market. But unfortunately, reforming education initially took a back seat to the issues of privatization and liberalization. Links between successful economic reforms and improvements in education were only recently recognized, and a greater emphasis on economic, business, and science education has only been seen in the last five years.

I. THE EDUCATION SYSTEM

Education reform in Latvia is guided by the following four goals, which became part of *The Education Law* in June 1991:

De-Politicization of Education

The revival of democratic principles for political and social structures has led to fewer government controls over educational content and methodology. The Soviet emphasis on conformity and uniformity of thought was the result of the single-party system, in which education was used as an instrument to form the goals and opinions of Latvian youth.

Freedom of Choice in Education

The main goal of Latvia today is to insure that all citizens have the opportunity to realize their aspirations based on their individual abilities and interests. For education, this means that a family can send their children to the school of its choice. The respect of personal choice is considered a basic principle of liberalizing education.

Abolishing the Governmental Monopoly in Education

Two of the main goals of the transition period are a return to democracy and the development of a market economy. A significant step in the transition process is to reestablish private and religious schools, while de-politicization improves the quantity, variety, and quality of educational programs in both public and private schools. This change has promoted healthy competition among schools.

Decentralization of School Boards and School Funding

Increasing responsibility for the operation of schools has been shifted to local governments, and to individual schools and their directors.

The systematic review of education as part of the transition to a market economy began in 1993. The goals of education were the topic of many formal and informal discussions, especially at the Congress of Latvian Educational Employees in 1994. These discussions led to the publication, *Educational Concept*, approved by the Cabinet of Ministers in 1995, which outlines the strategy of educational development in Latvia and the direction of educational reforms.

This document continues to be discussed and reviewed because there is some doubt that the *Concept* fully and truly reflects the needs and aspirations of the Latvian people, or that it has set the correct direction for educational reforms. The most recent changes in the educational system were made in 1999 with an eye toward closer alignment with education practices in the European Union.

Basic and General Education

Precollege education in Latvia beyond pre-school is divided into basic (primary) education and secondary education.

Basic education (grades 1-9) in Latvia is divided into two levels, grades 1-4 and grades 5-9. Level three or secondary general education include grades 10-12. Special institutions also exist in Latvia for children with special emotional and/or physical developmental needs. There were about 361,400 students enrolled in general schools in 1999-2000 and they were taught by about 34,800 teachers.[1]

School is mandatory in Latvia up to age 15 or completion of basic education (grade 9). Individuals over age 15 have the opportunity to continue in school or to receive their basic education in evening school or by correspondence. All children are guaranteed a basic level education regardless of their ethnic, social, or religious background. Children with special needs are guaranteed instruction meeting those needs.

The educational content of the basic program provides a solid basis for continued education. The choice after completing nine years of basic education is between general secondary, vocational secondary, or specialized secondary education. Secondary education is free but not mandatory in Latvia, and offered in a number of different types of institutions. General secondary education may be obtained in a high school (typically offering classes for grades 1-12) or in gymnasia (either offering classes for grades 7-12 or 10-12).

Professional education is offered in vocational schools, secondary professional education institutions, and schools for craftsmen. The Ministry of Education and Science is responsible for approving the classification of vocational and secondary professional educational programs by branch of study. The fields of study for vocational educational programs currently include teacher training and education, science, humanities, social sciences, natural sciences, engineering and technology, agriculture, health and welfare, and services.

Vocational education is offered in *arodpamatskola* (vocational basic schools), *arodvidusskola* (vocational secondary schools), *arodgimnâzija* (vocational gymnasiums), and *arodskola* (vocational post-secondary schools). These schools enrolled about 26,400 students in 1999-2000. Depending on the content level of a program it may take one to four years to complete. Only the four-year vocational secondary (*arodgimnâzija*) programs provide general secondary education that give students access to higher education. Graduates from other vocational education programs must complete their general secondary education before pursuing a higher education.

Secondary professional education institutions are usually named *tehnikumsor koledža* and offer four- to five-year curricula for students who have completed the nine-year program of basic education. These schools enrolled about 21,300 students in 1999-2000. Regardless of the curriculum selected, graduates of these schools are eligible to enter higher education institutions because these schools provide professional training at a higher level than vocational schools and simultaneously provide general secondary education.

Many secondary professional institutions have recently begun to offer special programs for secondary school graduates. These programs require two or three years of schooling after completion of general secondary schooling and are often high-level. Reorganization of the secondary professional education institutions into institutions of vocational (or non-university) higher education, along the lines of German *Fachhochschulen* or Dutch *Hogescholen*, is becoming one of the key points in the overall education reform program for Latvia.

Private schools exist at every educational level in Latvia. There are relatively few private schools today, but they are rapidly becoming a well-organized educational network. At the preschool level there are private kindergartens, art and music schools, and aesthetics programs. At the basic and secondary levels there are private general education schools, art and music schools, and alternative schools. Private educational facilities are under the oversight of the National Educational Inspector and must comply with all national regulations; all schools must be licensed by the Ministry of Education and Science.

Latvian is not the only language of instruction in schools. There are institutions where Latvian, Russian, and even a third language (English, German, Polish, Hebrew, Estonian, or Lithuanian) are all languages of instruction. These schools strive to offer equality of educational opportunities regardless of the native language of the students. Schools with dual-language instruction are established based on regional needs, and all students are required to take Latvian language classes. In addition, at least two subjects in humanities and science are required to be taught in Latvian.

Higher Education

Extensive changes have taken place in higher education in Latvia since 1991. These changes include reforms and reorganizations at existing institutions and the establishment of new colleges and universities. The total number of universities has grown since 1991 because no schools ceased operations and several new ones were opened. Overall student enrollment in higher education institutions grew from 46,000 students to 89,500 students. There are 19 national colleges and 15 licensed colleges founded by juridical entities in Latvia.

Higher education in Latvia is divided into three different levels. The first level is undergraduate study of from three to four-and-a-half years, including the preparation of a thesis, leading to a *Bakalaurs* (Bachelor's degree). The second level is the *Magistrs* (Master's) degree, which requires two years of study beyond the *Bakalaurs* and involves the presentation of a second thesis. The third level is a Doctor's degree that is typically awarded three to four years after completion of the *Magistrs* degree, following the public defence of a thesis (see Table 9.1)

Presently the national universities in Latvia offer more than 300 courses of study. One of the directions of higher education reforms has been to increase the number of available programs of study and the quality of these programs, to better fit with Latvian economic, political, and cultural priorities, and to be competitive within the European Union.

The *University and College Law* provides for the opportunity to switch from a professional program of study to an academic one, and vice versa. For example, after an individual has earned his professional qualification he may choose to continue in a master's program, or after receiving his bachelor's degree he may wish to continue in a one or two-year professional training program.

Table 9.1: Number of higher education students by degree levels, 1999-2000

| Type of Institution | Total | First Level (Undergraduate) | | Second Level | | Third Level |
		Bakalaurs Program	Professional Program	Professional Program	Masters Program	Doctoral Studies
State	29,647	10,936	9,278	2,826	4,480	282
Private	4,446	114	4,034	128	59	4
TOTAL	34,093	11,050	13,312	2,954	4,539	286
Percent	100	32.4	39.0	8.7	13.3	0.8

Source: Statistical Yearbook of Latvia, 2000, p. 95.

Teacher Training

Following the restoration of the independent Republic of Latvia, teachers' opportunities to acquire academic education changed radically. A teacher may obtain higher professional education by enrolling in professional study programs that comply with the *Classification of Occupations of Latvia*, offered by the different higher education institutions. Higher education institutions now also provide the opportunity for teachers to update their knowledge or, if necessary, to develop a new field of specialization to teach.

Minimum educational requirements for those who teach at all levels of education are specified in *The Education Law*: pre-primary and basic teachers must complete higher professional pedagogic education; secondary teachers must complete higher professional pedagogic education and academic training in the subject they will teach. There is currently a serious shortage of teachers in Latvia, however, and because of the shortage school principals have been given the right to sign contracts with teachers who do not currently meet minimum educational requirements. These teachers are required to acquire higher professional education as soon as possible.

Ministry of Science and Education figures on the level of education of teachers working in educational institutions indicate that, on average, only 65.5 percent of teachers meet the minimum educational requirements. Specifically, only 27.7 percent of pre-primary teachers meet the requirements; 63 percent of teachers at the basic education institutions; and 80.1 percent of teachers in secondary institutions. Providing adequate training for teachers is becoming easier because Teacher Institutes have been converted into higher education institutions or merged with other higher education institutions, which should allow future teachers to acquire higher education that complies with qualification requirements.

II. ECONOMIC EDUCATION IN LATVIA

During the Soviet period economics in Latvia was a combination of political economy and Marxist-Leninist philosophy. Neither market nor business economics was a required or even an elective course in grades 1-12. The economics curriculum at the university level focused on Marxist-Leninist political economy, and was modelled after the program at Moscow State University.[2]

The lack of experience (real or classroom) in market economics posed a serious problem for teachers when the Latvian economy began the process of transition. As the links between successful economic reforms and improvements in education were recognized, a greater emphasis was placed on economics and business courses. Economics first entered the Latvian curriculum in 1992 as an optional course at grade 11 or 12, titled Principles of Business Economics. But many of the teachers of this course had inadequate backgrounds and poor instructional materials to use with their students.

Current Instruction

Latvia has now set itself apart from many of the other transitional economies by mandating two courses in economics. The first compulsory course in economics, Introduction to Economics, was legislated in the 1997-98 school year for students in grade 8. Prior to grade 8, economics is a social science elective topic. The Introduction to Business Economics course for eleventh and twelfth-grade students became mandatory for the 1999-2000 school year.

At the undergraduate level university economics programs are becoming decidedly more western in their structure and content. The Bachelor's degree program in economics at the University of Latvia has been revised to include compulsory courses in macroeconomics, microeconomics, statistics, mathematics, the theory of money and credit, accounting, entrepreneurship, business law, and an introduction to the national economy. This core is almost identical to that required for a Bachelor's degree in economics offered in a school of business at any large US university.

Delivering courses that will prepare students for life in a market economy requires more than mandates, however. It depends on the level of economic knowledge and experience of the teachers of these courses and the quality of the instructional materials that are available for them to use with their students.

Teacher Training

The Ministry of Science and Education has been given the responsibility of coordinating the continuing education of Latvian teachers. A critical step in the process was the establishment of organizations to oversee and coordinate the educational programs in each region. In 1996, 27 adult education centers were opened to offer courses in methodology, including courses and seminars for economics teachers. The adult education centers are run by local governments and partner with local school boards and educational institutions to provide teacher training.

With the adult education centers to coordinate regional programs, the Ministry of Science and Education needed to provide incentives for teachers to seek continuing education. The *Regulations on the Improvement of Teacher Professional Qualifications*, passed in 1997, state that it is the teachers' duty to improve their education by participating in further education programs for at least 36 hours every three years. As a result, the demand for continuing education among economics teachers is high. Teachers have the choice of taking courses at colleges and universities, inservice seminars, special regional courses, or self-education followed by an examination.

The content of the training is also specified by the Ministry, which organizes regular seminars for regional school board directors. The regional school boards are responsible for setting up methodical societies in each area of specialization (such as economics). The methodical societies coordinate educational resources, determine content and methodology, and offer continuing education opportunities for their teachers. The regional methodical societies of teachers of economics offer inservice seminars and special courses in coordination with partner organizations specializing in economic education.

Partnerships

To overcome the shortage of domestic resources in market (or business) economics, a number of foreign partnerships were developed to provide training for Latvian teachers. The first were TEMPUS JEP projects with European universities. These are programs that bring representatives from leading European universities to work with Latvian professors to improve the quality and content of higher education. The second partnership was with the EU PHARE project, Business Education Reform in Latvia. This project was designed to promote the development of study programs at the first (*Bakalaurs*) level of higher education. The two remaining partnerships are with American economic education programs that are widely used in Latvian schools.

Until 1995 the only organized courses and seminars for pre-university economics teachers were provided by Junior Achievement of Latvia. In addition to teacher training, Junior Achievement of Latvia developed and translated economics and business curriculum materials for classroom use. Many of these materials are still used in the required eighth-grade economics course and the eleventh or twelfth-grade business economics courses.

The National Council on Economic Education (NCEE) began cooperative programs in Latvia in 1995 with support from the Office of Educational Research and Improvement of the US Department of Education. The initial focus of the programs is teacher training, with the goals of increasing the economic knowledge of participants and improving their pedagogy skills. The centerpiece of the

NCEE's work in Latvia is its 'Training of Trainers' program. This program has the additional goal of preparing Latvian teachers and university faculty to train teachers at schools in their region. During the six years of NCEE involvement in Latvia, 38 economics teachers and professors have completed the series of four one-week Trainers workshops. Most of these participants have now become highly skilled economics teacher-trainers and managers in the field of economic education in Latvia.

Six of the Trainers graduates have also completed the NCEE's Training of Curriculum Writers program to enhance their skills in curriculum development. Three other graduates of the Trainers program have completed the NCEE Economic Education Evaluation Workshop to develop research and evaluation skills. Yet three other graduates of the Trainers program participated in a program on Training on Non-Profit Management and Organizational Development and in a seminar on Creating National Examples in economic education instructional materials for use in the transition economies.

Training of Latvian teachers by graduates of the NCEE's Trainers program is now typically being carried out through the establishment of Centers for Economic Education at Latvian universities. Three graduates of the 1995-97 Trainers programs set up the Center for Economic Education at the University of Latvia and began to organize a wide variety of cooperative activities. Fifty-one Latvian teachers of economics have participated in two one-week workshops organized by the University of Latvia Center and conducted by NCEE faculty from US universities. The University of Latvia Center is also actively involved in conducting economic education workshops with regional methodical societies of teachers of economics. More recent graduates of the Trainers program are now organizing a network of Centers for Economic Education at Vidzeme University (in Valmiera), Ventspils University, Rezekne University, Liepaja University, Jelgavas University, and Daugavpils University. These six new Centers will make economic education more accessible to teachers outside Riga.

An economic education network needs a coordinating organization to develop cooperative agreements, raise funds for workshops, and lead the effort to develop content standards in economics for the primary and secondary levels. In 1998 the Baltic Council on Economic Education (BCEE) was created with financial support from the NCEE. The BCEE was formed to provide support for programs to prepare leaders in economic education in all three Baltic countries. In August 1999, 13 graduates of the Trainers program and one US faculty member representing the NCEE led a workshop for Russian-speaking economics teachers from Estonia, Latvia, and Lithuania. This was the first program of the BCEE involving teachers from all three nations. The BCEE and its affiliated centers play a major role in conducting Economic Olympiads and essay competitions. Currently these competitions are conducted on a national basis, but Latvia is taking a leadership role in the process to have competitions involve students from all three Baltic states.

The Role of Universities

Providing training for current economics teachers only addresses one part of the teacher problem. The shortage of qualified teachers in Latvia is serious and the problem is getting worse, because many teachers are finding more lucrative opportunities outside the classroom and a large number of teachers have reached or are about to reach retirement age. The growing shortage must be addressed by developing new programs to train teachers, increasing the number of graduates with teaching credentials, and retaining good young teachers. The mandated economics courses in grades 8 and 11 or 12 have created a demand for economics teachers that did not exist before 1997. Meeting this demand will require universities to develop and expand undergraduate and graduate programs to prepare economics teachers.

To address this problem the faculty of Economics and Management and the faculty of Pedagogues and Psychology of the University of Latvia created a new master's study program in the methods of teaching economics. Prior to the inception of this program, no teachers in Latvia held a master's degree in the methods of teaching economics. The training received by the graduates of this program will provide them with pedagogical training and tools to teach mainstream economics. Since its inception in 1996 the program has graduated 15 economics professionals. One of the graduates of this program has organized the Association of Economics Teachers. This organization works closely with the University of Latvia Center for Economic Education to provide seminars and workshops for economics teachers.

The University of Latvia's master's program is an important addition to teacher preparation, but most Latvian teachers do not have the luxury of only teaching economics. The teachers responsible for the mandated economics courses in most Latvian schools are typically only presenting a few lessons on economics each week and have an area of specialty that is usually not economics.[3] Because economics concepts in the basic and secondary grades are likely to be taught by instructors who have completed at most one economics course, economic content must also be integrated into the curriculum used to train primary and many secondary teachers. Teachers in basic education (grades 1-9) need to be prepared to teach the Introduction to Economics course by completing at least the equivalent of the principles of economics course. At the secondary level students studying to teach history, geography, math, and even physics should be prepared to teach the Introduction to Business Economics course. This will require completion of courses on the principles of economics, business law, and an introduction to the national economy, or the completion of extensive teacher training courses in economic education after graduation.

Higher academic and pedagogical education can be acquired at universities, academies, and professional higher education institutions. The number of venues offering training for teachers is expanding as former Teacher Institutes are converted into higher education institutions or merged with other higher education institutions.   Future teachers can now receive teaching credentials at three institutions in Riga and three institutions in regions outside the capital.[4]

Curriculum Guides and Instructional Materials

After providing well-trained teachers, the second necessary component for successful implementation of the mandatory courses in economics is quality instructional materials.   Latvian materials in market economics and business economics have been in short supply, so partnerships with international organizations have been the main source of curriculum materials.   Until 1995 textbooks and other materials translated by Junior Achievement of Latvia served as the main texts in economics and business economics classes.

Since 1995 teachers have been provided with supplementary lessons from the NCEE that have been translated from English to Latvian.   The NCEE funded translations of five of its guides from English to Latvian, including scope-and-sequence guidelines with economic content statements for grades K-12, a glossary of economic terms, a translators' dictionary and discussion guidelines for economics terms, the NCEE *Voluntary National Standards in Economics*, and the NCEE's *Framework for Teaching Basic Economic Concepts*.

A second aspect of the NCEE program was training Latvian economists to develop their own materials.   These training programs have proven very successful and the graduates have developed a number of texts and curriculum guides that are now used by Latvian economics teachers, including *TESTbook – Introduction to Economics; Teacher Workbook: Active Learning Methods; Student Workbook for Introduction to Economics; Textbook in Economics* (for grade 12); *What is an Essay in Economics?; Tests for Secondary School Students; Tests for Eighth-Grade Students; Introduction into Economics* (a textbook for grade 8); *Textbook: Active Learning Methods for Fourth to Sixth-Grade Students; Me in My Family, School, and Society* (for grades 4-6); and *Textbook in Economics* (for grades 10-11).

Development of National Standards

The introduction of common content standards in Latvian schools is extremely important to equalize and increase the quality of economic resources across all schools. The adoption of national content standards in economics will also allow the development of textbooks and teachers' manuals that are tied to those standards.   In 1998 the Ministry of Science and Education introduced and implemented the *National Standards of Compulsory Education* and *Project of National Standards of Secondary Education*. These are mandatory standards for each school to follow in preparing educational programs and for teachers to use in developing their lesson plans. Now the main objective is to develop not only the curriculum in economics, but to prepare national standards in economic education like the NCEE *Voluntary Standards*.

Each content standard has two parts: 1) what students should know, and 2) what students will be able to do with this knowledge. While many US educators believe both parts need to be developed simultaneously, the Ministry of Science and Education has focused on developing the first part of national standards in economic education. The next step is extensive discussion between legislators, ministry officials, and educators concerning appropriate concepts. The discussion will address: 1) What economic ideas should be taught? 2) In which classes can they be taught? 3) How can they be taught? and 4) How many economic concepts should be taught at various grade levels? It is also necessary to improve the second part of the content standards – to explain why these economic concepts are so important for secondary students to know and understand. In other words, how will students be able to use this knowledge in their adult lives?

Once the content standards are completed, the next step is to begin work on grade-level benchmarks: statements that identify what students will know and be able to do at three levels (grades 1-4, 5-9, and 10-12) as they move toward attainment of the broad content standards.

Survey of Economic Teachers in Latvia

In 1998-99 the Center for Economic Education at the University of Latvia developed and conducted a survey to determine the background level of economic knowledge and experience of Latvian teachers of economics. The survey was sent out to 270 teachers of the basic and secondary economics courses from the area served by the Center (the Cēsu, Valmieras, Kuldīgas, Jelgavas, Krāslavas, Preilu, Tukuma, Bauskas, Rīgas, Valkas and Ziemelu regions of Riga, and the city of Liepāja). The survey group represents approximately 35 percent of the total economics teachers in Latvia. Given the relatively recent mandate of economics this was a surprisingly large number of economics teachers. Some data were also collected from administrators in the school districts.

There were 265 completed surveys returned, for a response rate of 98 percent. The survey group was similar to the overall population of Latvian economics teachers in terms of age, gender, or other demographic characteristics. One possible source of potential bias may be related to the use of teachers in the Riga area. Teachers closer to Riga are more likely to be familiar with the Center or other economics training programs provided by other educational institutions in Riga. The result of this potential bias would be to overestimate participation in training programs.

The results showed that 93 percent of the responding teachers had completed higher education, five percent had completed special secondary education, and only two percent had general secondary education certificates as their highest degree. By comparison, in Latvian schools providing general education the percentage of teachers who have completed higher education is only 78 percent.[5]

While the teachers of economics are more likely to have completed higher education, their area of specialty is usually not economics. In most cases the teachers responsible for economics lessons also teach other subjects, and are only presenting a few lessons on economics each week. As a result, economics is typically taught by historians, physicists, mathematicians, geographers, and others. Only 12 percent of the economics teachers in the survey group had a specialty area in economics. The breakdown of specialties for these teachers is shown in Table 9.2.

Table 9.2: Specialty areas of teachers who teach economics classes

Field of Specialization	Percent
History	24.5
Physics, mathematics	14.3
Geography	12
Economics	12
Engineering, agronomy, veterinary science	9.5
Philology (linguistics)	7
Elementary education	6.8
Chemistry, biology	4.9
Handicraft	1.5
Other	7.5

The survey also asked about years of experience in teaching economics. Because economics is a relatively new subject in the curriculum of many schools, most teachers have little experience in teaching economics. Over three-fourths (76 percent) of the respondents had only one or two years of experience; 14 percent had three to four years of experience; and only 10 percent of the teachers had five or more years of experience. The majority of the teachers did not begin teaching economics until it became a compulsory subject in the 1997-98 school year. As for the share of economics classes in the teachers' total workload, only 12 percent of the teachers taught more than 10 hours of economics classes per week. Specific breakdowns are reported in Table 9.3. These results indicate that for 88 percent of the responding teachers economics is not a major portion of their total workload.

The final section of the survey dealt with teachers' participation in inservice seminars and courses for economics teachers. Over half (61 percent) of the respondents had improved their qualifications by attending different courses and seminars. The remaining 39 percent characterized themselves as self-taught in economics.

Teachers indicate that they prefer training organized by the methodical societies of their school boards because these seminars are organized on off-days and holidays.   The organizations providing training in economics and the percentage of respondents who had attended seminars offered by those groups are shown in Table 9.4. Many of the institutions offering these seminars cooperate in the development and presentation of their programs, so this table is more reflective of training received than competition among organizations.

Table 9.3: Economics teaching as a share of teachers' workload

Hours of Economics Classes per week	Percent of Total Class Time
1-3 hours	63.3
4-9 hours	24.5
10-20 hours	9.4
21 or more hours	2.6

The overall results of the survey indicate that the typical teacher of economics in Latvia has a relatively high level of education, but a specialty outside of economics. These teachers have only recently begun to teach economics and spend less than half of their time teaching economics. These results indicate a serious need for teacher training in economics in the Riga area, and the more limited availability of training programs in economics suggests an even greater need outside the capital city.

Table 9.4: Participation in inservice seminars and courses

Institutions Offering Seminars and Courses	Percent of Teachers Who Had Attended
Methodical societies of district or city	71.1
Junior Achievement of Latvia	51.1
Association of Economics Teachers and the Center for Economic Education at the University of Latvia	24.2
NCEE and the Center for Economic Education at the University of Latvia	11.1
Others	15.9

III. CONCLUSION

After regaining independence in 1991, Latvian educational reform initially focused on the most urgent tasks: the decentralization of school governance structures and essential changes in the contents of study programs. Latvian schools attempting to teach economics were confronted with a variety of conflicting terms and definitions, and teachers with little or no training. For those reasons, the introduction of American economic education materials in Latvian schools was extremely important, as was the demonstration of US teacher training programs. Without the help of the international organizations, especially the National Council on Economic Education and Junior Achievement, Latvia would not have been able to rapidly improve the quality of its economics curriculum and prepare highly qualified specialists to meet the new demands of the market economy.

Program delivery of this scale requires the creation of a sustainable economic education network. The Center for Economic Education at the University of Latvia has been providing teacher training and material development since 1996, and six new Centers for Economic Education are starting at regional universities outside Riga. Coordination and support is being provided by the Baltic Council on Economic Education and the National Council on Economic Education. Recruiting and workshop development assistance is provided by the Adult Education Centers and the regional methodical societies for teachers of economics. The institutional framework now seems to be in place for sustainable program delivery, but success of the program ultimately depends on the resources and commitment of the Ministry of Science and Education.

A major problem facing pre-university economic education in Latvia is the preparation of a sufficient number of highly-qualified economics teachers. Meeting the demand for economics teachers created by the addition of the two nationally mandated courses will require the development of undergraduate programs for preparing economics teachers at universities all across Latvia. Institutes of higher education training for basic (primary) and secondary teachers in history, geography, physics, and mathematics should also offer courses in economics. These changes will help improve the economics background of the new teachers, but still do not address the huge need to provide more training for current teachers.

While developing a new group of well-trained economics teachers is critical, improving the level of economic knowledge of current teachers may be an even bigger challenge. Training more qualified economics teachers will require a substantial commitment from a number of institutions. Faculties at universities will have to expand existing programs and develop new programs. The Ministry of Science and Education must work out the procurement and financing for these additional training programs. Funding must be provided for salaries high enough to keep current faculty and for programs to recruit and train new teachers. Inservice seminars and courses are necessary for current classroom teachers to improve their qualifications. The national system of Adult Education Centers must work more closely with national and international partners to assure the availability of quality teacher training in economics.

Research and evaluation will be necessary to determine the effects of economic education programs on teachers and students. Periodically, surveys and other kinds of studies of economics teachers and students should be conducted to provide a more comprehensive assessment of the state of economic education in Latvia.

NOTES

1. National enrollment data for all levels of education taken from the *Statistical Yearbook of Latvia*, 2000, p. 94.
2. See Kovzik and Watts (2001) for a complete discussion of the role of Moscow State University as the flagship university in the Soviet bloc.
3. The results of a survey by the Center for Economic Education at the University of Latvia on the specialty areas of teachers who teach economics classes are presented in Table 9.2.
4. The institutions in Riga are the University of Latvia, the Sports Pedagogy Academy of Latvia, and the Riga Pedagogical and Education Management Higher School. The institutions in regions outside Riga are Daugavpils Pedagogical University, Liepaja Pedagogical Higher School, and Rezekne Higher School.
5. Statistics provided by the Ministry of Science and Education.

REFERENCES

Avotina. G. (2000). *Textbook: Active Learning Methods for Fourth-Sixth Grade Students. Par Mūsu Ielas Bērniem un Ekonomiku. Sociālās Zinības 4-8 klasei*, Riga: RAKA.
Avotina, G., M. Sinicins, M. Karklina, I. Valaine, V. Melbarde, and M. Burge (1998), *Introduction to Economics for Eighth-Grade Students. Ievads ekonomikā, Sociālās zinības. 8.klasei. Eksperimentāla mācību grāmata*, Riga: RAKA.
Bikse, V. (1998), TESTbook − *Introduction to Economics. TESTI. Ekonomikas Pampatprincipi. Zvaigzne*, Riga: ABC.
Bikse, V. and I. Kullesa (1999), *Student Workbook for Introduction to Economics. Uzdevumi vidusskolai. Ekonomikas pampatprincipi.Zvaigzne*, Riga: ABC.
Birzniece, J. (1999), *The Textbook in Economics for Twelfth-Grade Students*, Riga: RAKA.
Birzniece, J. (1999), *What is an Essay in Economics*, Riga: RAKA.
Birzniece, J., I. Jornina, E. Lukjanska, M. Sincins, and V. Krievins (1999), *Tests for Secondary School Students*, Riga: RAKA.
Central Statistical Bureau of Latvia (2000), *Statistical Yearbook of Latvia 2000*, Riga.
Dike, V. and V. Krievins (2000), *Me in My Family, School, and Society. Es Gimene Pasaule. Sociālās Zinības Sākumskolai. Skolotāja grāmata*, Riga: RAKA.
Ekonomists (1998), *Student Workbook for 8th Grade Students Introduction to Economics. Ievads ekonomikā. Sociālās zinības 8.klasei. Darba burtnīca*, Riga: RAKA.
Ekonomists (1999), *Teacher Workbook: Active Learning Methods. Aktīvās mācību metodes. Ekonomikas pamatprincipi. Skolotāja grāmata. Zvaigzne*, Riga: ABC.
Jornina, I. (1999), *Tests for 8th Grade Students*, Riga: RAKA.
Kovzik, A. and M. Watts (2001), 'Reforming undergraduate economics instruction in Russia, Belarus, and Ukraine,' *Journal of Economic Education*, 32(1), pp. 78-92.
Ministry of Economy, Republic of Latvia (2000), *Economic Development of Latvia*, Riga.
Ministry of Science and Education (1996), *Education and Culture*, Riga.
Ministry of Science and Education (2000), *National Dossier on the Educational System in Latvia*, Riga.
National Council on Economic Education (1997), *Voluntary National Content Standards in Economics*, New York: NCEE.
National Observatory of Latvia (1998), *Country Report on the Vocational Education and Training System*, Riga.
Saunders, P. and J. Gilliard (1995), *Framework for Teaching Basic Economic Concepts*, New York: National Council on Economic Education.
Sinicins, M. (2001), *Textbook in Economics for Tenth to Twelfth-Grade Students, Biznesa ekonomiskie pamati 10-12 klasei*, Riga: RAKA.
United Nations Development Programme (1999), *Gender and Human Development in Latvia*, Riga: UNDP.

10. Poland: Teaching Economics Before, During, and After the Transition

Jacek Brant, David Lines, and Stefania Szczurkowska

The Republic of Poland is one of the largest countries in central Europe. It is roughly square in shape, measuring 650-700 kilometers across and covering some 300,000 square kilometers, making it approximately as big as the United Kingdom and Ireland together, but less than half the size of Texas. Poland's northern frontier is open to the Baltic Sea, which provides access to Scandinavian and North Sea ports, but on the remaining three sides it is surrounded by Russia, Lithuania, Belarus, Ukraine, Slovakia, the Czech Republic, and Germany.

Poland's history has been marked by frequent invasions, most especially over the past 200 years by its powerful and competing neighbors, Russia and Germany. From 1795 to 1918 the Polish state ceased to exist altogether, and even though it regained its statehood in 1918 its independence proved short-lived. In 1939 Germany invaded from the west and the Soviet Union from the east, and although Poland was in theory 'liberated' by Soviet troops in 1945 it effectively became a satellite of the Soviet Union until the late 1980s.

Compared to some other Soviet nations and satellites, the regime in Poland was relatively tolerant and progressive. The church remained a powerful influence, particularly after the archbishop of Krakow, Karol Wojtyla (later Pope John Paul II), was appointed head of the national Roman Catholic Church in 1978. But it was labor unrest, centered in the shipyards of Gdansk, that finally broke the communist stranglehold. In 1980 strikes led to the formation of the independent trade union Solidarity. which over time became a potent political force. Nevertheless, it took nearly a decade before the 'Round Table Negotiations' took place between the Communist-dominated authorities and the opposition. These discussions resulted in significant agreements including the legalization of Solidarity and free elections, the first of which was conducted on 4 June 1989. These agreements were the prelude to the development of a new system of government, with a President as head of state, a legal parliamentary opposition, and a second chamber of Parliament, the Senate.

I. CONTEMPORARY POLAND

Today Poland stands out as one of the most successful and open of the transition economies. The early and swift privatization of small and medium-sized state-owned companies, and a liberal law on establishing new firms, promoted the rapid development of a private sector that is now responsible for 70 percent of the nation's production. High rates of inflation were experienced during the early period of transition, but are now significantly lower (seven percent in 1999), though still above US and EU levels. In contrast to the vibrant expansion of private non-farm activity, however, the large agricultural sector remains handicapped by structural problems including surplus labor, inefficient small farms, and a lack of investment. Some key indicators of economic activity are shown in Table 10.1.

Table 10.1: Poland: GDP and population statistics

GDP (in purchasing power parity US $)	$276.5 billion (1999 est.)
GDP – real annual growth rate	3.8 percent (1999 est.)
GDP per capita (in purchasing power parity US $)	$7,200 (1999 est.)
GDP – composition by sector (1998)	agriculture: 5 percent industry: 35 percent services: 60 percent
Population (July 2000 est.)	38,650,000 0-14 years: 19 percent 15-64 years: 69 percent 65 years and over: 12 percent

Sources: World Bank and Polish government statistics

Reforms in Education

Alongside conventional economic reforms such as privatization, radical changes were carried out in education, which involved not only institutional and programmatic restructuring but also basic philosophical realignments. These changes reflect the continuing success of the national economy and a growing confidence among the citizenry, as well as the acceptance of market reforms at a fundamental level.

It must be remembered, however, that in the early 1990s the current situation could by no means be seen as an inevitable outcome. At that time, to help cement the early political and economic reforms, governments, charitable organizations, and other groups from the United States and the European Union rapidly dispatched economists and education specialists in economic education to Poland, to act as ambassadors of western economic philosophy and practice. Later in the chapter we will examine and evaluate the impact these groups had on the Polish educational system.

First, though, it is helpful to understand the structure of the Polish educational system as it exists today. Elementary schooling (*szkola podstawowa*) starts at the age of seven (non universal pre-school education exists for six-year-olds) and lasts until the student is 13. This is followed by three years of lower secondary school (*gimnazjalne*) up to the end of compulsory schooling at the age of 16. After that, students opt either for three years in a general secondary education school (*liceum ogolnoksztalcace*) or two years of technical and vocational education (*techniczne i zawodowe*). For those following the general secondary education route, university studies can begin at 19 years of age, or there is an option to pursue a further two years of vocational education in a post-secondary school. Post-secondary vocational education is also available for students in the vocational track who wish to go to universities; they must complete two years in a post-secondary school before entering a university.

Table 10.2 provides data on the Polish educational system and some of the changes that have taken place since 1989. Note that lower secondary schools did not exist before 1999.

The sections that follow provide a background on the Polish educational system as it operated prior to 1989, especially with regard to economic education. Changes made during the 1990s are then reviewed and some of the work performed by leading western agencies during that period is described. Finally, we look toward the future and discuss reforms that are soon to be introduced.

II. ECONOMICS AND ECONOMIC EDUCATION BEFORE 1989

Economic Systems and Education

Prior to the watershed year of 1989, vocational education and training in Poland were designed to meet the needs of the country's centrally planned economy, which was itself integrated within the trading structures of the Soviet Union. Education was compulsory for pupils between seven and 14 years of age. These students attended elementary schools and studied a common curriculum. Secondary education, for students 15 and older, was free of charge to candidates who passed an entrance examination. Pupils would then attend either a technical, vocational, or general secondary school.

Table 10.2: Poland: Education statistics

	1990/91	1995/96	1999/2000
Number of students (thousands):			
Pre-school education (ages 6-7)	651.3	537.2	469.4
Elementary (ages 7-13)	5,287.0	5,104.2	3,958.0
Lower secondary (ages 13-16)	NA	NA	615.3
Secondary	1,896.1	2,251.3	2,416.4
General secondary (ages 16-19)	445.0	683.0	864.1
Technical and vocational (ages 16-18)	1,451.1	1,568.3	1,552.3
Post secondary (ages 18+)	108.3	161.0	205.5
Tertiary (ages 19+)	403.8	794.6	1,431.9
Adults	224.9	263.7	325.7
Number of schools:			
Elementary	20,533	19,823	17,743
Lower secondary	NA	NA	6,121
Secondary	7,702	9,160	10,222
General secondary	1,100	1,705	2,156
Technical and vocational	6,602	7,455	8,066
Post secondary	893	1,432	2,328
Tertiary	112	179	287
Adults	2,065	1,900	2,713
Number of teachers (thousands):			
Elementary	329.1	323.5	274.6
Lower secondary	NA	NA	28.4
Secondary	110.6	123.4	133.0
General secondary	25.1	34.7	43.1
Technical and vocational	85.5	88.7	89.9
Tertiary	64.5	67.0	78.1

Source: Polish government statistics

Secondary education was dominated by vocational schooling. In 1990-91, 48 percent of all students attended basic vocational schools and a further 26 percent were placed in more specialized vocational schools. Of the remainder, 23 percent of all students opted for general secondary education, while only three percent left school at the end of the elementary stage.

Teaching Methods

Within schools teaching displayed many of the characteristics found in other countries of the former Soviet Union (Kovzik and Watts, 2001). Fundamental shortcomings included, among others:

- An excessively ideological approach to education. This manifested itself in the selection and interpretation of what was taught, in the development of teaching programs, the criteria used for the selection of teaching staff, and the methods used to assess students.
- The maintenance of a state monopoly over education, which resulted in the stifling of many public educational initiatives, especially those that were considered 'dangerous.'
- The preference for 'traditional,' authoritarian methods of teaching, which were deemed most 'appropriate' by the authorities. This structure led to significant restrictions in the freedom of activity enjoyed by individual teachers. The result was a technical, routine. and sterile pedagogy, allowing little scope for creativity.
- The separation of education from its social and economic context. As a result of this isolation, when students ended their schooling they found it difficult to adapt to the real world. Shortcomings in the vocational preparation of young people were acute, although this fact was hidden by the artificially supported system for mass employment. (Szymanski, 2000)

Teaching Economics

At the end of the communist era, economics instruction was only offered in vocational schools for students beyond the age of 15. Conventional, four-grade general secondary schools offered no economics coursework at all, which meant that students in these schools – nearly a quarter of each yearly cohort – had no exposure to the subject.

The content of the economics that was taught was shaped to serve the state-owned monopolistic enterprises and centralized economy. Vocational schools offered instruction exclusively within the framework of a subject called 'basic economics,' which was taught a maximum of four hours per week. In addition, one school year was dedicated to 'industry economics,' with an emphasis on 'organization economics' – a term used to describe the ways enterprises were structured, how they organized production, and how they acquired revenues and productive resources. This instruction was also highly segmented into sub-disciplines. Preference was often given to narrow and highly specific areas of study, such as the economics of industrial plants, transport, and trade, and to general business subjects such as accounting and statistics.

By the mid-1980s this level of detail and specialization became almost unmanageable, and financial stringencies had limited instruction in each specialty area to a single hour per week. The approach did, however, reflect a curriculum followed by vocational education and training throughout Poland, namely one based on very narrowly focused occupational profiles. As an illustration, the classification of occupation fields and specializations adopted in 1982 consisted of no fewer than 527 categories. By 1986 this number had been reduced to 241, and by 1993 to 168. Even today this is too many – the current objective is to cut them down to approximately 130 (Bogaj, Kwiatkowski, and Szymanski, 1999).

Teacher Training

Higher education for future Polish teachers was organized in five-year courses leading to Master's degrees, offered by university departments and specialist academies. Following the Polish tradition students took just one subject throughout the five years. Thus a very strong emphasis was given to subject mastery, although in the case of economics the content was not in the western tradition.

Students pursuing a teaching career had to complete a degree in educational studies, which amounted to 270 hours of coursework. Training on teaching practices usually took place in the fourth and fifth years of the degree.

It is generally acknowledged that the academic preparation of teachers in their content areas was of a very high standard (though in economics it would have been Marxist), whereas aspects of pedagogy, didactics, and methodology were not sufficiently developed. The mainstream model of preservice teacher education was dominated by a formal lecture approach, with very little emphasis on active learning techniques (Polish Ministry of Education, 1996, pp. 91-6).

III.   THE YEARS OF TRANSITION 1989-99

After 1989 wide-ranging educational reforms were introduced, although initially these did not represent a structural change to the overall system of education. This piecemeal approach was partly determined by a lack of financial resources for education and training, and partly because there was not a fully determined development strategy for the country's economy, including education as a whole. Nevertheless, one result of the Round Table Negotiations between the communists and the Solidarity movement in the spring of 1989, after the first democratic elections of that year, was to encourage state authorities to create a new statutory basis for the reform of schooling. Over the following decade structural changes did take place, based on:

- The *Education System Law* of September 7, 1991, with amendments in 1995;

- The concept of general education drawn up by the ministerial Bureau for School Reform Matters (in operation until the mid-1990s);
- A government discussion document entitled 'A good and modern school – the continuation of educational changes' (Ministry of National Education, Warsaw, 1993);
- The *Statute of 28 July 1998*, amending the law concerning the education system; and
- Amendments to the *Law on the Teachers' Charter* adopted by the Parliament of the Republic of Poland on 18 February 2000.

The overall effect of these reforms was to increase significantly the level of democratization within the school system and to allow more competition from the private sector. Teachers, students, and parents became far more engaged and involved in running their schools and decision-making was increasingly devolved to the local level. For example, the appointment of school principals became more openly competitive, replacing the system in which such appointments were made by the central authorities. In turn, the main role of principals was shifted to emphasize pedagogy and student attainment rather than the exercise of control, intervention, and supervision, which had been their prime function under communism. There were also structural changes, which will be dealt with in more detail below, as well as the development of a core curriculum that provided teachers with the basic knowledge components of their subjects.

Structural Change

The effect of these changes can be summarized as follows. They:

- removed the restrictive Marxist ideological corset imposed on schools and training institutions;
- released schools from the pervasive influence of state monopoly, central control, and authoritarian management;
- introduced revised curricula with the aim of providing broader vocational streams and new career opportunities in the light of emerging sectors of activity, chiefly banking and finance. A particular stress was given to areas of knowledge that improved vocational mobility, namely, financial law, understanding the workings and operations of private enterprise organizations, and computer science;
- updated textbooks and modernized school equipment. especially by providing students with access to computer technology.

Economics Instruction

Similar kinds of changes were both necessary and evident in economics instruction. In order to improve the responsiveness of education to the often unpredictable requirements of the emerging free labor market, as well as increasing the employability of school graduates, reforms were launched with the intention of:

- implementing changes to the professional preparation of economics teachers within the scope of preservice education at the university level;
- offering further inservice training opportunities for practicing teachers; and
- developing professional qualification standards in economics that better reflect employers' needs.

The impact of these reforms has been beneficial. Recent studies have shown that where education and training is focused on changing workplace demands resulting from new technologies and forms of organizations, employability and competitiveness increase (Bialecki and Sikorska, 1998; Bialecki and Drogosz-Zablocka, 1999; Rutkowski, 1996).

The value of education in Poland generally is further confirmed by national data on unemployment. Despite the fact that unemployment among people with higher education rose by nearly 14,000 persons in 1999, those in this category were, with an unemployment rate of only two percent, still the educational group least likely to be without jobs. In contrast, graduates of post-secondary and secondary vocational schools made up 20.6 percent of all unemployed Poles, while persons with only elementary education constituted 33.1 percent (*Bezrobocie rejestrowane w Polsce w I-IV kwartale 1999 roku*, 2000).

Given this context, it is not surprising that Polish students show increasing interest in economics courses. From the 1993-94 school year to 1998-99, the number of young people studying economics and business subjects in secondary vocational schools rose by 189 percent, while the number of students in general secondary schools taking these subjects rose by 166 percent (*Oswiata i wychowanie w roku szkolnym*, 1994/95 i 1998/99).

Pilot Projects in Economics during the Transition Period

The first stage of changes to economics instruction took place from the early to mid-1990s, and was generally characterized by experimental or pilot projects. In 1992, for example, there was an attempt to reshape the basic vocational school model and replace it with a three-year experimental vocational school for those who left school beyond the age of 15. The curriculum in the first and second years covered both general and vocational subjects. while general vocational knowledge and skills applicable to different kinds of careers were taught in the final year. The vocationally-oriented block of subjects integrated such fields as computer technology, accounting, and the economics of small businesses. Students also took courses in marketing, labor law, and the rules of employment (Szczurkowska, 1995).

In the 1995-96 school year, another pilot project introduced an innovative four-year secondary vocational school, called a 'technical lyceum.' Among 14 fields of study in the curriculum, which corresponded to the principal areas of the country's economic activity, 'economics and finance' was of primary importance. Soon, minor modifications reduced the number of fields from 14 to 12, but the economics stream remained central, renamed 'economics and business administration.' The other 11 subjects are: power engineering, chemistry, environmental protection, mechanics, agriculture and food industry, social services, other service sectors, electronics, forestry and timber economics, textile engineering, and transportation. Students were also offered elective courses on entrepreneurship, aimed basically at shaping positive attitudes to entrepreneurial activities – something unheard of in communist times (Bogaj, Kwiatkowski, and Szymanski, 1999).

Within vocational schools specializing in economics, pilot projects have modified the curriculum in response to changing demands in the labor market. Old-fashioned courses on Soviet/Marxist fields of economics and the organization of enterprises have been replaced by a curriculum targeted at preparing future 'economic technicians.' A new course entitled 'basic economics' combines three subjects that used to be taught separately – elements of commerce and management, economics, and law – into one broad stream that includes innovative elements of banking, business, finance, and stock exchange operations.

Reforms in Higher Education

Just as elementary and secondary schools have gone through a period of intense reform, so too have universities. For example, in 1991 a new Faculty of Economic Sciences and Management opened at the Nicholas Copernicus University of Torun. It offers courses across a number of departments:

- The Department of Economic Theory, which offers a wide range of courses in macroeconomics and microeconomics.
- The Department of Human Resource Management, which is particularly concerned with issues of the labor market, employment policy, demography, and the sociology of work.
- The Department of Econometrics and Statistics, which teaches mathematical economics, general and economic statistics, econometrics and its applications, information technology, and computer science.
- The Department of Marketing Management. formed in September 1996. which offers courses in such fields as marketing, marketing research, marketing strategies, business negotiations, and commodity and stock exchanges.
- The Department of Agrarian Policy and Management of Food Industry Units, which covers food policy and economics, the economics and management of the food industry, and food marketing.

- The Department of General Management, which focuses on administration and management; organizational, managerial, and control methods; and strategic management techniques in competitive work environments.
- The Department of Economic Policy and Regional Development, which emphasizes economic and land development policies as well as the economics of urban areas. It also includes aspects of environmental protection and the financial economics of business units.
- The Department of Finance and Accounting, which provides education in corporate and public finance.
- The Department of Management of Investment and Innovation Processes, which includes the areas of assessment of economic efficiency, land development, ownership changes, and the administration of real estate.
- The Department of Industrial Enterprise Management and Industrial Policy, which covers issues of product strategy within industrial companies and examines the general direction of the country's industrial development in the context of rapidly changing technological innovations (Faculty of Economic Sciences and Management, Nicholas Copernicus University, 1998).

These reforms are typical across Polish universities, reflecting the objective 'to free economics from the Marxist-Leninist ideology as soon as possible' (Zajicek et al., 1997, p. 279). Certainly from 1990 onwards the economics curriculum became ambitious, not only in terms of credit hours that had to be passed but also because of the breadth of courses and an emphasis on quantitative skills.

Despite such positive changes, however, Zajicek et al. (1997) identified structural problems within Polish higher education. First, they note a continued reliance on pre-reform pedagogical methodology – namely lectures and drills, although they acknowledge that the number of more student-centered interactive seminars has increased (p. 280). Second, the lack of prerequisite knowledge for courses that are ostensibly taught at a higher level means that, in practice, 'there is a tendency to increase the variety of course offerings and to decrease the depth of covering' (p. 280). Then there is the dearth of textbooks generally, and specifically a lack of textbooks written originally in Polish for the Polish market. This shortcoming, combined with a lack of agreement across universities about what constitutes a core curriculum (in contrast to the secondary school sector) results in courses with the same name covering quite different topics. Finally, there is the problem of pay. Qualified academic staff are able to earn three or four times their salary in the private sector, so the difficulties of recruitment and retention are self-evident.

Teacher Training

In light of the widespread school reforms that occurred both during and after the transition period, preservice and continuing teacher education and training face totally new challenges. Inservice training of economics teachers in Poland is chiefly organized under the auspices of the National Center for the Professional Development of Teachers and its regional branches, as well as the newly created National Center for the Promotion of Vocational Education and Training. Teachers are offered a variety of courses in the fields of market economics and entrepreneurship. They are also trained in selected companies across the country, using simulation techniques to familiarize them with updated practical skills, which are now widely demanded in response to changing labor market requirements. In addition, inservice training centers provide teaching materials that match modern European standards.

The Influence of Western Organizations

A large number and wide variety of activities were undertaken in Poland by outside organizations during the decade of the transition period. Not surprisingly, the United States and the European Union were eager to support ventures that would cement reform, partly out of altruism, partly for reasons of ideology and national and international security, and partly because Poland represented a growing market for their exports. Inevitably, therefore, the subject of economics received particular attention, although the courses that were offered were targeted at different groups, ranging from university lecturers to those teaching in vocational schools. The content of the courses varied as well, with some emphasizing subject content and others stressing pedagogy.

There is insufficient space here to detail all of the activities that took place during this period, but three prominent examples typify the type of work that was (and in some cases still is) going on.

The Stefan Batory Foundation. George Soros created this foundation in 1988, with the aim of supporting 'the development of a democratic open society in Poland' (*www.batory.org.pl/english/aims.html*, 2001). From 1989 until 1992 the Foundation supported an economic research program that focused on observing and analyzing the changes that were taking place in the transition economies, with a particular emphasis on Poland. When this research was completed the Foundation concentrated on economic education.

In 1992 two programs were sponsored by the Foundation, both aimed at schoolteachers. One was the Junior Achievement program and the other was titled Enterprise Education. These programs were offered in cooperation with the University of Durham's Business School (UK).

In the following year a team from the Warsaw School of Economics (WSE), headed by Professor Janusz Beksiak, started a new project sponsored by the

Foundation entitled 'The Modernization of Economic Higher Education in Poland.' This program examined traditional teaching schemes, handbooks, and methods, and then set out to introduce a new curriculum at WSE. This work was complemented by a series of summer schools offered between 1991 and 1998. These schools were open to young faculty members in universities across central and eastern Europe, and taught by leading economists from both European and US universities. The focus of this work was subject knowledge and understanding (Chalasinka, 2001).

National Council on Economic Education (NCEE). Founded in 1949 with offices in New York, the NCEE's guiding philosophy is that well-prepared teachers are the cornerstones of educational excellence. In its international programs the NCEE prefers to concentrate on preparing teacher trainers rather than on teachers directly, because it believes this approach has more long-term effects on teacher quality, is more cost effective, and provides a faster way for national groups to achieve independence from outside sources. The key program in the NCEE's International Education Exchange Program is its series of four week-long 'Training of Trainers' seminars, which cover the fundamental concepts of micro- and macroeconomics but also emphasize pedagogy. Many classes in this series are taught using classroom and computer simulations, role-playing activities, small-group cooperative activities, and other active learning instructional formats. Participants are also videotaped and debriefed by the faculty and other participants in two 'microteaching' lessons that they deliver. Some of these training of trainers seminars have been offered in Poland (in Krakow and Gdansk) for participants from Poland and more than 20 other nations.

Despite its preference for training trainers, the NCEE has also worked directly with teachers in 'demonstration workshops.' For example, in 1996 a group of 42 participants from 42 Polish cities attended a weeklong seminar. The make-up of this group was interesting, and typical of the experience found by another team from the United Kingdom working under the auspices of the Thatcher Foundation at the same time (see below). The participating teachers were not fluent in English, with 71 percent saying their level was 'poor.' They were experienced teachers, however, with 59 percent having eight or more years in the classroom and 57 percent aged 40 or over. On the other hand they were not experienced in teaching economics – 21 percent had three years or less subject teaching behind them.

To judge its impact, the NCEE administers cognitive tests and attitude surveys to participants at the start and at the end of its courses. Judged against the aim of much of the overseas work in Poland, namely to cement the reform program in place, the seminars could be counted a success. For instance, in the 1996 teacher workshop sessions, to the statement 'A rapid reform would result in a better outcome than a slow transition,' 48 percent agreed on the pretest but 88 percent on the posttest; and 'In the movement from a non-market to a market economy, it is important that ownership of productive resources be privatized at the onset,' 55 percent agreed on the pretest and 88 percent on the posttest.

Similarly, in relation to pedagogy, participants ended the course recognizing that diagnosing and incorporating the learning needs of students were crucial. While knowledge of economic principles remained the participants' highest perceived priority, the week-long course convinced teachers that it was relatively less important than they had thought at the beginning. In short, there was a transformation of attitude away from a monofocus on subject transmission towards a more participatory methodology.

The Thatcher Foundation. Because of her own beliefs in the strength of free enterprise and the market, Lady (then Mrs) Thatcher was a strong supporter of the reform movement in eastern Europe. Her Foundation was therefore keen to assist academicians and others going to the country to 'spread the message.' Between 1994 and 1996, academics from a number of UK universities, but mainly from the Institute of Education at the University of London, traveled to Gdansk (in 1994 and 1995) and Krakow (in 1996) to deliver coursework and materials to economics and business teachers. The summer schools took place at the end of August and were organized by Professor Marion Turek of Gdansk University.

The participants came from across Poland but were mainly from the region in which the school was located. The focus of the work was initially two-fold: economic subject knowledge and pedagogy. But the direct input of the former proved not a great success, mainly because of the limited ability in English of the course members. In contrast, the emphasis on pedagogy was highly successful, especially because the active-learning approaches used were also vehicles for acquiring subject knowledge that might otherwise have been lacking. The issue of language was a problem for the program, but this was in part resolved in the final year, according to the course evaluations, by the inclusion of a bilingual lecturer on the team.

Current and Future Reforms

Since September 1999 students have been legally obliged to attend school until they are 16. Elementary schools now cater for pupils until they are 13, and a new lower secondary school (*gimnazjalne*) has been introduced for pupils between 13 and 16. Following that, as outlined above, a number of routes are available for pupils wishing to continue their education.

In the new model students have some choice as to what they study. Programs are organized in blocks and pupils choose which block, and to some degree which subjects, they follow. Under this revised structure economics is strongly evident. It appears in the curriculums of the now compulsory three-year lower secondary schools, and again in the two-year vocational schools that follow, as well as in the three-year general secondary schools (*lyceums*). This is an important shift in attitude towards the subject, which as we have seen used to be regarded exclusively as 'vocational.'

Following the second wave of reforms that, though still out for consultation are likely to come into effect by September 2002, a particular emphasis is also placed on 'entrepreneurship' both in the lower secondary and the general secondary curricula.   One priority is shaping entrepreneurial attitudes among students by offering knowledge and skills in a number of areas (Polish Ministry of Education, 2000).   But arguably the most radical element is the change in philosophy from an encyclopedic, content-driven approach to a more process-oriented model.   'Theory,' 'practice,' and 'social outlook' are given equal weightings, so for the first time the social and emotional needs of pupils will become an important educational aim.

Currently students are assessed by their subject teachers, but in another radical change, in the future there will be external examinations. Similar to the French *Baccalauriate*, the *Matura* will consist of Polish, a foreign language, mathematics, and one additional subject of the student's choice. Passing the entrance exam will become the gateway to higher education, unlike the present system in which students take an entrance examination for each university to which they apply. Such a system is common practice in many countries and is a means of ensuring equality of opportunity (Lambert and Lines, 2000). It is also further evidence of the Polish system being brought more in line with the rest of Europe.

The Future

By any measure, whether social, legal, institutional or economic, Poland is now a fully democratic, 'westernized' nation. It has applied for membership in the European Union, and were it not for fears in other member states about the impact of Poland's agricultural sector on the Common Agricultural Policy, acceptance would be imminent. Without doubt, the spectre of communism is now simply another chapter in the country's chequered history.

The question, then, is what has caused or enabled such a transformation in little more than a decade?   Historians might argue that the foundations for successful change were laid well before the end of the 1980s, citing the depth and significance of the church's influence, even within an ostensibly atheistic communist state. Some might emphasize the role of the trade unions, whose militancy allied to political awareness proved a thorn in the side of successive Polish communist leaders. Others would suggest that it was the moral, ethical, and intellectual corruption of Marxism-Leninism that ultimately caused it to implode. though this does not explain the success of replacing such a system in Poland compared to other former communist countries. For that, sociologists might point to Polish nationalism, which over the centuries has, in the face of invasion by foreigners and foreign ideas, become used to accepting the situation and quietly waiting for it to go away, confident in the knowledge that Polish cultural and social values will, inevitably, re-emerge.

Yet such historical determinism is flawed, because it relies on hindsight. Self-evidently, the economic failures of all the former communist countries, compared to nations in the West, contributed to their downfall. But the strength of the Polish model (echoed in the Czech Republic and Hungary) is the way institutional change was effected so swiftly and relatively painlessly. For that, education and specifically economic education must have played a part, including that which was 'imported' from North America and western Europe.

The extent to which foreign educators influenced the outcome we see in Poland and Polish schools today will probably never be known, but reading curriculum documents, noting reforms in university, vocational, and other schooling, as well as in assessment systems, it is apparent that Polish teachers and educational administrators have both absorbed and adapted knowledge, information, and ideas from overseas, especially in economics and economic education. As a result, economic or business-related courses are now more sophisticated, there are more students taking them, and the ever-increasing market value placed on individuals with strong qualifications in economics reflects these improvements. All the evidence suggests that cementing reform was at least in part achieved through the efforts of overseas educators, even if the building blocks were themselves already in place.

Yet it would be wrong to paint too rosy a picture. Polish schools are often technologically backward, money is frequently short and unevenly distributed, and some teachers are inadequately prepared. Furthermore, regional differences are becoming increasingly apparent and stark. Rural areas, and in particular north-eastern Poland, are disadvantaged compared to regions in which the major cities are located (Warsaw, Cracow, Wroclaw, Poznan, Gdansk, and Lodz). This situation is worsened by the decreasing share of public expenditure allocated to schools – often below five percent of GDP.

There is also a need to increase participation rates in post-compulsory education, to better reflect structural and technological changes in the labor market since 1989. This requires a strengthening of the links between all levels of schooling, industry, and society in general. Such shifts are by no means exclusive to Poland, and many countries are increasingly recognizing that schools have a responsibility to help students to become self-learners. Only when this is achieved will graduates be equipped for the new, dynamic, and ever-changing work environments that exist within a globalized, market dominated, information-rich world economy.

IV. CONCLUSION

The notion that a confident, self-assertive Poland no longer has any need for overseas assistance in education, and more specifically economic education, is naïve. While the country certainly does not require the kind of help that it received in the early days of transformation, there are still unresolved issues – not only those at a national level concerned with inequality, but also from a subject perspective, and in how the training of teachers in economics can be made more sophisticated and relevant to today's world. Simply leaving the Poles to 'get on with it' might have an appeal given the achievements of the last ten years, but such an attitude must be avoided. Much still remains to be done.

REFERENCES

Bezrobocie rejestrowane w Polsce w I-IV kwartale 1999 roku [Unemployment registered in Poland in the I-IV quarters of 1999.] (2000), Warszawa: Glowny Urzad Statystyczny.

Bialecki, I. and E. Drogosz-Zablocka (1999), 'Vocational education in Poland,' *International Journal of Sociology*, **29**(2), pp. 66-93.

Bialecki, I. and J. Sikorska (1998), *Wyksztalcenie i rynek* [Education and the market]. Warszawa: Wydawnictwo TEPIS.

Bogaj, A., S.M. Kwiatkowski, and M.J. Szymanski (1999), *Education in Poland in the Process of Social Changes*, Warsaw: Institute for Educational Research.

Chalasinka, E. (2001), e-mail (*echalasinka@batory.org.pl*), Feb. 6.

Faculty of Economic Sciences and Management (1998), *The Nicholas Copernicus University of Torun, 1968-1998*, Torun.

Glowny Urzad Statystyczny. [Polish Statistical Department] *Oswiata i wychowanie w roku szkolnym, 1994/95 i 1998/99* [Education and upbringing in the 1994/95 and 1998/99 school years], (1995, 1999), Warszawa.

http://ciesin.ci.uw.edu.pl/poland/poland-home.html (accessed 2/1/2001).

Kovzik, A. and M. Watts (2001), 'Reforming undergraduate instruction in Russia, Belarus and Ukraine,' *Journal of Economic Education*, **32** (Winter), pp. 78-92.

Lambert. D. and D. Lines (2000). *Understanding Assessment: Purposes. Perceptions and Practice* London: RoutledgeFalmer.

Ministerstwo Edukacji Narowowej (2000), *Reforma sytemu edukacji, szkolnictwo ponadgimnazjalne.* [Polish Ministry of Education (2000), *Reform of the Education System of the Post-Middle School]*, Warsaw.

Ministerstwo Edukacji Narodowej (2000), *Reforma systemu edukacji. Szkolnictwo ponadgimnazjalne* [*Reform of the education system. Post-gymnasium schooling*], Warszawa.

Ossowski, R and J. Rulka (1996), *Wiedza o zyciu w spoleczenstwie* [*Knowledge of Life and Society]*, Warsaw: BGW.

Polish Ministry of Education (2001), *www.men.waw.pl* (accessed 2/1).

Polish Ministry of Education (1996), *Reviews of national policies for education. Poland*, Paris: OECD.

Rutkowski, J. (1996), '*Wyksztalcenie a perspektywy na rynku pracy dziesiec rysunkow pokazujacych, ze warto sie uczyc,*' [Education and job prospects. Ten drawings showing that study is worthwhile], in *Science and Higher Education*, No. 7.

Stefan, M., S. Kwiatkowski, and Z. Sepkowska, (eds) (2000), *Developing Professional Qualification Standards in Poland*. Warsaw: Institute for Educational Research and Radom: Institute for Technology.

Szczurkowska, S. (1995), 'Restructuring vocational education in Poland within the context of a free market economy,' in *Managing Vocational Education and Training in Central and Eastern European Countries*. Paris: UNESCO Institute for Educational Planning, pp.131-91.

Szymanski, M.J. (2000), 'Democratic changes in Polish education: aims, achievements and problems,' in S.G. Murdoch, S. Szczurkowska, and P.T. Slowinski (eds), *Examining Educational Trends in the United States and Poland. Comparative Studies*, Warsaw: Institute for Educational Research: pp. 183-96.

www.batory.org.pl/english/aims.html, 2001.

Zajicek, E.K., T.P. Steen, and S.R. Domanski (1997), 'The Reform of Higher Education in Poland,' *Journal of Economic Education*, **28** (Fall), pp. 377-82. ·

11. Economic Education Reform in Romania

Jane S. Lopus and Dan Christian Stoicescu

Romania, historically a poor agricultural country in south-eastern Europe, suffered through an unusually repressive communist era and is today struggling to emerge as an independent and viable member of the European community. Although progress has been made toward this goal, the *2001 Index of Economic Freedom* characterizes the Romanian economy today as 'mostly unfree' with high levels of government regulation, very high inflation, and financial turmoil (O'Driscoll et al., 2001, pp. 311-2). Occupying an area of about 92.000 square miles with a population of 22.4 million, Romania continues to be one of the poorest countries in Europe with 22 percent of its population living below the national poverty line in 1999 (*www.worldbank.org*). Against this background, economic education is poised to play a critically important role in Romania's reform process. Economic theory and economic understanding may well provide the foundation for Romanians to be able to function successfully in their emerging market economic system, and the foundation for the success of democracy in Romania (Niculescu and Adumitracesei, 1999, p. 187).

This chapter focuses on the evolution of economic education in Romania from communist times through the present. After providing background on Romanian communism and transition, we discuss the structure of education in Romania, the state of economic education during the communist era and today, and programs to train economics teachers in post-communist Romania. We conclude by assessing what has been accomplished and what remains to be done with respect to economic education in Romania.

I. BACKGROUND

Romania's communist experience was markedly different from that of other countries in the Soviet bloc. Although it became a communist state in 1947 it practiced a 'national communism' largely free of Soviet influence from the early 1960s through 1989, under the reigns of Gheorghe Gheorghiu-Dej and Nicolae Ceausescu. Ceausescu's reign was marked by severe repression of civil liberties, censorship, destruction of villages and ethnic minorities in the name of agricultural collectivization, and attempts to establish a cult-like family dynasty. These policies took a severe toll on Romanian society and on the economy, and eventually discredited the government.

Romania's transition to a market system differed in many respects from that of other Soviet countries. The end of the Ceausescu regime in 1989 was both sudden and violent, and the period following was politically, socially, and economically tumultuous. Former communist party officials who ruled Romania through 1996 were pledged to a slow transition to a market economy. This 'go slow' modernization and the delays in the privatization process translated into a massive decline in GDP in the 1990s, with dramatic social repercussions (Elster, Offe, and Ulrich, 1998, p. 195). The election of Emil Constantinescu in 1996 was accompanied by attempts to implement more market reforms, but these reforms met with limited success. According to World Bank figures, Romanian GNP was $41.5 billion in 1989 and decreased to $34 billion by 1999[1] (*www.worldbank.org*). Per capita GNP fell by an average of 1.4 percent during this period to $1,520 in 1999, compared to an index of $2,150 for Europe and central Asia.

II. CURRENT STRUCTURE OF EDUCATION IN ROMANIA

The problems of economic reform in Romania are mirrored in attempts to reform education. Emerging from communism with one of the most centralized education systems in central and eastern Europe, the totalitarian mentality of education officials initially impeded the reform process (OECD, 2000, pp. 13-14). With assistance from the World Bank, however, serious and systematic education reforms began in 1994-95. The World Bank support, and support from other organizations and individuals, has also played a role in the reform of economic education in Romania. But the structure of education remains highly centralized and the reform process is ongoing.

There are several principal actors in control of the Romanian education system today. The Ministry of Finance allocates and monitors monthly budget credits to the Ministry of National Education (MNE), which 'has final authority for school governance and ensures general education administration' (OECD, 2000, pp. 17-23). The MNE controls school budgets, establishes curricula, approves textbooks, conducts research. and takes the leading role in establishing reform strategies, training and evaluation programs, international agreements, national examinations, and quality assessment. The School Inspectorate administers a geographical region (*judet*) for the MNE, which officially names all inspectors. Inspectorates are responsible for overseeing curriculum compliance, teacher performance, and finances in their region. Budget Centers, although without decision-making authority, are responsible for transferring money from the School Inspectorate to the schools, and oversee the finances and accounting for up to 15 schools. School Directors (principals), along with local Teachers' Boards and Administrative Councils, make local decisions for their schools relating to expenses, infrastructure, staff duties, and payroll. Each school's Administrative Council is the highest authority at the school level. Administrative Councils are made up of from five to 11 members including the School Director, a Chief Accountant, teachers, and parent representatives. The Chief Accountant represents the school and Director in negotiations outside the school. Local public authorities are elected to represent the 42 *judets*, but their authority vis-à-vis that of the School Inspectorate is not clearly defined. Finally, 10 teachers' unions, representing about half of Romania's teachers, promote the well-being of teachers and play a consultative role with respect to educational reform and innovation.

School attendance is compulsory in Romania from ages six through 15. Compulsory education consists of the school preparatory group (ages six to seven), primary school (ages eight to 11; grades 1-4), and lower secondary school (ages 11 to 15; grades 5-8). Romania essentially has a three-tiered high school system today. Academic high schools prepare students for higher education, commercial high schools prepare students to become skilled workers for jobs such as store employees, and vocational high schools require students to take classes relating to mechanics and industry. After completing lower secondary school students take an examination to determine which type of high school they will attend, if any. Due to a declining birth rate, the total school population fell from 5.6 million in 1985 to 4.7 million in 1995 (out of a total 1995 population of 22.8 million). This represents approximately 65.5 percent of those aged three to six, 96.7 percent of those aged seven to ten, 94.3 percent of those aged 11 to 14, 61.1 percent of those aged 15 to 18, and 24 percent of those aged 19 to 23. Education participation rates are roughly equivalent for males and females (OECD, 2000, pp. 62-3).

Post-secondary, or tertiary, education in Romania dates back to the middle of the seventeenth century and came under communist control in 1948. There were 42 institutions of higher education, including seven universities, in the 1970s. After 1989 the institutions took charge of their own reforms in programs and management, and legislation affecting them continues to evolve (OECD, 2000, p. 125). A major change affecting higher education in Romania following the fall of communism is the proliferation and growth of private universities. In 1989-1990 there were 44 state institutions and no private institutions of higher education. By 1993-94 there were 48 state institutions and 67 private institutions (Sadlak, 1994, pp. 15-17). Before 1990 when all universities were public, the number of students was strictly limited and admission was very competitive. Given this history it is still common for people to think that public universities are better than private ones. In fact, the first students who attended private universities after 1990 were those who could not pass the entrance exams to public universities. But after 10 years of private higher education the situation and attitudes are changing. Many graduates of private universities have found very good jobs, and consequently people are beginning to trust in private education. This change in attitudes is a good development for supporters of economic education because private universities typically have departments of economics.

III.   ECONOMIC EDUCATION UNDER COMMUNISM

During the communist era education in Romania was one of the main instruments for the ruling communist party to spread its values into Romanian society. The aim of the communist party was to create an economy with people fully committed to communism and working according to the basic Marxist principle 'From each according to his ability, to each according to his needs.' Educators were politically supervised to ensure their commitment to communist ideology, and the communist party used the education system and political youth movements to communicate its own views of history and other school subjects (Miller, White, and Heywood, 1998, p. 36).

Because of its subject matter, economic education was also viewed as a vehicle for instilling communist ideals in Romanian youth and for providing an opportunity for the communist party to extol the superiority of communism over capitalism, which was regularly described as being in a state of crisis and dissolution. Students were taught that a market economy was an instrument for class exploitation and should be replaced with a planned system. Although this ideology was the fundamental approach to economic education at all levels, there were important differences between kindergarten through twelfth grade (K-12) education and university economic education.

K-12 Economic Education Under Communism

In regular Romanian high schools during the communist era, students took a tenth-grade course in scientific socialism, an eleventh-grade course in economics, and a twelfth-grade course in Marxist philosophy. These social science courses were intended to form a new type of human being who would be able to transform the concept of a socialist society into reality. The eleventh-grade economics course met for two hours per week, and students completed a final in-class written assignment each trimester that counted for half of their final grade. In the high schools that prepared students to enter the work force immediately after graduation, students studied economics for three hours a week in the tenth grade.

There was one required textbook, used in both regular and commercial high schools, which aimed to indoctrinate students with propaganda about the superiority of planned economies over market economies. The textbook was divided into two sections: the first presented Marxist perspectives on economic concepts such as markets, capital, and the means of production. The second section was mainly a collection of ideas and documents issued by the Romanian Communist Party, emphasizing the ideas of Nicolae Ceausescu on various five-year plans. Most economics teachers had degrees in philosophy, which at that time meant that they studied the social sciences from a Marxist perspective blended with Stalinism and nationalism.

University Economic Education Under Communism

Economics was an even more important instrument for indoctrination in higher education. Regardless of their academic discipline, all students were required to study economics for one year. All courses focused on socialism – initially on the works of Marx, Engels, and Lenin, but later on works attributed to Ceausescu (Sadlak, 1993, p. 78). To obtain a university degree in economics students usually studied economics for four years with mandatory class attendance. It was also possible to obtain an economics degree in five years by attending evening classes, or in six years without attending classes but by passing annually scheduled exams.

During the communist era the Academy for Economic Sciences in Bucharest was the main institution for higher education in economics. The primary academic programs offered were finance, economics for industrial production, cybernetics, and domestic and international trade. There were also academic programs in economics at Jassy University, Babes-Bolya University in Cluj, and Timisoara University. The competition to attend these universities was high because degrees led to employment in domestic commerce and were seen to be a means of survival. This situation was especially true during the 1980s when dramatic shortages of food and essential goods were evidence of the rapidly deteriorating economy. Corruption was pervasive in Romanian society under communism, however, and this affected the possibility of succeeding even with an education in economics or other fields.

Communist party control of academic and student life was a basic feature of higher education in Romania in this period. Several social science disciplines, including sociology and psychology, were dissolved because they were deemed to be useless to the Romanian people. Including favorable references to Ceausescu was a prerequisite for the publication of any academic textbooks (Woodard, 1995, p. A37-8). Perhaps one of the most destructive innovations of the era was a uniquely Romanian doctrine implemented in the 1970s that viewed education, research, and production as a unitary process. To carry this out, after 1976-77 students and staff in institutions of higher education were required to undertake 'productive activities' such as working in agriculture or industry for certain periods of time. Universities had production plans and contracts, and became vehicles for training workers at the expense of focusing on academic studies and research. Higher education had to be justified by its relation to production, and thus became more vocationally and application oriented (Sadlak, 1990, pp. 58-65).

Another peculiarity of economic education in Romania under communism was that it did not prepare leaders for the communist economy. Instead, the Academy of Social and Political Sciences was created for this purpose in 1970. Access to this academy was restricted to those who met established political criteria; other students need not apply.

IV. ECONOMIC EDUCATION IN ROMANIA TODAY

Romania has undergone several phases of education reform since 1989 that affect economic education. Overall, significant reforms have resulted in revising the curriculum to eliminate communist ideology and introduce new electives, reducing class size and teaching loads, allowing minority language education, and revising the assessment process. At the precollege level decisions about the national curriculum and textbooks remain largely under the control of the MNE, although an effort has been made under the World Bank project to privatize textbook publication (OECD, 2000, pp. 79-83).

K-12 Economic Education

Policy-makers appear to be more interested in economic education today than in the past, although to some extent they still ignore the importance of economic education at the pre-university level. K-12 economic education coursework follows roughly the same pattern that existed under communism, but there is now an attempt to begin to teach some basic economic knowledge in elementary and middle schools. Since 1993-94 the curriculum for civic education (which is taught in third grade for one hour a week and in fourth grade for one half-hour per week) has included some economic issues. For example, in a chapter in a civics textbook about the relation between children and their social and natural environments there is a section on the family budget and how to use and save money. In the eighth grade elements of economics are also taught as a form of civic education, with two hours per week allocated to economics over approximately thirty weeks. For one hour these students discuss economic problems and democracy, and for another hour they learn about major economic, social, and political issues around the world. One of the eighth-grade operational objectives in the civics education course emphasizes that students should be able to explain factors determining an economic crisis, describe the current economic situation in Romania, and identify the means by which Romania can become a market economy. This overly ambitious goal may reflect a lack of awareness on the part of education administrators in Romania of the complexities of teaching about economic transition and market economics. Or it may result from a continuing emphasis on normative ideology rather than positive economic concepts and analysis.

In Romanian academic high schools, economics is studied in the eleventh grade for two hours per week, the same time frame as under communism. In commercial high schools students study economics in the tenth grade for one hour per week and in the eleventh grade for two hours per week, again paralleling the pre-1990 structure. There is currently only one textbook available and required in both types of schools, *Economics Textbook for High Schools* (Cosea et al., 1999), which was originally published in 1991 but systematically revised through 1995. The authors of the textbook are professors of economics, and one, Mircea Cosea, was also a member of the Romanian government from 1992-96. The content of the textbook is dramatically different from the textbook used under communism, and reflects the economics curriculum adopted by the MNE in 1990 under the first wave of education reforms.   The content centers on the topics of markets and a market economy, factors of production, cost, productivity, economic competition, profit, efficiency, equilibrium, inflation, and unemployment. Many of the chapters also contain applications for students to complete as homework, issues to be discussed in the classroom, and excerpts from the writings of famous economic thinkers.   The MNE has announced that more economics textbooks will be available beginning in fall 2001, and that teachers should be able to select from a list of pre-approved books.

The economics curriculum is set at the national level and in many respects overlaps that of the voluntary national standards and state standards in the United States (Lopus and Lacatus, 2001, pp. 3-4). There are differences in emphasis and terminology, however, and the similarities to the US curriculum may be due to both countries' curricula addressing standard economics concepts rather than US programs that directly influenced Romania.   According to the high school economics curriculum established by the MNE in 1994, the major goals are for students to be able to achieve the ability to analyze and interpret economic realities, develop a logical way to think about economic issues, develop practical social economic habits for their own life, and function under the requirements of a market economy (Ministry of National Education, 1994). This last goal refers to the need for those raised under communism to learn to accept market ideas such as competition, promotion based on merit, income inequality, and other possible market outcomes such as layoffs and bankruptcy.

Specific cognitive and operational objectives from the required curriculum are outlined in Table 11.1. These objectives are designed to help students understand how the Romanian economy functions and form and develop abilities that will help them succeed in the future.

Economic education is all but absent from the vocational education curriculum in Romanian high schools (Ministry of National Education, 1994), which may further demonstrate that economic education still receives only peripheral attention from education policy-makers.   Students who attend vocational schools are given instruction that includes knowledge about consumer rights, but the curriculum does not address the functioning of a market economy.

University Economic Education Today

Enrollment in institutions of higher education has nearly doubled in Romania since 1989, although access to universities is still highly competitive. These increased enrollments are accompanied by shifts from fields such as science and engineering toward fields in demand in the new economic environment, including economics, law, and commerce. Between 1989-90 and 1992-93, enrollment in economics programs (broadly defined to include business) increased from nine percent to 20

Table 11.1: Economics objectives for Romanian high schools

After a high school student studies economics for one year (or two years in a commercial high school), he or she should be able to:

Cognitive Objectives

1. Understand the significance of economic concepts (principal concepts include markets and the market economy, factors of production, cost, productivity, competition, profit, efficiency, equilibrium, inflation, and unemployment).
2. Analyze economic phenomena and processes characteristic of a market economy.
3. Demonstrate, on the basis of knowledge achieved, that he or she has the capability to synthesize and evaluate different effects of economic processes.
4. Formulate mathematical economic laws or be able to transfer statistical or mathematical formulas with economic content into the language of economics.
5. Achieve the ability to analyze, comment on, and interpret an economics textbook.
6. Solve exercises with economic content.
7. Achieve an interrogative way of thinking about interrelations between economic processes and social processes, and between objective and subjective factors in any economic activity.

Operational Objectives

1. Define concepts and economic categories correctly, and be able to distinguish among them.
2. Formulate hypotheses and decide on optimal solutions.
3. Identify and argue the correct answer among a set of answers to different questions.
4. Analyze economic phenomena from a general and specific perspective, internal and external.
5. Make comparisons and analogies between economic phenomena.
6. Explain argumentatively the dynamics of different economic perspectives.
7. Distinguish between what is rational and irrational from an economic perspective.
8. Present and solve problems or practical applications with economic content.
9. Present and defend a personal point of view regarding an economic issue.
10. Use graphs, diagrams, economic models. and applications correctly to explain relationships among diverse economic processes.

Source: Ministry of National Education, 1994

percent of total university enrollments. This increased demand for economic education, along with that for management and other applied social sciences, is no doubt due to the perceived importance of the field for succeeding in the emerging market economy. There is evidence that graduates in law, economics, and business-related fields are in short supply and thus able to find jobs in the private sector. Unfortunately, growing enrollments are coupled with serious shortages of qualified professors in these fields, resulting in dramatically increased faculty-to-student ratios and the employment of under-qualified instructors (Eisemon et al., 1995, pp. 139-41).

As in communist times, there is great interest in studying economics in Romania today. The most prestigious institution remains the Academy for Economic Studies in Bucharest. Traditionally, universities in Romania were only located in large cities. After 1990 the number of cities with universities increased greatly, and now many cities have both private and public universities. These cities include Arad, Oradea, Subiu, Blaj, Baia Mare, Brasov, Constanta, Ploiesti, Galati, Pitesti, Targu Jiu, and Petrosami. Other universities that traditionally did not have economics departments now offer majors in economics, including the Polytechnic University, the Constructions University, and the University for Agricultural Sciences, three of the most important universities in Bucharest. Private universities in Bucharest typically have departments of economics. management, marketing, finance, or international economics.

Today the content of university economics courses has changed greatly from the politically controlled curriculum of communist times. Reform of all study programs – but most profoundly those in economics and other social sciences – involved the removal of ideology from the curricula (Sadlak, 1993, p. 95). Table 11.2 outlines the required and elective courses for the economics degree with a specialty in a foreign language from the Academy for Economic Studies in Bucharest (*www.ase.ro*). From the standpoint of curricular reform, this program is notable for its lack of courses focusing on Marxism (with the possible exception of the history of thought course) or the philosophy of the Romanian Communist Party. It is also noteworthy that for the most part the course titles reflect courses commonly found in an economics/business curriculum in universities in the United States.

This curriculum includes many more required business courses than would be required for an economics degree in the United States unless it was offered in a school or college of business, and appears to be more of a combined business/economics/foreign language degree than one in economics per se. It also differs in this regard from the economics curriculums from the top universities in other formerly communist countries such as Russia, Belarus, and Ukraine (Kovzik and Watts, 2001).

Table 11.2: Curriculum for economic studies with a speciality in foreign languages at the Academy for Economic Studies, Bucharest

Required Courses	Options Within Requirements	Optional Courses Relating to Teaching
Year 1		
Economics (two semesters)	Second language (two semesters)	Logic
Economic mathematics	Technology and innovation	Psychology of education
Data processing	Economic geography	Introduction to culture and civilization (French, English, German, Romanian)
Fundamentals of accounting	Economic history	
Introduction to economics (in first foreign language)	History of economic thought	
Birotica*		
Physical education		
Year 2		
Financial mathematics	Introduction to economics in second language (two semesters)	Pedagogy
Financial administration for databases		World economy
Statistics (two semesters)	Philosophy	Physical education
Financial accounting (two semesters)	Economics for enterprises (two semesters)	
Civil law (two semesters)	International economic relations	
Business communication– first language (two semesters)	Sociology	
Public finance		
Databases for financial administration		

Table 11.2 (continued)

Year 3

Marketing (two semesters)	International financial	Sciences learning
Analytical accounting	relationships (two	methodology
(two semesters)	semesters) OR	Pedagogy (practical
Finance for business (two	International financial	training)
semesters)	transactions (two	Sociology of education
Commercial law (two	semesters)	
semesters)	Business investment OR	
Business communication–	Economic decision	
first language (two	making	
semesters)	Business communication–	
Accounting (practical	second language	
training)		

Year 4

Financial economic	Business communication–	National economy
analysis (two semesters)	second language	Pedagogy (practical
Techniques and operations	Comparative accounting	training)
in banking (two	OR Financial auditing	Microeconomics
semesters)	Database systems for	
Insurance and re-insurance	management negotiating	
Economic projects and	techniques	
management games	Data analysis for market	
(two semesters)	capital and stock	
Human resources	exchanges	
management		

*Romanian word for course dealing with office organization and technology
Source: www.ase.ro

V. PROGRAMS TO TRAIN ECONOMICS TEACHERS

If economic education is to prepare students in the former communist world to function in emerging market economies, a key element of this education is to provide instruction for teachers on market economics and how to teach the subject to students. Unfortunately, teaching and other public sector professions are becoming less popular in Romania due to expanded job opportunities in the private sector, particularly for economics and similar majors (Eisemon et al., 1995,

p. 141). This was different under communism, when it was important to have graduated from a university, but then job choice was not so important because those with the same education generally received the same salary. In fact, in that system teaching was more desirable than many other positions because it offered shorter working hours and a better work environment.

Teacher training in Romania has two components: preservice training and inservice training. Preservice training is primarily done at universities in departments that prepare teachers. These departments offer pedagogical courses including courses in the methodology of teaching economics. They also work with schools to assign preservice teachers to work with current economics teachers who serve as mentors.

Inservice economic education, for those already working as teachers, is a relatively new concept in Romania. Some of the institutions that offer inservice training are universities, centers for professional development of teachers, private business schools, and different private organizations. The MNE has begun a program for the continuous training of teachers, although this program is not yet well developed and does not focus on economics. The School Inspectorate from Bucharest implemented a government-sponsored program involving economic and entrepreneurial education in February 2000 by sponsoring a conference on these topics. The goals were to inform teachers about these programs and to find ways to implement them.

One of the more extensive inservice economic education programs to train teachers in post-communist Romania to date took place in Mangalia in May 1999. Funding was provided by a World Bank loan to the government of Romania as part of the Romania Education Reform Project, which is jointly administered by the World Bank and the MNE. The Education Development Corporation (EDC) was in charge of the economic education component of the program and, through a subcontract with the National Council on Economic Education (NCEE), set up a six-day economic education workshop for teachers. The stated purpose of the program was to train teachers to help prepare them to train others to teach economics (Schoener and Spiro, 2000, p. 10). During the seminar participants were introduced to innovative and interactive methods for teaching basic economic content and given curriculum materials and a handbook designed to help them organize their own training programs. A total of 42 teachers participated, 36 of whom were currently teaching high school economics in different areas of the country. Overall workshop evaluations were strongly positive, with participants indicating that the content and pedagogical methods were useful and that, on the whole, the seminar was valuable (EDC, 1999, p. 2). Participant scores on a modified version of the *Test of Economic Literacy* (Walstad and Rebeck, 2001), administered before and after the workshop increased significantly, as did teachers' perceptions of their ability to use active learning methods of instruction.

The NCEE has also conducted a series of multinational economic education programs with participants from Romania since 1995-96, with major funding from the US Department of Education, Office of Research and Improvement. The

NCEE's flagship program has been its 'Training of Trainers' seminars, in which university professors and secondary teachers are trained in economic concepts and active-learning teaching methods, with the goal that they will then train other teachers in their own countries. In four week-long programs, Training of Trainers participants learn methods for teaching basic economic concepts, microeconomics, macroeconomics, and international economics. One of these seminars was held in Bucharest in 1996. To date, seven Romanian educators have graduated from the NCEE Training of Trainers program.

In 2000 some of these graduates offered a teacher-training program for 30 elementary teachers and designed an elective economic education course. They developed a curriculum (mainly consisting of objectives and activities) and sought to persuade teachers to apply the program in their schools. They are currently seeking support from local and national institutions for these programs.

Junior Achievement (JA) of Romania, founded in 1993, offers its economics education curriculum to K-12 schools with financial support from businesses. According to its website (*http://domino.kappa.ro/ja/home.nsf*) a sequence of optional social science programs is available to K-12 schools, resulting from an agreement between JA and MNE. Materials include teacher and consultant textbooks, student textbooks, maps, school supplies, questionnaires, tests, and posters. When business or government sponsorship is available, these materials are provided to schools at no financial cost. Generally the instructor for these classes is a teacher assisted by a JA consultant. The JA consultant may be an employee of JA, a manager of a business, or a student. JA training programs are offered to teachers, as well as annual evaluation and feedback seminars.

The elementary (K-6) curriculum offered by JA Romania includes 'Ourselves' for kindergartners, 'Our Family' for first grade, 'Our Community' for second grade, 'Our Town/City' for third grade, 'Our Region' for fourth grade, 'Our Nation' for fifth grade, and 'Our World' for sixth grade. The length and number of classes may vary depending on student age, interest, and academic ability. At the middle school level the JA programs offered are 'The Economy and Me' for seventh grade, and 'How an Economy Works' for eighth grade. The high school JA curriculum, designed to supplement the regular social studies and economics curriculum, includes the programs 'The International Market' for ninth grade, 'Applied Economics' for tenth and eleventh grades, and 'Connections' for twelfth grade. The JA website indicates that a goal for JA is to increase the number of students involved in JA programs from 11,000 in 1998 to 650,000 by 2002.

VI. CONCLUSIONS

Economic education in Romania has come a long way from recent decades when it essentially provided a forum for indoctrination and communist party propaganda. Today, the objectives of the mandated high school economics curriculum for tenth and eleventh grades contain market economic concepts and require analysis of economic problems. Market economic concepts have been introduced into the elementary and middle school curricula. Optional economics curriculum programs offered by Junior Achievement of Romania and others provide the opportunity for K-12 schools to introduce economics content at all grade levels. At the university level the introduction of academic freedom has resulted in the proliferation of private universities and in curriculum revision at state universities, leading to the growth of economics programs and the number of economics graduates. Several teacher-training programs in economics have provided teachers with opportunities to learn and practice the teaching of economics. Programs to train teachers to train other teachers are providing substantial multiplier effects.

Despite these significant accomplishments in economic education reform in Romania, much remains to be done. Education reforms in general face significant obstacles against the background of slow privatization, high inflation, and increasing poverty. Even ten years after the fall of the Ceausescu regime, many people remain uncomfortable with ideas of political participation and reform (OECD, 2000, p. 147). Education decision-making remains highly centralized, although progress is being made in this area to introduce new policies and new policy-makers. Of particular importance to economic education is the introduction of choice in textbook selection, planned for fall 2001.

International organizations such as EDC, NCEE, and JA are likely to continue to play important roles in the development of economic education in Romania, and their efforts appear to be providing the foundation for a self-sustaining network of economic education professionals. Teacher training and curriculum development by graduates of NCEE programs and extensive in-country efforts by JA indicate that efforts to improve economic education probably would continue at some level even if international support were to cease. MNE acceptance of these programs is further evidence of their self-sustaining nature. But although it is difficult to assess the number of teachers who have been reached by economic education reforms in Romania to date, it is likely that only a small percentage, mostly in urban areas, have been affected. Therefore there is little doubt that economic education reforms in Romania would be greatly enhanced by continued international support.

Economic education stands to help Romanians cope with and address the problems of transition and achieve the goals of market systems. But before it can play a more significant part in this process, education policy-makers need to accept, understand, and support the importance of economic education. Important steps in this area would be to provide more training in economics for teachers at all levels, increase the time allocated to the required high school course from two hours a week, and introduce economic education into the vocational high school curriculum. Because of the power it wields, increased support from the Romanian Ministry of National Education is critically important for the continued development of economic education. When politicians and educational policy-makers come to appreciate its importance, economic education may become a major component of the process for both economic and educational reforms in

Romania, and may help all Romanians understand and function in their new economic environment.

NOTES

The authors thank Dorina Chiritescu, Maria Lacatus, and Paul Lacatus for providing helpful comments and information.

1. World Bank GNP and per capita GNP figures are calculated in US dollars using the Atlas conversion factor, which averages Romania's exchange rate for the three most recent years and adjusts for differences in relative inflation between Romania and the G-5 countries.

REFERENCES

Academy of Economic Studies, Bucharest website: *www.ase.ro*.

Cosea, M., I. Gavrila, D. Nitescu, C. Popescu, and P.T. Ghita (1999), *Economics Textbook for High Schools,* Ministry of National Education, Bucharest: Editura Didactica si Pedagogica.

Education Development Center, Inc. (1999), Summary Data of the Teacher Workshop: Romania-Level I, New York.

Eisemon, T.O., I. Mihailescu, L. Vlasceanu, C. Zamfir, J. Sheehan, and C.H. Davis (1995), 'Higher education reform in Romania,' *Higher Education,* **30**, pp. 135-52.

Elster, J., C. Offe, and U.K. Ulrich (1998), *Institutional Design in Post-Communist Societies,* Cambridge, UK: Cambridge University Press.

Junior Achievement Romania website: *http://domino.kappa.ro/ja/home.nsf*.

Kovzik, A. and M. Watts (2001), 'Reforming undergraduate instruction in Russia, Belarus, and Ukraine,' *Journal of Economic Education,* **32** (1), pp. 78-92.

Lopus, J. and M. Lacatus (2001), 'Economic education in the high schools: Comparing post-communist Romania to the United States,' working paper.

Miller, W.L., S. White, and P. Heywood (1998), *Values and Political Change in Postcommunist Europe,* London and New York: Macmillan Press Ltd and St. Martin's Press, Inc.

Ministry of National Education (1994), *Curricula for Socio-Human Sciences,* Bucharest: Editura Didactica si Pedagogica.

Niculescu, N.G. and I.D. Adumitracesei (1999), *Invatamantu Romanesc la o Rascruce* [Romanian Education Today], Isai, Romania-Publirom.

OECD (2000), *Reviews of National Policies for Education: Romania,* Paris and Danvers, Massachusetts. USA: Organization for Economic Cooperation and Development.

O'Driscoll, G.P. Jr., K.R. Holmes, and M. Kirkpatrick (2001), *2001 Index of Economic Freedom,* Washington DC and New York: The Heritage Foundation and the *Wall Street Journal*.

Sadlak, J. (1990), *Higher Education in Romania 1860-1990: Between Academic Missions, Economic Demands and Political Control.* Buffalo, NY: Graduate School of Education Publications, Comparative Education Center, State University of New York at Buffalo.

Sadlak, J. (1993), 'Legacy and change: Higher education and restoration of academic work in Romania,' *Technology in Society,* **15**, pp. 75-100.

Sadlak, J. (1994), 'The emergence of a diversified system: The state/private predicament in transforming higher education in Romania,' *European Journal of Education,* **29** (1), pp. 13-23.

Schoener, J. and J. Spiro (2000), Romania Education Reform Project: Technical Assistance to the Teacher Training Component: Year Two Project Report. New York: Educational Development Center, Inc.

Walstad W.B. and K. Rebeck (2001), 'Teacher and student economic understanding in transition economies,' *Journal of Economic Education,* **32** (1), pp. 58-67.

Woodard, C. (1995), 'Ceausescu's legacy,' *Chronicle of Higher Education,* **41**(45), July 21, pp. A37-38.

World Bank website: *www.worldbank.org*.

12. The Status of Economic Education in Russia

Thomas McKinnon and Sergei Ravitchev

Mikhail Gorbachov's declarations of *perestroika* and *glasnost* unleashed forces that within three years brought an end to almost seventy years of a command economic system. The process of transition and market reforms in Russia is far from complete, which has made it more difficult for citizens to understand and adjust to the changes that have taken place. Even with its shortcomings, the old order was familiar and understood by the people, and provided for their basic needs. While the transition to a market system is difficult under the best of circumstances (Bragiunsky and Yavlinsky, 2000), political, legal, and social conditions in Russia have made the transition especially difficult (Roland, 2000).

Understanding basic economics is not as crucial in a system in which central planners make economic decisions as it is in a market economy. Indeed, it can be disruptive, because individuals making choices in their own self-interest can undermine the central plan, leading the government to try to enforce conformity. Economic education in the Soviet Union reflected this viewpoint and consisted primarily of political ideology. A fundamental role of Soviet education was to socialize young people to accept the state's dominant role in economic planning and control.

The new reality in Russia requires individuals to make choices as consumers, workers, savers, investors, and citizens that were not required under the old system. For Russia, building the infrastructure and institutions of a market economy are necessary, but these reforms must be built on the foundation of a citizenry that understands and practices sound economic choices. This foundation is the best defense against those who would use and abuse the system to their own advantage. Efforts to build a comprehensive economic education program in Russia are well underway, but there is still much to be done. For many reasons, changes in education are especially difficult to make in Russia.

Russia is the largest country in the world in area, spanning two continents and eight time zones. It has a territory of over 8,647,000 square miles, compared to the United States' 3,615,000 square miles. It is technically a federation, with 89 federal administrative units. The population is 146 million, but continues to decline each year – by 0.38 percent in 2000. The population includes a wide variety of ethnic groups, but approximately 80 percent are Russian (CIA, 2000).

During the 1991-2000 period of transition, gross domestic product declined some 45 percent. The decline seems to have bottomed out recently, and the economy grew by 3.2 percent in 1999. But per capita GDP continues to be lower than that of most developed nations at $4,200. Inflation also remains a problem, but the outlook is improving somewhat with prices increasing 86 percent in 1999 but about 30 percent in 2000. Unemployment was estimated at 12.4 percent in 1999, but there continues to be considerable underemployment (CIA, 2000).

The education system in Russia has been generally successful for decades, with a current literacy rate of 98 percent. But educational reform in the areas of school financing, structure, and in some particular content areas – including economics – is extremely difficult to accomplish because of the vastness of the country, the size of the system, and the legacy of Soviet governance structures. There are currently an estimated 65,899 schools (Ministry of Education).

I. ECONOMICS AND ECONOMIC EDUCATION IN RUSSIA IN THE SOVIET PERIOD

Maintaining a universal educational system in the former Soviet Union was a formidable task, but one that was largely achieved in most curriculum areas. Despite its size and the number of different nations and internal colonies involved, the Soviet Union had an education system that was essentially uniform at the precollege level.

Control of the curriculum was centralized under national Ministries of Education, and designed to socialize youth for their roles in the communist state. Teacher training, teaching practices, textbooks, school organization, and the curriculum were all designed to achieve this socialization. Education received a high priority in society and government policy, and the members of the teaching profession were accorded considerably more prestige than their counterparts in the West (Rushing, 1994).

Typically, schools were not divided between elementary and secondary grades, but grades 1-11 were taught in the same building. There were some exceptions in rural areas, but more than 90 percent of Soviet school students attended this type of school. Advanced students could be admitted to specialized schools (mostly in physics, mathematics, or foreign languages), which were generally located in the major Soviet cities.

With minor exceptions, mostly related to learning native languages, the entire curriculum of the Soviet schools was identical. In the early 1990s some Soviet schools were allowed to offer classes on new subjects, but as a rule these classes were only offered as extra-curricular activities. The standard secondary curriculum did not include economics. Social studies education was based on three subjects: history (with courses on the History of the World and History of the Soviet Union), economic geography (emphasizing the spatial distribution of resources and industries), and a course on Society-Learning (including limited and very basic coverage of Marx's economic theories, as developed by Lenin). Marx's theory of surplus value was usually presented as his greatest achievement, and a cornerstone of economic theory. None of the concepts that constitute the basis of contemporary economics, such as scarcity, opportunity cost, trade-offs, demand, supply, or competition, were ever taught in Soviet schools.

It is useful to consider why some of these specific concepts were not taught. First, communist countries are ideologically opposed to teaching the concept of scarcity. The primary stated objective of Soviet communism was for all members of society to achieve complete satisfaction of all their needs. The contradiction between this ideal and the fundamental economic problem of scarcity made western economics ideologically unacceptable to teach in Soviet schools.

Another example deals with the concept of profit. In a command economy in which all businesses are owned by the government, the concept of profit loses its meaning. All of the enterprise's revenues are treated as part of the government budget. During the Soviet period, only private – meaning illegal – enterprises could make profits. As a result, the term profit took on a criminal connotation for the general population.

The Soviet system of education was highly regarded for its achievements in teaching physics, mathematics, biology, and other sciences. Compared to courses in physics or mathematics, the course titled Society-Learning was extremely feeble, lacking analytical rigor, an intellectual framework, internal logic, or any possibility of using numerical computations for analysis and demonstrations. Treated by many students and even some instructors as a soft, non-scientific subject, the Society-Learning course did not attract the attention or loyalty of leading educators, which left it as an even less viable substitute for western economics.

Political and economic changes in the Soviet Union in the early 1990s led to a rapidly growing demand for economic knowledge and instruction. As a new subject in Russian schools, economics entered the curriculum not through the Ministry of Education's main gate, but rather through the back door as individual schools began to offer economics courses and other kinds of economic education programs as electives or extra-curricular activities.

II. ECONOMIC EDUCATION AFTER 1989

With the breakup of the Soviet Union the education hierarchy in Russia was substantially weakened. Serious financial problems undermined the central authority as local schools' funding was cut and teachers were paid erratically. As the national Ministries of Education lost authority, regional and local education authorities filled the vacuum. Curriculum reform, however, took a back seat to issues of finance, structure, and central versus regional or local control. Consequently, economic education efforts became a grass-roots movement, with considerable regional variation.

As in the United States, there are advantages and disadvantages for those promoting economic education in this decentralized environment. The Ministry could mandate economic education across the country if it should be so inclined, but mandated curriculum reform often fails to generate enthusiasm from teachers in the classroom. Grass-roots programs are more likely to include a variety of creative approaches, and teachers who play an active role in formulating a program are more likely to invest in making it successful. In this system, however, many teachers or school districts are likely to minimize or avoid teaching economics if they are more interested or better prepared to teach other subjects that they may view as equally or more important.

The role of the Ministry of Education changed considerably under the new regime, mainly due to its loss of financial power. Under new regulations financing public schools became a part of the regional government budgets, rather than the national budget. Along with this freedom the Regional Departments of Education also obtained the right to make some changes in the curriculum, including instituting new subjects such as economics and using different instructional materials. The establishment of private schools in Russia also presented a new avenue to introduce new courses into the curriculum.

During this period the Ministry of Education could neither initiate nor seriously support this process of instituting economic education in the country. For one thing it did not have experts in the field of economics at that time, so there were no departments in the Ministry that could coordinate or supervise the implementation of economics in Russian schools. A series of internal reorganizations also prevented the Ministry from supporting economics during this period.

After 1991 the whole system of Russian education faced extreme financial problems that it had never experienced in Soviet times. One response to the financial crisis was to concentrate efforts on maintaining the level of teaching in traditional 'core' disciplines. It was therefore obviously not the best time to try to introduce new subjects in the public schools. Nevertheless, the Ministry eventually accepted the need to begin teaching economics and in 1994 hired a specialist to oversee the introduction of economics coursework in Russian schools. The Federal Expert Committee on Economics was organized to select the best instructional materials and to recommend them for publication. The Committee consisted of representatives of several leading Russian universities, nongovernmental organizations (NGOs), and prominent teachers active in the field of economic education. One of the main objectives of this Committee was to check the content accuracy of new economic instructional materials proposed for publication.

In 1995 the Ministry printed 50,000 copies of the economics curriculums recommended by the Federal Expert Committee for Russian high schools. The content of this material was largely based on economics textbooks from the United States. The Russian Federation, however, has more than 60,000 schools and about 20,000,000 school students, so the materials were only distributed to school libraries as general recommendations on the content of economics courses for high school students. To build on this effort, in 1996-97 the Ministry supported a Russian National Olympiad in Economics.

In 1999 a document entitled *The Minimal Content for Teaching Economics in High Schools* was developed under the supervision of the Ministry. One of the reasons for creating this document was the enormous variety of names and corresponding variety in the content of economic courses taught in Russian high schools. In 1998 St. Petersburg's teachers taught courses with 137 different names purporting to teach economics, but the actual course content ranged from accounting to the development of business plans. *The Minimal Content for Teaching Economics* was a list of about 90 basic economic concepts (see Appendix 12.A) that can be regarded as a first step toward the development of a national standard for economics instruction in Russia.

In 2000 the situation changed again. Several Russian pedagogical universities had initiated a program leading to diplomas designating graduates as teachers of economics. Even though the content of these programs varied somewhat they were largely sound economics courses. In the spring of 2000, by order of the Ministry of Education, this degree program was terminated for reasons that remain a mystery. Despite efforts by many Russian educators, the Ministry has continued to leave economics out of the mandatory curriculum.

A more promising development is the likely restructuring of the curriculum for Russian schools in grades 11 and 12 over the next three to five years. The general curriculum of Russian schools will consist of three parts: federal, regional, and school components. The new basic curriculum for schools with 12 grades is now under development, and after public discussion throughout 2001 the Ministry will consider the curriculum for approval. Economics is currently included in the draft version of the curriculum as a separate subject in grades 11 and 12.

III.   THE ROLE OF NONGOVERNMENTAL ORGANIZATIONS

Several nongovernmental organizations played key roles in the early stages of the development of economic education programs in Russia. Private organizations from the West, such the Soros Foundation, Junior Achievement, and the National Council on Economic Education, saw the need for understanding market economics among citizens of the former Soviet Union and began to provide materials, training programs, and financial assistance. Domestic groups of educators also mobilized to meet these needs, and in many cases partnerships were formed.

Junior Achievement-Russia

In March 1991 the Soros Foundation organized and funded the first international workshop for prospective economic educators from several republics of the former

Soviet Union. The workshop was devoted to the introduction of the Applied Economics program developed by Junior Achievement, Inc. (JA). In April 1992, the first pilot Applied Economics classes were offered in Russian schools. This launching of economic education occurred at a moment in Russian history when fundamental social and economic changes were taking place, and consequently there was enormous interest in any kind of business and economic education. Despite all the disadvantages of a centralized system of Soviet education, widespread resistance from local educational managers, and the intellectual and institutional barriers built up from 70 years of hostile attitudes and traditions, the economic education program was off to a promising start.

From January to May of 1992 a group of participants in the first international JA workshop (later named the Expert Group) coordinated the organization of the first seven Russian teacher training workshops. Working also as trainers they taught week-long workshops to more than 400 participants from 11 republics of the former Soviet Union. But potential teachers of economics were not the only ones interested in these training programs. In particular, people who wanted to start their own business were seeking any useful information, and also managed to attend. Up to 20 percent of the participants of the first workshops were actually new businesspeople pretending that they were teachers planning to teach economics. The successful start of Applied Economics in Russia can be explained not only by the enthusiasm and effective teamwork of the Expert Group, but also by the new content of the subject; the publication of an attractive package of instructional materials; and the creativity and flexibility of a self-selected, highly innovative group of Russian teachers who found their own ways of using these materials.

The initial success of the JA instructional package was short-lived, however, as a number of problems soon developed. In the summer of 1992 JA-Russia was officially registered by former leaders of the Young Communist League, who had little knowledge of either English or economics but were attracted by the international status of the program. Disagreeing with the Soviet style of the new management, the Expert Group left the program. Furthermore, several components of the JA materials were not translated in a timely manner, so teachers were hampered in their efforts to utilize them. Many teachers also came to realize that the JA curriculum included very few economics concepts, and began to switch to other materials that were becoming available.

In 1994-95 JA-Russia changed almost all its staff and again redirected its activities. It is still organizing seminars for teachers on some parts of the Applied Economics program, but the primary focus of JA-Russia is now business education activities in which students set up 'student companies' to produce and sell goods or services. The Ministry of Education has expressed some disappointment concerning the quality of training JA provides for teachers and its economic content.

The International Center for Economic and Business Education

In 1992 a group of Russian educators, mostly those who started and then left the JA program, contacted the Soros Foundation with an initiative to create a Russian-American center for economic education. They were impressed by six-day teacher workshops conducted by the National Council on Economic Education (NCEE) in Moscow and St. Petersburg during the summer of 1992. The academic level of the economics in these programs, the framework used to organize the content of those workshops, the pedagogical methods demonstrated by American professors, and the general approach to teaching economics were seen to match the needs of Russian educators and were immediately accepted by them. A combination of the most promising ideas obtained from NCEE and JA workshops was used as a basis for the development of the new center, which was initially funded by the Soros Foundation and named the International Center for Economic and Business Education (ICEBE). Through ongoing cooperation with the NCEE, developing its own permanent support staff, and cooperation with a network of regional centers and leading university professors, the ICEBE has become recognized as the leading organization involved in promoting precollege economic education in Russia.

Since 1992 ICEBE has been involved in a variety of activities, including teacher training, curriculum development, student programs, and network development. ICEBE offers both introductory and advanced seminars for teachers of economics, and to date more than 6,400 teachers have been trained at ICEBE seminars and workshops. Participants at these seminars receive certificates that authorize them to teach economics using the curriculum developed by ICEBE.

The curriculum is titled Contemporary Economics, and is offered in five versions according to different numbers of school hours that could be devoted to economics in a given school. Specifically, there are versions for 34 hours (one hour per week), and for 68, 102, 136, and 170 hours. The instructional packages for these programs include textbooks for elementary school and study guides, student workbooks, test banks, and problem banks for secondary schools. All of the instructional and evaluation materials developed and printed by ICEBE have been approved and recommended by the Russian Ministry of Education.

In addition to programs for classroom teachers ICEBE coordinates a number of programs involving competitions among students. Since 1994 ICEBE has organized Economics Olympiads for approximately 30,000 students from Russia, Belarus, Kazakhstan, Ukraine, Latvia, and Estonia. Regional winners compete in a face-to-face competition in Moscow where an overall winner emerges. The Olympiad includes a competition in economic theory, which consists of a multiple-choice test and economic problems, and a competition using a computer simulation involving decision-making in economic and business situations.

Perhaps the greatest achievement of ICEBE since its inception in 1992 is the development of a network of regional centers for economic education. By the summer of 2000 this network had grown to a total of 55 centers with staffs of two to four part-time employees.[1] Some of the centers are NGOs while others are affiliated with institutions of higher education. The regional centers conduct teacher-training programs, distribute curriculum materials, consult with local schools, and help local teachers develop their own educational materials.

Technical Assistance to the Commonwealth of Independent States

Another organization that had a significant impact on the development of economic education in Russia was the Technical Assistance to the Commonwealth of Independent States (TACIS). The Higher School of Economics in Moscow and the University of Rotterdam coordinated this project, which began in 1994 and ended in 2000. The main goal of the project was to spread contemporary economic knowledge and teaching methods throughout the Russian Federation and to create a viable curriculum of business and economic subjects.

The Secondary School part of the TACIS project included short-term courses for retraining secondary economics teachers. These courses were offered from 1995-2000 in Moscow (190 teachers participated), Novosibirsk (170 participants), Perm (364 participants), Nijniy Novgorod (124 participants), Krasnoyarsk (224 participants), and Tambov (117 participants). Courses dealt with teaching economics, math, and foreign languages. The program for economics teachers included study tours to universities in The Netherlands and Great Britain. Five economics textbooks and study guides for Russian high schools were written under the project.

The National Council on Economic Education

This organization has played a major role in developing an economic education program in Russia and for that matter all across the former Soviet Union and eastern Europe. With more than 50 years of experience in training teachers and developing curriculum materials in the United States, the NCEE was the logical organization to aid Russia in developing an economic education program. The first NCEE workshops were conducted with financial support from the Soros Foundation in the summer of 1992 in Moscow and St. Petersburg. These programs were well received and were followed by three more workshops in 1993 and 1994, offered in cooperation with several Russian educators and organizations.

In 1995 the EconomicsInternational program at the NCEE was begun, supported by funding from annual grants from the US Department of Education– Office of Educational Research and Improvement. The primary purpose of these programs was to work with educational leaders in the former Soviet Union and eastern Europe to train teachers and develop curriculum materials for the implementation of precollege economic education. The first efforts in Russia were six-day teacher-training programs to train teachers to teach economics and serve as models for their colleagues. The need to develop a cadre of in-country trainers to maintain a sustained program led to the intensive (four-week) Training of Trainers programs conducted for teachers in Russia and other countries in the region. Russian teachers participated in 11 of these programs between 1995 and 2001.

Good curriculum guides and instructional materials are also necessary for economic education. The NCEE materials that have been translated into Russian include *The Framework for Teaching Basic Economic Concepts* and *Focus: High School Economics*. Then, to develop curriculum materials that use Russian examples to illustrate economic concepts, five Train the Writers workshops were conducted for teams of Russian and American teachers. Other specialized NCEE programs have included study tours for Russian teachers to visit the United States and for US teachers to visit Russia. Special conferences on teaching and evaluation methods have also been conducted. All of these efforts are moving toward developing a self-sustaining Russian network for economic education. More than 6,000 teachers from Russia and other countries of the former Soviet Union and eastern Europe have taken part in these programs, and testing of these program participants from 1995-99, conducted by the Education Development Center, Inc., found that teachers exhibited significant improvements in economic knowledge and that teachers continued to use methods and materials from the programs one and two years after the workshops (Blais, McKinnon, and Parliament, 2000).

Russian economic educators often find the pedagogical methods modeled by the NCEE even more novel and innovative than the economics content of these training programs. Those pedagogical methods are distinguished by three features that have been emphasized almost since the founding of the NCEE: 1) economics instruction is integrated into virtually all subjects; 2) instructional methods are active, with lectures largely replaced by simulations, role playing, and cooperative learning activities; and 3) economic education programs frequently involve the community in class projects.

IV. CONCLUSION

During the past decade much progress was made in developing an economic education program in Russia. The initiative was frequently a joint effort of forward-looking Russian educators and several different western organizations. This role for nongovernment organizations is a major innovation in Russia, where for 70 years the government operated virtually all educational activities.

Methods of economic education in Russia have been greatly influenced by those developed by the NCEE over the past 50 years. Because teachers in Russia and the United States all too often do not have formal training in economics in their undergraduate or graduate degree programs, it is necessary to provide that training on an inservice basis. Veteran economic educators in both countries recognize this as the most difficult and most important task that they perform.

There are some notable differences in approaches, however. For example, most economic education programs in Russia focus on secondary schools. In the

United States some of the most creative and successful curriculum has been developed at the elementary level. Economic education in Russia seems to place more emphasis on student competitions (such as the national Economic Olympiads) than is typically done in the United States. These activities provide publicity for economic education efforts and motivate students to learn economics.

Russia still has much to do, mainly in training teachers and developing and disseminating more and better instructional materials. The NCEE has developed many exemplary materials for teaching economics, but more of these need to be translated into Russian, and in many cases these materials need to be revised to reflect economic institutions and conditions in Russia.

Russia is a vast country and, as in the United States, economic education is not yet a widespread and routine outcome in the nation's elementary and secondary schools. While there is much to be said for local initiatives, a comprehensive nationwide program will not come about until economic education is an integral part of what schools and other educational institutions in the country do. The most obvious way to ensure that all Russian students receive economic education is to include it in the required curriculum. The Ministry of Education can establish such a requirement, and there is currently a real possibility that this will happen. To require the teaching of economics without trained teachers, however, could be disastrous. Even with a universal requirement there will still be a crucial need to provide inservice training, develop curriculum, and build educational partnerships with the private sector.

APPENDIX 12.A: Minimum content standards in economics

Adopted by the Order of the Ministry of Education #56 on 30 June 1999.

Economy and Economics. Scarcity of economic resources, its origins and consequences. Free goods and economic goods, factors of production (resources) and income earned by factor owners. Basic goals of an economy and ways of achieving them in different economic systems. Types of economic systems.

The role of specialization and trade. Ways of exchange and markets. Demand. Determinants of demand. Quantity demanded. Law of demand. Demand curve. Individual and market demand. Price elasticity of demand and the ways of its measurement. Supply. Determinants of supply. Quantity supplied. Law of supply. Supply curve. Individual and market supply. Price elasticity of supply and the ways of its measurement. The meaning of market equilibrium. Equilibrium price.

Sources of family incomes. Principles of determining expenditures. Inequality of incomes and its origins. Methods of government regulation of incomes in Russia. Types of social aid to low-income population categories.

Firm and its economic goals. Types of firms according to Russian legislation. Economic costs, economic profit, and accounting profit. Fixed, variable, average, and marginal costs.

Competition. Types of market structures. Perfect competition. Monopolistic competition. Oligopoly. Monopoly. Natural monopolies. Means of anti-monopoly regulation and protection of competition.

Labor market and its specific features. Supply of labor. Wage determinants, origins of wage differentiation by industries and professions. Unemployment and types of unemployment. Origins of unemployment. Trade unions, their activities and impact on the labor market. Minimum living standard. Minimum wage. Forms of payment, wages and salaries, methods of increasing workers' motivation.

Capital market. Stock market. Markets for land and natural resources. Specific features of these markets.

Money. Functions of money. Types of money. Banks and their role. The central bank and commercial banks.

Inflation and its consequences.

Property rights and their role for organization of economic activities.

Market failures. Externalities. Public goods. The economic role of government.

Basic macroeconomic indicators. Aggregate supply and aggregate demand. Macroeconomic equilibrium. Gross domestic product (GDP). Business cycles. Measures of macroeconomic stabilization: fiscal policy and monetary policy.

Government finances. Government budget. Basic sources of government revenues and main items of government expenditures. Taxes. Principles and ways of taxation. Main types of taxes in Russia. Government budget deficits. Government debt.

APPENDIX 12.A (continued)

Economic growth and factors of increasing economic growth.
International trade. Free trade. Protectionism.

NOTE

1. ICEBE regional centers are located in Arzamas, Beloretsk, Berdsk, Cheboksary, Chelyaybinsk, Chelayabinsk (*oblast*), Davlekanovo, Divnogorsk, Dmitrov, Dubna, Kolomna, Kotlas, Krasnodar, Krasnoayarsk, Kronshtadt, Kursk, Lesnoi, Lysva, Moscow (East), Moscow (West), Moscow (Moscovskaya *oblast*), Novgorod, N. Novgorod, N. Novgorod (*oblast*), Novocherkassk, Novokuznetsk, Novosibirsk, Novouralsk, Obninsk, Oktayabrskiy, Omsk, Ozersk, Penza, Perm, Pestovo, Poltavka, Samara, Sarov, Seversk Sharypovo, Snezhinsk, Stavropol, St. Petersburg, Talnah, Tomsk, Trehgornyi, Tula, Tver, Ufa, Volgograd, Voronezh, Voskresensk, Yayroslavl, Zlatoust, and Zarechniy.

REFERENCES

Blais, J., T. McKinnon, and C. Parliament (2000), 'The status of economic education in Russia,' unpublished report prepared for the National Council on Economic Education.

Bragiunsky, S.V. and G. Yavlinsky (2000), *Incentives and Institutions: The Transition to a Market Economy in Russia*, Princeton: Princeton University Press.

CIA (2000), *World Factbook*, www.cia.gov/cia/publications/factbook/geos/rs.html.

Ministry of Education of the Russian Federation (1999), 'The minimal content for teaching economics in high schools,' appendix to Order # 56, issued June 30.

Roland, G. (2000), *Transition and economics: Politics, markets and firms, comparative institutional analysis*, vol. 2, Cambridge and London: MIT Press.

Rushing, F.W. (1994), 'The changing face of economics instruction in Russia,' in W.B. Walstad (ed.), *An International Perspective on Economic Education*, Boston, Massachusetts, USA: Kluwer Academic Publishers, pp. 233-54.

13. Economic Education in Ukraine

James Dick, Volodymyr Melnyk, and Sandra Odorzynski

This chapter provides an overview of economic education in Ukraine at the end of the Soviet period, followed by a review of changes in the curriculum and teacher education that have been introduced over the last decade. Programs supported by international organizations are then described and the subsequent creation and activities of the Ukrainian Council on Economic Education are outlined. The chapter concludes with a review of possible future developments in economic education programs in Ukraine, and how those programs and changes can support the broader social and economic transitions occurring in the country.

I. BACKGROUND

Since becoming an independent nation in January 1992, Ukraine, a former internal colony of the Soviet Union, has struggled to create a strong sense of national identity. The lack of such identity helps to explain the fragmentation of political parties along regional, historical, and personal lines, and the confusion that continues to exist about the relationship between central government and local governments. There continues to be a severe institutional deficit that also limits nation building. D'Anieri, Kravchuck, and Kuzio (1999, p. 45) described Ukraine as a 'quasi-state with minimum institutions and an ancient regime's ruling elites.'

Ukraine's economic conditions were already difficult at the time of independence, but worsened dramatically during the early 1990s. Official measures of GDP declined by over 60 percent and inflation in 1993 exceeded 10,000 percent. Since then overall economic activity has usually declined on an annual basis, but at a slower rate. GDP declined by 12 percent in 1995 and continued to decline through 1999 at a rate of 10 percent or less (World Bank, 2001). The National Bank of Ukraine reported that the economy grew for the first time since independence during 2000, at a rate of six percent; and it continues to grow in 2001 (Sych, 2001). Inflation has fluctuated, at 24 percent in 1995, 66 percent in 1996, 18 percent in 1997, 12 percent in 1998, and 24 percent in 1999 (World Bank, 2001). But in the first quarter of 2001 inflation fell to an annual rate of only 2.7 percent (Sych, 2001). Two particularly telling results of the economic decline in Ukraine have been a net loss in population during the past decade and a reduction in life expectancy.

In addition to GDP and inflation concerns, Ukraine continues to be regarded as one of the most corrupt countries by business leaders and academics. In the 2001 *Corruption Perception Index*, which is based on public perceptions of corruption among public officials and politicians, Ukraine ranked 83rd out of 91 countries. Azerbaijan was the only former Soviet colony to rank lower than Ukraine (Transparency International, 2001). In addition to facing these political, economic, and social problems, economic education reformers also had to deal with an educational system that continued to reflect its Soviet heritage.

II. ECONOMIC EDUCATION AT THE END OF THE SOVIET ERA

During the 1980s all university students in Ukraine had to complete one course in political economics. This course was mandated by the central government and emphasized standard Marxist-Leninist doctrine – the benefits of the Soviet system and evils of capitalism – with no review of concepts covered in western courses on micro- and macroeconomics. Students in this course took oral and written examinations to demonstrate their understanding of differences between capitalistic and socialistic economic systems. Industrial economics and agricultural economics were added as elective courses for college students in the late 1980s, but there were no specialized courses for teachers at the elementary and secondary levels.

During the Soviet period and continuing into the first decade of Ukrainian independence, students completed secondary school at grade 11. The Rada (the Ukrainian Parliament) recently approved school reorganization plans that require students to complete an additional year of secondary school. There were no specific courses or curriculum materials on western, market-oriented economics in the precollege curriculum in the Soviet era, but economic concepts such as production and specialization were included in geography courses and, of course, there was continuing instruction in Marxist-oriented political economics. In the high schools, history teachers typically taught the political economics courses and geography teachers taught courses on economic geography. Economics was not included in the elementary curriculum. Educational policies, materials, teacher training, school management practices, and assessment were all dictated by Moscow. Russian was the predominant language of instruction.

III. THE MINISTRY OF EDUCATION AND SCIENCE

In Ukraine today virtually all control over education still lies with the state. The Ministry of Education and Science issues mandates regarding curriculum standards, textbooks, school calendars, teacher credentials, entrance examinations, and academic competitions. In the past separate ministries existed for secondary education, higher education, vocational education, and scientific research, but in the restructured system adopted in 1996 these four areas became separate departments in the Ministry of Education and Science. Below these four departments are 27 regional boards and hundreds of district school boards that report to the regional boards.

Since the early 1990s the Ministry of Education and Science has struggled to develop an economics mandate that increases the amount of economics in the curriculum and encourages teachers to use new instructional strategies. The first official recommendation was issued in 1993 and suggested that schools should provide one hour per week of economics instruction in the eleventh grade. While the number of schools offering economics increased and a textbook was published, the Ministry cancelled this recommendation when it determined there were not enough qualified teachers to teach the course. In 1997 the Ministry expressed an interest in developing national standards for economics; consequently, a report was prepared by a committee of economists and educators, based on the US National Council on Economic Education's *Voluntary Standards in Economics*. The Ukrainian standards were widely circulated and are often used as a basis for curriculum development; but the Ministry has not officially endorsed these standards, so they remain only a draft in terms of influencing national policies.

In July 2000 the Ministry indicated an interest in developing the concept of continuous economic education. The following guidelines were announced in the *Methodological Instruction of the Ministry of Education and Science*:

- The economics curriculum in Ukraine is still being developed.
- Economics is an elective course that the Ministry is prepared to make mandatory.
- The proposed course would be 68 hours of instruction in the tenth and/or eleventh grades.
- Two years of economics instruction are also suggested for eighth and ninth grades.
- Teaching economics in grades 5-9 is encouraged, but left to school discretion.
- Applied economics courses, including entrepreneurship, management, and marketing, are recommended for inclusion in the secondary curriculum as separate courses in vocational training, but not as substitutes for a basic economic course.

The implementation of such a program has remained uncertain because of limited resources, and the mandated course has since been reduced to 48 hours of instruction in the tenth grade. The other courses are now considered electives, and even implementation of the mandated course depends on the availability of qualified teachers. A governmental reorganization in the spring of 2001, following a national election, led to further review of curriculum mandates and implementation policies.

It is difficult to see how the Ministry will ensure compliance with the new curriculum requirements. State funds have not been provided to assist in training teachers or preparing student materials, and some educators trained in the Soviet era disagree with the market economics orientation of the July 2000 mandate. Reaching teachers in rural areas will be even more difficult because, according to some educational leaders, village teachers tend to be generally more resistant to curriculum innovations in content and pedagogy, and are less well prepared to implement the economics mandate.

IV.   TEACHER EDUCATION IN UKRAINE

Some attempts have been made to reform teacher education systems and programs since the time of Ukrainian independence, but Soviet-era patterns still prevail. With few exceptions there is no economics major for preservice teachers at the pedagogy institutes, or in economics departments at universities where faculty members remain divided between those who continue to teach command-oriented political economics and those who teach market-oriented economics. The divisions among university economics faculty members will continue for some time, but should gradually diminish as younger professors replace older faculty.

Until the mid-1990s there was no demand for training economics teachers because economics was not required in the elementary and secondary curriculum. Ukrainian universities and other institutions of higher education do not have a tradition of providing inservice or graduate courses for teachers; instead, teachers meet re-certification requirements through regional Post-Diploma Institutes. It is unrealistic to think that these patterns will change in the near future. University resources are also extremely limited, making it difficult to create and support new courses and programs (Kovzik and Watts, 2001).

At five-year intervals all Ukrainian elementary and secondary teachers must complete 120 contact hours in retraining courses at a Post-Diploma Institute. Fifty hours must be committed to Ukrainian studies, pedagogy, and educational psychology; the remaining hours can be used for specialized subjects, including economics. The Institutes located in each *oblast* (political administrative regions) provide meeting space, recruit teachers, and offer consulting services to the schools in their regions. They also assist in testing programs for secondary students, including the preparation of materials for the recently developed Economics Olympiad, a national competition for secondary students. To provide additional training support, staff members from the Post-Diploma Institutes have been recruited for various economics training programs for professors and teachers, with the idea that these instructors would then provide additional teacher training programs at their own institutions.

Some western college textbooks (including *Economics* by Samuelson and Nordhaus, *Economics* by McConnell and Brue, and *Economics of Money and Banking* by Mishkin) have been translated into Russian and Ukrainian. The extent to which these materials are available and utilized is not clear, however.[1] The Ukrainian private publishing industry is still in its formative stages, and most libraries have few textbooks or other instructional materials.

V. INTERNATIONAL SUPPORT FOR ECONOMIC EDUCATION REFORMS IN UKRAINE

Much of the support for fostering changes in the economic content and teaching strategies utilized in elementary and secondary schools has been provided by grants from international foundations and organizations. The three major organizations and their key programs are briefly described in the following sections.

The International Renaissance Foundation

Funded by George Soros, the International Renaissance Foundation was the first international organization to act on the need to build the institutions of a democratic political system and a market economy in Ukraine, including the need to educate the citizens of the country to understand and participate in these new systems. The Foundation provided funds to support retraining programs in western economics for university professors beginning in 1994, and has continued to support the development of a national and regional economic education infrastructure. For example, it provided funds to support the initial programs of Junior Achievement and the National Council on Economic Education in Ukraine, and the development of the Ukrainian Council on Economic Education and a professional association for economic educators. Key personnel who once oversaw economic education programs for the Foundation later became leaders in the Ukrainian Council network.

Changes within the Soros organization and a reordering of funding objectives have reduced its level of support for reforms in economic education in recent years. This pattern is the typical pattern for Soros support – providing resources to get programs established with the expectation that, if the programs are successful, other organizations will join in providing support, or that support will be generated internally.

Junior Achievement International

In 1992 Junior Achievement International (JAI) began to train teachers and disseminate curriculum materials developed in the United States, first in Kiev and Kharkiv and then in other cities and regions. *Applied Economics*, a semester-long package of curriculum materials developed for US secondary students that included computer-based business simulations and a textbook, was the first JA program introduced in Ukraine. Additional materials disseminated by JAI in Ukraine include *Fundamentals of Market Economics* (a training program for business managers of private businesses), *Business Basics* (a curriculum package for elementary students), and *Project Business* (for upper elementary students). These materials are basically US-developed materials translated into Ukrainian, but Ukrainian examples have been incorporated in some of these materials (Davis, 1995).

JAI has a national office in Kiev, and teacher consultants who conduct regional teacher training workshops to promote and support the use of their curriculum materials. In 1999-2000 almost 200 teachers attended JAI training seminars, and over 6,000 textbooks were distributed. These seminars and materials are provided at no financial cost to teachers, with costs covered by sponsors of the JAI program (primarily US firms with operations in Ukraine and Ukrainian businesses, with additional support provided by the US Agency for International Development). JAI has high name recognition among some Ukrainian teachers and school leaders, but their teacher training efforts have been limited and there is little follow-up support to teachers who use these materials and programs.

The National Council on Economic Education

Since 1995 the National Council on Economic Education (NCEE) has become the major international sponsor of economic education programs in Ukraine. In 1992 the NCEE obtained modest support from the International Renaissance Foundation to conduct its first teacher workshops in Kharkiv. These programs were the basis for many of the developments in economic education that have occurred in Ukraine to the present day. Since 1995 funding for this program has been provided by annual International Exchange grants from the Office of Educational Research and Improvement at the US Department of Education (DOE).

With the DOE funding in 1995, the NCEE dramatically expanded its support for reform in economic education in Ukraine and other transition economies. These new programs were based on the NCEE's half century of experience with programs to improve the economic literacy of American students through teacher training programs and the development and dissemination of academically based curriculum guidelines and instructional materials featuring active learning strategies. In the teacher training programs the NCEE developed for Ukraine and other transition economies, the focus was on programs that offered large multiplier effects – meaning that participants would take the materials and knowledge they gained in these programs back to their own schools and colleagues. The major components of the NCEE's Ukrainian efforts include four basic types of programs.

Training of Trainers. Each year since 1995 Ukrainian professors, staff development specialists, and secondary teachers and administrators have been selected to attend this series of four week-long seminars, which provide intensive training on economics content and pedagogy. Through 2000, over 120 Ukrainian participants had attended these programs in Ukraine or in other countries. Two all-Ukrainian seminars were conducted in 1995-96 and 1996-97, while other seminars included educators from Russia and many other countries in eastern Europe and central Asia. Pre- and posttests were used to determine the participants' mastery of economics content, and videotapes of lessons presented by the participants were used to determine their mastery of the related teaching strategies. Program evaluations conducted by the Education Development Center indicated that the four Training of Trainers seminars significantly increased participants' understanding of micro- and macroeconomics. The participants also indicated on surveys conducted after the training programs that they were using more active learning strategies in their classes, including group work, simulations, and discussion. Participants also developed plans for conducting teacher workshops in their own schools or regions after attending the seminars (Education Development Center, 1999).

Training of Curriculum Writers. Ukrainians have participated in two training of writers workshops conducted in Ukraine to develop the skills required to produce new, Ukrainian-based instructional materials aligned with the content and strategies taught in the Training of Trainers seminars. Additional Ukrainian representatives attended other writers' seminars for professors and teachers from several former Soviet bloc countries. In these one-week workshops participants are paired with American teachers and learn more about curriculum development from experienced US curriculum writers. After the week of classes participants prepare lessons that are edited by the workshop instructors and then shared with other participants via e-mail. Curriculum materials produced by these educators from eastern Europe and the United States include two NCEE secondary curriculum guides (*Economics in Transition* and *From Plan to Market*), an elementary guide (*Roosters to Robots*), and a guide for developing a coordinated curriculum (*Connecting the Pieces*). Other NCEE publications, such as *Focus: International Economics*, have been translated into Ukrainian, in some cases by teams of past Ukrainian participants in NCEE training programs.

Specialized Training Workshops. Selected graduates of the Training of Trainers seminars were invited to attend weeklong workshops focusing on research and evaluation in economic education, economic education for elementary teachers, or the organization and management of non-profit, nongovernmental organizations (NGOs). To date, five Ukrainians have attended the research and evaluation workshop, 16 have attended the elementary workshop, and eight have attended the NGO management workshop.

Study Tours. The NCEE has sponsored three study tours that brought groups of American teachers to Ukraine to visit elementary and secondary schools, and others that brought Ukrainian economic educators to the United States to visit centers for economic education located at colleges and universities. Under this program Ukrainians have also attended and made presentations at annual meetings of economic educators in the United States, professional meetings in Europe, and regional planning meetings in eastern Europe.

The level of NCEE support and programming has been greater in Ukraine than in the other countries in the former Soviet bloc. There are several possible explanations for this: the initial success of the early programs developed in cooperation with the Soros Foundation; the interest in and commitment to the NCEE approach to economic education that developed originally in the Soros projects; and the committed, hardworking leaders, first in Kharkiv, and then other cities/regions, who created teacher workshops with very limited resources. The geographic size of the country was probably also an asset along with the support that emerged from the education Ministry, and the Council/Center network and the professional association of economics teachers that are described below.

In recent years, however, the NCEE's role in providing assistance in Ukraine has changed. In 1998 the NCEE began to send observers/consultants to work with Ukrainian economic educators as the Ukrainian educators (rather than US faculty) conducted workshops for teachers. The NCEE also began to provide financial assistance to the Ukrainian centers to support their program efforts. With a Council/Center network in place in Ukraine and the large cadre of educators who have received training in the various NCEE programs, it seems realistic and appropriate to expect that Ukrainian economic educators must now develop and implement their own programs at the regional and national levels, and begin to secure the funding to support teacher training and curriculum development.

VI. THE UKRAINIAN COUNCIL ON ECONOMIC EDUCATION

Patterned on the US National Council on Economic Education, the Ukrainian Council on Economic Education (UCEE) was organized in 1998. The UCEE is a nongovernmental, non-profit, non-partisan organization that seeks domestic and international funding to coordinate and support economic education across Ukraine. Major support for the Council was provided by the Soros Foundation through 1999, and continues to be provided by the NCEE through grants from the US Department of Education. Additional funds to support teacher training and curriculum development have been provided by Cargill-Ukraine, Credit Lyonnais, the Ukrainian Ministry of Science and Education, the US State Department, and Students in Free Enterprise.

The UCEE is governed by a board of educators and business leaders from Ukraine. US representatives from the NCEE and Cargill-Ukraine are also members of this governing board. The Council interacts with the Ministry of Science and Education at various levels: for example, a Deputy Minister serves as a director of the Council, and a UCEE board member was appointed as the chairman of the Ministry's Economics Methodological Commission, which reviews and approves all economics textbooks and other curriculum materials that may be used in Ukrainian schools.

The UCEE provides resources to its national network of centers for economic education and coordinates their efforts to bring economic education and curriculum resources to teachers and students. The Council also works with the All-Ukrainian Association of Economic Educators (AUAEE). Founded in Kharkiv in 1996, the AUAEE's members are the professionals at institutes and universities who deliver economic education programs, consult with schools and educational leaders, develop curriculum materials, and conduct related research. In 2000 there were more than 200 AUAEE members from all regions of Ukraine.[2] The AUAEE sponsors the Ukrainian National Economics Olympiad, a competition for secondary students, and also a student research program to help promote the importance of economic education.

UCEE Economic Education Programs

Most of the economic education programs for Ukrainian teachers in the last decade have been carried out at centers for economic education in Kharkiv, Lviv, Dnipropetrovsk, Simferopol, Kiev, Odessa, Donetsk, Ivano-Frankivsk, Zaporizhia, Chernivtsi, and Cherkassy. The centers were developed through discussions between the President of the Ukrainian Council, local educational institutions, and educators and economists who were interested in promoting reform in the teaching of economics at the elementary and secondary levels. Many of these educators had participated in the NCEE training programs described earlier. These 11 centers are modeled after the centers for economic education that are part of the NCEE's US network of state councils and university-based centers, which supports and promotes economic education in K-12 schools. The institutional support for centers in the US will not be duplicated in Ukraine, however, because of the limited resources at universities and pedagogical institutes in Ukraine, and the divisions that still exist among the university economics faculties.

The achievements of two centers for economic education – the oldest and newest centers in the country – offer an overview of the teacher education programs and curriculum resources provided by the Ukrainian centers. The center at Kharkiv, the second largest city in Ukraine, was created by professors and teachers who participated in workshops conducted by the NCEE beginning in 1993. Over 30 teachers and professors from Kharkiv have since participated in the NCEE's Training of Trainers program. These trainers have offered over 700 teacher workshops and courses that incorporate the content and strategies presented in the NCEE courses to teachers who teach over 60,000 elementary and secondary students in the Kharkiv region.

The Kharkiv center also provides consulting services to teachers and school administrators, maintains a library of curriculum materials, and has developed professional linkages with the Ukraine Ministry of Education, the Kharkiv Institute for Advanced Teacher Studies, and the Kharkiv Academy of Pedagogical Science. Staff members have authored textbooks and student materials at several grade levels, including a state-approved textbook for the secondary level. The center has received financial support from the Eurasia Fund, the Ukrainian Council on Economic Education, the government of The Netherlands, and the International Renaissance Foundation.

The newest center for economic education in Ukraine, in Cherkassy, has offered programs for teachers since 1997 through the regional Post-Diploma Institute. The Cherkassy center has sponsored a four-week summer course for secondary teachers that was taught by three university professors and an educational administrator from the Post-Diploma Institute, who all participated in the NCEE Training of Trainers program. The center also conducts short seminars and workshops during the school year. In addition to offering programs for teachers in the Cherkassy region, special efforts have been made to attract teachers at the junior and technical colleges in the city, as well as teachers from neighboring small towns and rural areas. The center has organized a group of geography teachers who are infusing economics content and strategies into their courses, and hosted two international economics education conferences, a Fulbright lecturer, and the All-Ukrainian Economics Olympiad. Funding for this center has been provided by the Ukrainian Council for Economic Education.

The success of the Kharkiv and Cherkassy centers has depended to a large degree on the talents and commitments of university faculty who attended the NCEE Training of Trainers seminars. Both centers provide a variety of teacher education programs with minimal resources, and have built a cadre of teachers who are anxious to participate in training programs and share new teaching materials and methods with their colleagues. At both sites there are strong leaders in the local universities or Post-Diploma Institutes who believe in, and support, economic education. These local educational leaders also help the center staff members find resources to conduct programs and carry out other center activities.

Although programs at the other centers are not identical to the two described above, there are many similarities. Staff members are usually faculty members at higher education institutions who have attended NCEE workshops and courses and have a strong commitment to economic education. Some centers are aligned with regional Post-Diploma Institutes. A 1999 report prepared by the Ukrainian Council indicated that the 11 Ukrainian centers conducted a total of 50 workshops reaching over 1,000 teachers, with another 500 teachers receiving various types of consultation services in that year. About two-thirds of the 120 professors and teachers trained in the NCEE Training of Trainers programs participated actively in center programs. The Council estimated that 45,000 high school and college students were taught in 1999 by the trainers themselves, or by the teachers who completed seminars and workshops offered by trainers at the centers.

VI.   THE FUTURE OF ECONOMIC EDUCATION IN UKRAINE

A true national network has been established in Ukraine in its first decade of independence.   This work progressed from a loosely connected group of individuals interested in economic education to the creation of the Ukrainian Council for Economic Education and the centers for economic education that work in conjunction with the Ministry of Science and Education. It ultimately led to the development of the All-Ukrainian Association of Economic Educators and the establishment of strong relationships with the Post-Diploma Institutes of teacher education.   That network now regularly promotes economic literacy through teacher training programs, curriculum development, and student competitions.

Economics is now offered in secondary schools in all regions of Ukraine, although student and teacher involvement has been stronger in specialized high schools (lyceums, gymnasia, collegia) than in regular schools. Surveys of 21,274 regular secondary schools (16,191 responding) indicated that four percent offered economics in 1997, while over eight percent offered economics in 1999. In 460 specialized schools (377 responding), 27.1 percent offered economics in 1997, compared to 63 percent in 1999. A growing number of universities are offering entrance examinations in economics.

While these accomplishments are noteworthy, particularly in light of the severe resource limitations facing Ukraine, and education in particular, the current situation is, in truth, not as positive as this brief summary might indicate. Some economics education programming is offered in all regions of the nation, but in many regions the level of classroom instruction on economics is very low. It is almost non-existent in most rural areas.

Additional challenges for the next decade remain. Complying with any form of Ministry course mandates will require the training, or retraining, of many teachers. Geography and mathematics teachers may have to be trained to deliver economics instruction in addition to their initial teaching areas, but in any case resources will be needed to help the centers for economic education and the Post-Diploma Institutes organize and conduct staff development programs. Providing training will be more difficult in rural areas, where special incentives may be needed to insure that a uniform level of economics teaching exists in all parts of the country.

If economics content is introduced in the elementary curriculum – particularly if it is mandated by the Ministry – there will be an even greater increase in the demand for teacher training and instructional materials. It will also require teacher trainers with additional skills and understandings, because the NCEE Training of Trainers seminars focused on teaching economics at the secondary and college levels.

To guarantee the quality of the teacher training programs at the Post-Diploma Institutes, there is a need for workshop curricula developed by outstanding economists and pedagogy specialists in Ukraine.   The adoption of national education standards on economics could provide additional incentives to help improve economic education in Ukraine, especially if the interest in infusing economics into the elementary curriculum expands in future curriculum mandates.

Even though the NCEE has sponsored curriculum projects and had some of its materials translated into Ukrainian, the need for additional high quality Ukrainian-based materials that emphasize market economics and utilize active learning strategies remains strong. There is a pressing need for appropriate textbooks and other student materials. The Ministry of Education and Science has made this a high priority. Some of the Training of Trainers participants have authored materials, and some of the Ukrainian centers have published student and teacher instructional materials. What may prove to be even more difficult than developing the materials, however, is paying for, or at least heavily subsidizing, publishing costs so that schools can afford to provide teachers new materials to use in their classrooms.

In just three years, student interest and participation in the national Economics Olympiad has grown dramatically. Much of the work to organize and conduct the contest has been provided by volunteers, but if this event is to maintain a high profile additional funding will be necessary. This Olympiad is similar to national academic competitions conducted in other curriculum areas, and generates a broader awareness of, and support for, economics in the secondary curriculum.

The need for technological support is enormous in all areas of Ukrainian education, including economics. Computer access and related services are non-existent or outdated by US standards. Internet service is expensive and slow, and there is little instructional software available. There are also staff development costs connected with the introduction of new technology, and there are no provisions for distance education that would deliver economic education to rural areas. The Ukrainian Council and its national network could also use this technology to improve their ability to communicate with each other, store and share information, and provide additional administrative support to new and existing Centers.

One can reasonably ask whether economic education in Ukrainian schools will end when the NCEE and other external funders end their support for teacher training and curriculum development. While Ukraine has a tendency to move forward and backward in all of its reform efforts, and to make even the simplest things complex, we believe that economic education in Ukraine will continue to grow and develop. And while external support has made the change process less difficult and more consistent, curriculum reform in economics will continue with or without that support because of the fundamental changes that are taking place as the national transition toward a market economy accelerates.

NOTES

Much of the information for this chapter was obtained from a 'Report on the Status of Economic Education in Ukraine,' a report of a conference sponsored by the National Council of Economic Education. The authors of the report were Sandra Odorzynski, James Dick, and James Grunloh. At that conference presentations on Ukrainian economic education were made by Natalia Chepurnaya, Victor Chuzhikof, Ihor Hubatiuk, Vladimir Humennyk, Lidia Kozhina-Bahata, Olha Kramareva, Larisa Krupskaya, Lyudmyla Kutidze, Yuliya Lelyuk, Volodymyr Melnyk, Irina Parkhomenko, Elena Reshetnyak, and Igor Shymkiv. In addition to the Moscow Conference, Olga Kramareva, Larisa Krupskaya, Volodymyr Melnyk, Irina Parkhomenko, Elena Reshetnyak, and Volodymyr Gummennyk also made presentations on economic education in Ukraine at an NCEE conference in Dubrovnik, Croatia, in May 2001. Information from these presentations was also incorporated into this chapter. Nancy Keel, the Director of Junior Achievement in Ukraine, also provided information that was used in preparing this chapter.

1. One professor from Cherkassy described his discovery of a Samuelson textbook in a library in Kiev at the time of independence. To learn more about market economics he would transcribe portions of the text because there were no copy machines available. After returning to Cherkassy, a friend would translate the notes into Russian, and only then could this professor learn more about market economics.

2. The AUAEE is similar to the US National Association of Economic Educators (NAEE). Most members of NAEE are professional staff members at the state Councils and college and university Centers affiliated with the NCEE.

REFERENCES

D'Anieri, P., R. Kravchuk, and T. Kuzio (1999), *Politics and Society in Ukraine*, Boulder, CO: Westview Press.

Davis, J. (1995), 'Fundamentals of market economics,' *Social Studies*, **86**(5), pp. 227-30.

Education Development Center (1999), *International Educational Exchange Program Results 1995-1999*, New York: Education Development Center.

Kovzik, A. and M. Watts (2001), 'Reforming undergraduate economics instruction in Russia, Belarus, and Ukraine,' *Journal of Economic Education*, **32**(1), pp. 78-92.

Kiev Post (2001, May 17), 'Business wrap' [on-line], *http://www.thepost.kiev.va.*

McConnell, C.R. and S.L. Brue, (2002), *Economics*, 15th ed. New York: McGraw-Hill Irwin.

Mishkin, F.E. (2001), *Economics of Money, Banking, and Financial Markets*, 6th ed. Boston: Addison Wesley.

Odorzynski, S.J., J. Dick, and J. Grunloh (2000), 'Report on the Status of Economic Education in Ukraine,' New York: National Council on Economic Education.

Samuelson, P.A. and W.D. Nordhaus (2001), *Economics*, 17th ed. New York: McGraw-Hill Irwin.

Sych, V. (2001), 'Ukraine's economy poised for further growth,' *Kiev Post* [On-line], *http://www.thepost.kiev.va.*

Transparency International (2001), 'New index highlights worldwide corruption,' [On-line], *http://www.transparency.org/documents.*

Ukrainian Ministry of Education and Science (2000), *Methodological Instructions of the Ministry of Education and Science*, Kiev, Ukraine.

World Bank (2001), *World Development Indicators* [On-line], *http://dev.data.worldbank.org.*

PART THREE

Conclusion

14. Reforming Economics and Economics Teaching in the Transition Economies: Agents of Change and Future Challenges

William B. Walstad and Michael Watts

As the nations of central and eastern Europe and the former Soviet Union undertook the transition from centrally planned to market economies, the academic transition from teaching Marxist economic analysis to teaching western-style, market-based economics also became accepted as useful, necessary, and even inevitable.[1] This sweeping academic reform in a single discipline was affected by broader educational reforms, by economic conditions in the transition economies, and by the uneven and often sporadic progress of the economic and political reforms.

Economic circumstances and public policies now vary considerably across the transition economies. And the question of how to accomplish the reform of economics instruction was, in its own way, as unprecedented and uncharted as the broader democratic and economic reforms. Not surprisingly, therefore, despite starting from a uniform Soviet-style curriculum and educational structure with its remarkably standardized coursework in economics at the secondary and university levels, these nations chose alternative routes and different rates of change to accomplish this academic transition.

There are several key reasons for the differences across nations beyond the political and economic conditions, including differences in cultural heritages that date back to the pre-Soviet periods, which ended for some nations in 1917 and for other nations at much later dates. Geographic locations also lead some nations to identify more closely with cultural and economic practices in the West. Educational policies and some educational institutions – including international organizations – have also differed significantly across the nations, although many of both the domestic and international institutions are more alike than they are different.

Perhaps the major similarity that made the academic transition possible in all of the transition nations was the eagerness to teach market economics by many instructors, both at the university level and in secondary schools. There were some holdouts – especially among older faculty members – but it is clear that among most instructors and students western economics is viewed as more useful, rigorous, and scientific than the old Soviet-style political economy. The reformed economics courses and units are therefore a better fit with the rest of the curriculum and high educational standards in these nations, as well as with their new economic systems.

The instructional problems that must be faced are also similar across the transition economies when the decision is made to offer new kinds of economics coursework: teachers must be trained or retrained, new educational materials must be found or developed, and somebody has to pay for all the training and new resources. For the efforts to improve economic education to be successful and sustaining, institutional support must be built up in each nation. Especially at the elementary and secondary level that support requires the involvement of organizations other than schools and government agencies, and in particular international nongovernmental organizations (NGOs) that serve as 'change agents' because they exert considerable influence in shaping the goals, methods, and pace of the academic transition.

The first and most important group of these change agents, however, are the domestic or in-country organizations, including Ministries of Education, universities, pedagogical and faculty retraining Institutes, and a variety of NGOs such as the national Soros Foundations, national councils and associations of economics teachers, and local or regional centers for economic education that are sometimes housed at universities.[2] The second group of change agents are the international organizations or sponsors of economic education (and often civic education) programs, including the National Council on Economic Education, national affiliates of the US Junior Achievement program, government agencies from western nations and the European Union, and other organizations that have offered programs in a smaller number of the transition economies. The remainder of the chapter briefly summarizes the role of each of these major organizations in the academic transition, and offers an assessment of their influence and effectiveness in this arena.

National Ministries of Education

The Soviet heritage of national control over education remains strong across the transition economies in all areas of the curriculum. Indeed, with few exceptions, the major factor leading to less national control over education in the post-Soviet period seems to have been the severe financial constraints facing the ministries. There is, of course, extensive debate about the proper role and scope of the national government in education in the West, particularly in the United States. Philosophical issues such as parental or local control over the educational process will, undoubtedly, also become more prevalent in the transition economies in the future. At the time of the collapse of the Soviet Union the curriculum inherited by universities and secondary schools was certainly not based on local or parental control, or a competitive response to market demands for education and training by prospective employers.

Since the breakup of the Soviet Union most of the national ministries of education have followed one of three approaches to changes in the economics curriculum. Some countries – such as Kyrgyzstan, Poland, and Latvia – responded to widespread criticisms of Soviet instruction that reflected earlier mandates by political officials who were responsible for enforcing the former official state ideology, and moved quickly to mandate new courses in western-style economics.[3] In a few former Soviet republics, such as Bulgaria and Romania, short, formal courses on Marxist economics that had been mandated were replaced with short, mandated courses on market-oriented economics. In many other countries, however – including Russia, Ukraine, and Belarus – ministries have announced plans to consider or eventually adopt new mandates for economics courses or national standards for elementary and secondary economic education, but have not yet acted to implement such policies.

A key reason for the delays in these latter cases is the cost of providing new textbooks and other instructional materials, and of training or retraining teachers who will teach the new courses. Other problems include severe financial shortfalls for buildings, maintenance, staff salaries, and providing textbooks and newer instructional technologies in all subject areas. It is also difficult to find time in the curriculum to introduce a new subject area, particularly when the new economics coursework appears to be considerably more demanding and rigorous than the material that was covered during the Soviet period. Coursework on math, science, and foreign languages is already more demanding than in many western nations – particularly the United States – so the decision to add another rigorous course to the student load cannot be made lightly.

Taken together, these problems suggest that without mandates from the national ministries, or perhaps the new regional and local authorities that are acquiring more control over elementary and secondary education in some of the transition economies, economics courses are not likely to become a standard part of the school curriculum taken by most students. Nevertheless, student demand for economics coursework and training seems strong, and at many schools or other organizations offering extracurricular programs economics is already a popular 'after-school' elective.

Universities

Colleges and universities in the transition economies have moved quickly to offer undergraduate economics and business courses and programs that are now similar to what is taught in leading western universities. Most departments are now made up of faculty representing three different groups.[4] The first group is the older, long-time faculty members whose training and inclination is to teach the old, Soviet-style political economy. The second group includes mathematical economists who studied problems of central planning systems but not western economics, or retooled mathematicians who often have little or no grounding in the structure, logic, and application of basic economic ideas and models. The third group are the usually younger economists who were willing and able to drop Soviet political economy in favor of western economics, largely by retraining themselves using English or translated western textbooks, or in some cases by attending training or faculty exchange programs in the West sponsored by national governments or by international organizations such as the World Bank, the International Monetary Fund (IMF), or the European Union.

Students at universities in the transition economies are likely to take some courses taught by professors from all three of these groups, at least until the older professors retire and are replaced by faculty members who are trained under the new system.   That obviously creates problems for the students during their undergraduate studies. It has also created a 'brain drain' problem in the transition economies, because top graduates of these schools realize that, for a solid graduate education in economics or business, they must attend a western university, or perhaps one of the programs recently established in eastern Europe or the former Soviet Union featuring western faculty members, such as the Central European University in Prague and Budapest. Among the many top students who now go to programs in the United States or western Europe, most graduates try to stay in the West, to use their training more intensively and earn salaries that are several times higher.

It is clear, however, that universities will remain a major stimulus for continuing reform and modernization of the economics curriculum in the transition economies.   There is widespread support and interest in learning western economics and establishing curriculum standards that are similar to those found in EU and US universities. The strong mathematical training of most students in the transition economies also provides a solid foundation for the study of economics both at the undergraduate and graduate levels. In the short run faculty retraining remains a key issue for teaching graduate-level courses, improving the quality of graduate education in economics, and engaging in economic research.[5] Another area of concern is the pedagogical approach to teaching undergraduate economics courses. This instruction is typically didactic, almost exclusively lecture, and even less interactive than undergraduate economics instruction in the United States.[6] There are many opportunities for promoting innovative teaching practices in these universities if the educational culture in these institutions will permit and encourage such changes.

Pedagogical and Retraining Institutes

With a few possible exceptions such as Ukraine and Latvia, pedagogical universities in the transition economies have not yet begun to offer degree programs for future secondary teachers of economics, or even significant coursework in economic education for future teachers of geography, history, or other social sciences.   University faculty members still regularly return to retraining institutes to update their training and skills, in economics as well as other subjects; but few instructors who teach at the retraining institutes are themselves formally trained in western economics at the graduate level. This situation will obviously need improvement if new methods of teaching economics and the knowledge base of the instructors of economics are to be systematically strengthened in the transition economies.

In time, university economics instructors will be able to make this transition, learning new material as they teach their courses, conduct research, and hire younger colleagues with western-style training in economics. Retraining and faculty exchange programs can no doubt speed up that process, but eventually the changes that are already well underway will be completed, and university economics in the transition economies will likely become indistinguishable from what is taught in the West at both the graduate and undergraduate levels.

On the other hand, it will be especially difficult for secondary and elementary teachers in the transition economies to teach the subject well if they do not get substantial coursework in economics and on teaching economics. Like their counterparts in the West, these teachers are typically not full-time economics teachers even if they teach secondary courses in economics, nor were their undergraduate majors in economics.

National Soros Foundations

The national foundations established under various names in the transition economies by George Soros have played a major role in promoting civic and economic education in many countries, especially Kyrgyzstan, Russia, and Ukraine. The typical pattern for these foundations is first to support programs offered by organizations from the United States and western Europe, such as Junior Achievement programs for students and teacher training and materials development programs sponsored by the National Council for Economic Education. This work is then followed by the development of national, regional, or local organizations for the teaching of economics. Eventually the Soros foundations reduce their support for these new organizations and encourage them to operate as independent units.

Special programs in individual nations, such as the Model Schools program in Kyrgyzstan, the International Center for Business and Economic Education in Russia, and student Olympiads in several countries, have also been developed by or with major support from individual Soros Foundations.[7] These programs have all been successful in terms of attracting sustained and enthusiastic participation from teachers and students. Despite the successes, these approaches to building an institutional structure to sustain economic education have not been adopted in all of the transition economies, or at the same level, partly because the level of cooperation between national governments – especially Ministries of Education – and the Soros Foundations has varied widely. For example, in Kyrgyzstan there were explicit agreements and strong cooperation between the Ministry of Education and the Soros Foundation, while in Belarus the Soros Foundation was expelled by the government. In most cases the national Soros foundations have faced similar, but more moderate, opportunities and concerns. They have usually played important roles in educational reforms, including reforms in economics, but not as central or certainly as well publicized as the polar cases in Kyrgyzstan and Belarus.

Councils for Economic Education and Teacher Associations

Another promising development has been the creation of national councils for economic education, which serve as umbrella organizations sponsoring economic education program in various nations. These councils have been formed primarily in countries where a large number of university and secondary teachers of economics have completed training programs sponsored by the National Council on Economic Education (NCEE), and where national Soros Foundations have been willing to provide financial support for economic education programs. There is even one multinational council, the Baltic Council on Economic Education.

These organizations have been most successful in establishing delivery networks of local offices, usually called centers for economic education as in the United States, but not always housed and supported by colleges and universities as in the NCEE network of some 270 college and university centers in the United States. Of course, colleges and universities in the transition economies face far more severe financial constraints than most US institutions of higher education. Numerous teacher training and materials development programs have been conducted by the various national councils, and in some countries the organizations have also been able to begin working closely with the Ministry of Education.

Financially and administratively, however, the nationwide councils are still small, fledgling operations. In some cases these organizations receive limited financial support from the NCEE through its funding from the US Department of Education and other public and private organizations, as well as in-country sponsors. It is especially difficult for these councils to raise public or private funds given overall economic conditions and the lack of tax incentives for charitable contributions or an established corporate culture to support educational programs. It is not yet known if these councils can become self-sustaining institutions to advance economic education or if their existence will be largely dependent on funding from a few other non-profit or private organizations.

Teacher associations have also played key roles in improving the professional development of economics teachers in many of the transition economies, by conducting or helping to coordinate and recruit teachers for retraining programs. These associations are usually focused on either university or pre-university teaching, but in the countries where university faculty have been more directly involved in training programs for pre-university teachers of economics, such as Belarus and Ukraine, these organizations also reflect these joint interests and activities.

The teacher associations are typically not as involved in the day-to-day search for funding and administration of programs as the national councils on economic education, and consequently they have less direct influence over the delivery of economic education materials and programs. They operate more like the US and UK professional associations of economics teachers who are involved in pre-university and university instruction, or at least in training elementary and secondary teachers in economics. In this sense the professional associations offer teachers a network to belong to and serve as a major resource base that complements the work of the national councils on economic education. The success of these associations, however, often depends on the organizational skills and enthusiasm of unpaid leadership, which varies over time and across countries.

Junior Achievement (JA)

JA was one of the first international organizations to offer specific economics programs for secondary schools in the transition economies. In 1991 the Soros Foundation helped organize and fund a workshop for teachers from the nations of the former Soviet Union to learn about the JA Applied Economics program. By 1992 Applied Economics classes were being conducted in schools in Russia and in other nations that were formerly Soviet republics.

A significant factor contributing to the initial acceptance and use of the JA programs in many of the transition economies was a standard package of curriculum materials for different grade levels. The translated materials were available to teachers who wanted to teach basic business and economic concepts to their students, so schools and teachers did not have to spend time developing an economics curriculum. The relatively easy content level of the materials also limited the amount of teacher training or retraining required to begin teaching these units. Of course it was also a major advantage that the materials were provided at no financial costs to teachers or schools, because they were initially paid for through contributions from private foundations and sponsors, and in some cases by US companies with operations in a particular transition economy.

Some of the features that contributed to the initial success of JA in the transition economies have not worked as well over time, however. For example, the standardized sets of curriculum materials at different grade levels are not always sufficiently flexible for teachers and schools. The curriculum packages cover only a limited amount of business and economic content, and the teacher training component is not extensive. As a result, schools and teachers seeking a more flexible curriculum, a wider and deeper range of economics content, and more intensive teacher training have often turned to other sources.

In addition to these issues, the major obstacles to the expansion of the JA international programs are those that also affect other economic education programs and organizations: getting courses accepted into the curriculum, and finding funds to pay for materials and teacher training. As funding from US-based firms and other early sponsors has become more difficult to find and maintain, some of the national JA programs have cut back on their programs. In other cases the national JA programs have been able to partner with other organizations, such as Ministries of Education or other non-profit groups with external sources of funds.

National Council on Economic Education

NCEE representatives first traveled to the transition economies to participate in an international conference on reforming undergraduate economics hosted by Moscow State University in February of 1992. That concern with university economics reflects the NCEE national delivery network of some 270 centers for economic education located at US colleges and universities. The primary program initiatives of the NCEE itself are, however, to train elementary and secondary teachers in economics, using active learning approaches and instructional materials that cover the same basic economic concepts and issues taught in principles of economics classes by academic economists.

Unlike JA, the NCEE does not publish or base its programs on any particular set of textbooks, although it does publish curriculum guidelines and standards that set out a core set of material for elementary and secondary teachers to cover, and a set of nationally normed, standardized exams to help assess and measure student learning. Its focus is also limited to economic education, whereas JA and some other organizations also provide materials on business education. Given these goals, the limited training of elementary and secondary teachers in economics, and the limited time available in the curriculum for teaching economics, the NCEE has understandably stressed teacher training programs since it was formed in 1949. Ideally that training would include both preservice courses, taught as part of future classroom teachers' undergraduate program of study, and inservice programs for current classroom teachers to provide remedial or updated training in economics and new methods of teaching economics.

The NCEE's focus on academic economics, teacher training, active learning, and formal testing and evaluation has been well received in the transition economies, where academic standards are generally high in most subject areas (particularly math, science, and languages), but also because the pedagogical and evaluation procedures and emphasis were seen as innovative and effective. The NCEE's strategy of finding local partners to work with in these nations, rather than setting up its own national franchises and operations, has achieved success over time, although it is initially a slower process than the JA approach. It also results in greater variations across countries, and is probably even more dependent on outside funding from groups such as the Soros Foundations, the Eurasia Foundation, US corporations, and since 1995 especially from the US Department of Education.

The general range and pattern of NCEE program activity seems to change in the transition economies in predictable and intentional ways, although the timing is more variable depending on when the initiatives begin in a particular country and differences in economic conditions, and on the strength of the personnel and funding available to the national partners who work with the NCEE in different nations. The more or less typical scenario, however, seems to be that some local agency such as the national Soros Foundation initially asks or agrees to invite the NCEE to offer demonstration workshops for a group of 25-50 secondary teachers, then helps to organize the program and recruit teachers, and in some cases provides partial funding. After one or more of these teacher workshops, and often after the NCEE has established ties with additional groups or organizations, participants are selected to attend the NCEE's flagship program in the transition economies, its Training of Trainers program. When some critical mass of trainers has gone through this and perhaps additional NCEE workshops they begin to offer training programs for secondary and sometimes elementary teachers themselves, using NCEE materials and often textbooks or other materials developed in their own countries.

Subsets of the trainers are likely to continue in more specialized NCEE programs, on curriculum and instructional materials writing, teaching economics in elementary schools, assessment and evaluation, or managing a nongovernmental organization. In the more successful cases the participants form – if it did not already exist – a national organization of economics teachers, with local centers for economic education that may or may not be housed or affiliated with a university or pedagogical institute. The NCEE often provides some funds to help these organizations begin operating, and also sends US faculty to participate as co-faculty, advisors, or mentors in teacher training programs.

In some of the countries, particularly Ukraine, Latvia, and Russia, an extensive translation program is undertaken to provide NCEE instructional materials and curriculum guidelines for the teacher training programs, schools, and national and local curriculum planners. The Russian translations of these materials have also been widely used in other transition economies where direct translations into the local language have not been undertaken. Occasionally the NCEE will become involved in more specialized programs developed in particular countries, or take a more direct and permanent role in working with a particular organization. Examples of this include the programs for parliamentarians, ministry officials, and journalists offered in Latvia, and the NCEE representative's seat on the Board of Directors of the Ukrainian Council for Economic Education.

The NCEE has also conducted numerous exchange programs for university and secondary economics teachers. US teachers have visited many of the transition economies where the NCEE has offered programs, and teachers from those countries have visited the United States. These programs usually include presentations in schools and classrooms, as well as visits to private homes, businesses, government offices, and various social and cultural activities. In one NCEE program, the Training of Curriculum Writers workshop, teams of teachers from the United States and the transition economies work together to write instructional units, often featuring international comparisons of economic conditions and institutions.

There are, of course, problems or limitations with this program model, as with the models used by other organizations. With no standardized textbook or other mandated instructional materials for students, the ultimate classroom results of NCEE programs are particularly dependent on the knowledge, skills, and dedication of the teachers and teacher trainers who complete its training programs. That approach puts a greater premium on recruiting well-qualified participants, and on the participants retaining their commitment to improve economics instruction after attending NCEE programs. Those objectives are difficult to achieve in any country at any time, but especially in the transition economies where teachers are poorly paid and beginning to see many new career opportunities as their nations' economies become more market oriented, and where the NCEE's recruiting must be done working with other organizations and in languages other than English.

As with all of the programs promoting the reform of academic economics, there are serious obstacles to overcome in moving beyond demonstration programs to reach most schools, economics teachers, and students. These costs are related to the costs of training a large number of teachers, distributing many sets of instructional materials, and getting the organizational support to include economics as a basic part of the curriculum. The effectiveness of this work depends on the acceptance of economic education programs by government and education officials, and by the willingness of university faculty and other teachers or administrators who assume leadership positions to continue this activity in their country. While the NCEE programs show what is possible and demonstrate various methods that can be used to teach economics more effectively at the elementary and secondary levels, the NCEE is not directly responsible for sustaining programming or the level of teacher training or classroom activity in each nation.

Moreover, the major funding for NCEE's work in these countries since 1995, from the US Department of Education, is only appropriated on a year-to-year basis. That makes it difficult to plan for, and impossible to commit to, specific sustained, long-term initiatives. The major effect of this uncertainty in funding and the other problems noted above is a higher degree of variability in the level and effectiveness of programs across the many different nations where the NCEE is attempting to promote the academic transition to market-based economic education, and also variability in the level and quality of programs in a particular country from year to year.

Other Western and International Organizations

A number of other western and international organizations and governments have sponsored economic education programs in some of the transition economies at various times over the past decade. Programs were conducted or sponsored by, among others, the European Union, the Thatcher Foundation, the World Bank, the International Monetary Fund, the United Nations, the Foundation for Teaching

Economics, many western universities, and various national governments. Although these groups were not the main agents of reform in academic economics because they sponsored programs that were often highly specialized, did not operate across many nations, or paid little attention to the systematic reform of economics in elementary and secondary schools, as a group they had the effect of reinforcing the other efforts to transform economics and the teaching of economics. Just as people in competitive markets make independent decisions that lead to a common outcome with many social benefits, the work of these organizations, though often done independently, has helped to transform economic education in the transition economies.

Future Challenges

The economics that is taught today in the nations of eastern and central Europe and the former Soviet Union bears little or no resemblance to what was taught at the end of the 1980s. That transformation is found both in cases where the people and organizations now teaching economics are different from those who taught it at the end of the Soviet period, and where the organizations and even individual instructors have not changed. What makes these academic reforms especially impressive is that they occurred despite the dire financial circumstances facing people and schools in these nations, and that they involved extensive international cooperation and support that could not realistically have been envisioned just 10 to 20 years ago. The reform of economics and the teaching of economics in the transition economies is historic and unprecedented.

As remarkable as this story of an academic transition is, however, what remains to be done is even more daunting. It has proved to be even more difficult than expected to transform authoritarian governments and centrally planned economies into democratic market economies, and also to transform the economics curriculum and the teaching of economics across all of the schools and universities in the transition economies. The most optimistic prospects are at the university level, where there is strong interest in establishing a curriculum based on the current thinking in western economics, and indeed a professional vested interest for both institutions and individual faculty members in meeting academic standards like those at leading universities in the rest of the world.

At the elementary and secondary level the challenges are enormous: millions of students are waiting to be taught market economics under comprehensive curriculum plans; thousands of teachers require training in economics and how to teach the subject; and hundreds of new textbooks and other educational materials must be written, published, and distributed to help students learn economics and help teachers provide high quality instruction. This will require substantial financial resources and a commitment to change that is made more difficult for international agencies that want to help by the differences in languages across nations. All of these challenges are set against the even more historic and unprecedented backdrop of the economic and political reforms in these nations, which makes the work both more challenging and more important.

Many of these same challenges still confront the United States and other western nations, although on a lesser scale and under significantly better financial circumstances. For example, the basic problem in the United States is that economics is not an integral part of the school curriculum, and academic standards in many key subjects are lower than they are in western Europe, Japan, and other nations. Less than half of US high school graduates take at least a full semester course in economics during their secondary education. Teachers are also often poorly prepared to teach the subject because they receive little training in economics or how to teach the subject in their undergraduate education, and because they are more likely to be specialists in teaching other subjects, such as history or government. With or without a course in economics, US high school students score relatively low on a national test of understanding of basic economics and in international comparisons of economic understanding. So although the transition economies have a long way to go in reforming economics teaching at the pre-university level, they are by no means hopelessly behind other nations.[6]

The prospects for sustaining the academic reforms in the transition economies are considerably less optimistic at the pre-university level than at the university level. The acceptance and reform of economics in elementary and secondary schools that has been achieved to date has often depended on external funding from both domestic and international educational organizations. If that support ends or decreases sharply in the near term, there is a very real question as to whether economics would continue to be accepted, let alone considered as worthy of becoming a core part of the curriculum, at least in some of the transition economies. That concern is based more on the resources needed to continue teacher training programs and the development and dissemination of instructional materials than on any residual ideological opposition, and there is also the issue of finding time in an already crowded and demanding curriculum.

And yet there are compelling reasons to believe the academic transition of economics will succeed even at the pre-university level. First, at least some of the support from private and public educational organizations is likely to continue, based on the personal interests of some donors, the strong perception of strategic interests in the West in supporting the economic and educational transitions in these nations, and the interest of individual western educators and organizations in working in this interesting, educationally advanced, and once-forbidden part of the world. Even more important, in the transition economies there is clearly widespread concern among educators and policy-makers about the role economic understanding can play in supporting economic reforms. In these nations economic policies and the variable progress of market-based reforms are a constant source of debate, confusion, frustration, but ultimately hope. In that setting, many more people seem to feel that economics is simply too important to be left out of the curriculum at any educational level – especially the thousands of teachers who have already begun to teach it. That commitment and enthusiasm is a powerful force that will not go away. So the real questions are how much economics will be taught and how well it will be taught. The academic transition in economics and the teaching of economics has been uneven across the transition economies, and there is still far to go; but substantial progress has clearly been made and is likely to continue.

NOTES

1. It is also interesting to consider how public knowledge of differences of standards of living in the former Soviet Union and the West contributed to the breakdown of the former Soviet Union and its economic system, and beyond that knowledge by some Soviet officials and academics of western economics and economic policies. But that lies well beyond the scope of this volume.
2. In many cases these organizations have formally or informally cooperated to develop and offer programs on economics and economic education in one or more of the transition economies. Examples are noted later in this chapter, based on the more detailed discussions provided in earlier chapters.
3. In economic terminology, in these circumstances mandates for western-style economics courses or training can be considered an example of the 'theory of the second best' — a policy response to a situation that is already far from ideal.
4. The exception is the former East Germany where the faculty members who taught Soviet-style economics were simply fired.
5. For an assessment of the capacity of universities, government agencies, and private institutions in transition economies to prepare economists, assist economic policy-makers, and conduct economic research, see Pleskovic, Aslund, Bader, and Campbell (2000). They reported good progress in about a third of the 24 countries they reviewed, but judged that significant improvement was still required in the other nations.
6. Although lecture methods are also widely used in undergraduate instruction in the United States (see Becker and Watts, 2001), the method is more often supplemented with discussion and other teaching strategies during a lecture. In addition, there has been extensive innovation in teaching economics at the undergraduate level — at least at the level of experimentation or demonstration projects — through active learning techniques, cooperative learning, writing, discussion, and computer technologies. For a discussion of these alternative approaches see Walstad and Saunders (1998) and Becker and Watts (1998).
7. Academic Olympiads, or national student competitions, are one area in which programs in the United States have now been modeled after national and international economic education programs first launched in the transition economies. While many states and universities have long sponsored social studies fairs or quiz bowls in economics and other areas, national competitions featuring exams and team problem-solving on written and computer programs were done first on that scale in Russia and other transition economies, usually under the auspices of Ministries for Education or other educational organizations. These competitions were commonplace at the end of the Soviet period, although the competitions in market-based economics obviously began later, in the 1990s.
8. For further discussion of the condition of economic education in US high schools see Walstad (2001). For comparisons with other western nations see Walstad (1994).

REFERENCES

Becker, W. and M. Watts (2001), 'Teaching economics at the start of the 21st century: Still chalk and talk,' *American Economic Review*, **91** (2), pp. 446-51.

Becker, W. and M. Watts (eds) (1998), *Teaching Economics to Undergraduates: Alternatives to Chalk and Talk*, Cheltenham, UK and Northampton, Massachusetts, USA: Edward Elgar.

Pleskovic, B., A. Aslund, W. Bader, and R. Campbell. (2000), 'State of the art in economics education and research in transition economies,' *Comparative Economic Review*, **42** (2), pp. 65-109.

Walstad, W.B. and P. Saunders (1998), *Teaching Undergraduate Economics: A Handbook for Instructors*, New York: Irwin/McGraw-Hill.

Walstad, W.B. (2001), 'Economic education in U.S. high schools,' *Journal of Economic Perspectives*, **15** (3), pp. 195-210.

Walstad, W.B. (ed.) (1994), *An International Perspective on Economic Education*, Boston, Massachusetts, USA: Kluwer Academic Publishers.

Name Index

Subject Index